EIGHT SACRED HORIZONS

EIGHT SACRED HORIZONS

The Religious Imagination East and West

VERNON RULAND, S.J.

MACMILLAN PUBLISHING COMPANY
A Division of Macmillan, Inc.
NEW YORK

Collier Macmillan Publishers
LONDON

Macmillan Publishing Company
A Division of Macmillan, Inc.
866 Third Avenue, New York, N. Y. 10022

Collier Macmillan Canada, Inc.

Library of Congress Catalog Card Number: 84-21291

Printed in the United States of America

printing number
1 2 3 4 5 6 7 8 9 10

Library of Congress Cataloging in Publication Data

Ruland, Vernon.
Eight sacred horizons.

Includes bibliographies and index.
1. Religions. I. Title.
BL80.2.R85 1985 291 84-21291
ISBN 0-02-927320-X

Contents

Preface

This work is an essay on selected motifs from the major extant world religious traditions. It is not a factual encyclopedic textbook, nor an apologia blueprint for interfaith dialogue. It centers on a few decisive personalities, rites, or themes from each world spirituality, and by exploring their range of implication, converges gradually toward the unique vision pervading that tradition. Its aim is less to judge than to grasp, share, and appreciate the religious imagination behind faiths other than one's own. Cantwell Smith characterizes this approach as an imaginative sympathy directed, for instance, not toward Buddhism but toward Buddhists—how it feels in the pulse to believe and worship as Buddhists.

A crucial interpersonal factor underlies this present study. First, we pursue the vital Hindu adjective and adverb modifying basic ethical and ritual behavior in a society, not the muddled substantive called Hinduism. Moreover, it is not Judaism and Islam that intersect, but specific Jews and Muslims who befriend or despise one another. Second, the most plausible basis for opening oneself to the faith of another person is affection first for the person, and then readiness to hear out and respect the most cherished convictions of that person. Exposure to library research, world travel, and a few exotic liturgies might facilitate understanding but scarcely suffices. It is hard to find people who so live and articulate their faith that they can be said to represent their own tradition with authority. Even fewer know how to discern and interpret with empathic accuracy a tradition that is not their own. Yet no matter how cursory and fallible, mediation of this type must always be attempted—with modest candor, of course, cautioning readers of the pitfalls into which human ignorance and incurable religious bias might lead them.

My interest in comparative religious traditions, first aroused by two seminars under Mircea Eliade at the University of Chicago, did not intensify until recent friendships and counseling experiences with international students prompted me to explore beyond my own tacit cultural, spiritual boundaries. The present book emerges from a decade of teaching introductory courses on world faiths and of residence as priest and counselor in student dorms at the University of San Francisco. I have been neighbor to a wide ethnic range of dialect, dress, music, and aromas from portable hotplates. Requested often to ease the strain of culture shock or to mediate quarrels with someone's distant lover or parents, I learn daily, for example, not to project my own limited bourgeois norm of adult individuality upon a person trained to form major decisions only after sounding out the consensus of a clan or tribe. Mistakes in my class lectures have been set right repeatedly by devout students from various spiritualities, including a Kashmir Śaivite who seldom ceased mumbling his prayer beads, Chinese Buddhists with tales of ghosts and miraculous divination, and a feisty group of Saudi Muslims whose devout Friday *ṣalāt* prayers I attended an entire semester in their campus mosque. Often stalled before some apparent fallacy or idiocy in a specific religious tradition, my imaginative sympathy has been revived consistently by this acid test: how would my friends Toshi, Fatima, or Ananda have lived out this phenomenon and made sense of it?

Since every religious symbol is an expression of both the sacred phenomenon and also the symbol-maker, my method in the following chapters will be interdisciplinary, charting the inclusive human frontier where theology converges with anthropology, social psychology, and aesthetics. Formal reflections on the fivefold method that gives unity to this study are summarized in the final pages. Précis of a Dostoevski novel or Kurosawa film script, an anecdote about Ramakrishna or Marx, a genre sketch from Tibetan Buddhist iconography—varied illustrations are introduced whenever appropriate. Each crucial new concept is carefully defined and exemplified. The style attempted in this book is consciously nonsexist or inclusive, though the patriarchal flavor of scriptural quotes has sometimes been retained. To standardize variant spellings, the Asian chapters in particular adopt a format of scholarly transliteration. Every chapter concludes with a useful description of materials for further reading.

I acknowledge gratefully the helpful critiques and encouragement of my colleague in the field of world spiritualities, Fr. Paul Bernadicou, S.J., and cordial assistance from the Gleeson Library staff at the University of San Francisco. Behind the vision and resources in this book are the many people who have helped shape me spiritually, experientially, and intellectually. Most patent here are the challenging interests and needs of my student friends from many nations.

V.R.

1

Primal Hunt

Contemporary world maps registering the distribution of major world spiritualities leave huge geographical swaths unnamed. These are the divergent self-contained civilizations of indigenous peoples scattered through Central Africa, the Amazon basin, northern Australia, Melanesia, Siberia and the Arctic, the reservations of North America. Acknowledging this astounding diversity, and the limited ethnographic data accessible, we must still try to discern the threads of some common underlying pattern. To name something is to pass judgment on it, and thus to affect its destiny. Labels of psychopathology, for instance, have been known to create symptoms in the patient and predetermine diagnosis. When we sum up whole civilizations as undeveloped or underdeveloped, or again as preliterate or illiterate, we enshrine the implicit criterion of technological proficiency or the written word. It is instructive that sensitive adherents within indigenous cultures also deplore, for one reason or another, terms like *tribal, local, ethnic, folk,* and especially *primitive,* with its gamut of colliding connotations from Hobbes's barbarism, or Freud's infantile regression, to Rousseau's romanticized simplicity.

This loosely encompassing horizon shall be called *primal* for three reasons. The term calls attention to a basic dimension in all spiritualities, it suggests continuity but not simplistic identification with the conjectured rituals of earliest Paleolithic hunting cultures, and the label at present seems least obnoxious to the persons described. Living in small-scale communities cemented by kinship and locale, deprived or enhanced by their marginal encounter with urban values, these societies learn the urgency of intercommunion with natural forces which they lack the technology or inclination to dominate. Like the Tao to be discussed in the next chapter on China and Japan, the primal vision recognizes a balanced symbiotic cosmos, vibrant with magic forces, with interpenetrating spiritual and human and physical worlds. This is something to be lived and danced out, more than intellectualized in a preached creed.

Links with some specific clan, group worship pattern, or sacred neighborhood often get such emphasis that many primal cultures cannot survive export or family dispersal. Legend and rite handed down orally from master to disciple take the place of sacred scripture—the secret word might be endangered or profaned by capturing it in print, even if a written language happens to exist. Anthropologists of religion, once prone to spot fetish cults and polytheism in almost any unfamiliar ritual, have more recently favored the so-called *African triangle* presumption. The numinous is divided, first, into a godhead source at the apex, often unapproachable and left awesomely unnamed. Then radiating from this source are two legs of the triangle, ancestral spirits and nature spirits, accessible to popular devotion.

This hypothesis at least opens an observer's mind to the possibility of a tacit and diffusive monotheism, but it also projects an inchoate monotheism where it may not actually exist. I prefer an approach alert to the comprehensive way a people not only explain but also implicitly live out their faith, and to the interplay also between their religious rationale and the horizons shaped by their language, polity, and social psychology. For example, with the graded levels of social behavior and custom in Nuer society, Evans-Pritchard correlates the Nuer concept of *kwoth* or numinous power, refracted into separate spirits ranked in a complex hierarchy. Leon-Portilla observes the Aztecs' dual language patterns—"water and hill" stand for a town, "shirt and blouse" for an attractive woman—and questions whether the Nahuatl godhead in this linguistic universe could be anything but dualistic or at least polytheistic.

We shall observe in the next chapter how Shinto spirituality stakes out its own theological identity the moment Buddhist missionaries threaten to absorb it. This defensive reflex is common also to many primal cultures. Even after conquest by a more aggressive tradition, the primal dimension may survive as a recognizable residue. Note, for instance, the striking primal Bon imagery and ritual that distinguish Tibetan Buddhists from other Buddhists, or the unique sacrificial rites shared by Toraja primal and Toraja Christian funerals in Indonesia.

Black Elk dictated his celebrated shamanic visions to Neihardt and Brown because he wanted the Oglala Sioux to preserve and appreciate their own dying traditions. It may not be widely known that once his first book appeared, Black Elk decided to issue a statement in Sioux and English reaffirming his Catholic faith for forty uninterrupted years since his conversion, so readers would not mistake him for a "pagan medicine man." A far different Sioux voice, the feisty saboteur of all enforced acculturation, is recorded in *Lame Deer, Seeker of Visions*. Informed of plans to build a great tipi Catholic chapel on the reservation, with a peace pipe hanging next to the cross above the altar, John Lame Deer complains, "It is dishonest. . . . There will always be a difference, as long as one Indian is left alive. Our beliefs are rooted deep in our earth, no matter what you have done to it and how much of it you have paved over. And if you leave all that concrete unwatched for a year or two, our plants, the native Indian plants, will pierce that concrete and push up through it."

The primal umbrella stretches over so much vague geography and history that it seems wise to focus on one indigenous people as a paradigm. I have selected the Huichol Indians from the rugged Sierra Madre area of north-central Mexico, mostly because of the scholarly, varied, and recent anthropological materials about them. There are monographs by Mexicans and Americans on Huichol religion, economy, medicine, family structure; an hour-long ethnographic film of their annual peyote hunt; extensive displays of Huichol culture and yarn paintings I have seen at the Mexico City Anthropological Museum, and especially the renowned 1979 Huichol exhibit at the San Francisco De Young Museum. Similar terrain is explored in the Carlos Castaneda series, with its teasing concealment of ethnographic sources, its constant spoof of the academician's inflexible apparatus. From an analysis of the annual Huichol peyote pilgrimage, I shall extract four motifs essential to an appreciation of the primal horizon: the hunt, shaman, gift, and mask. These four combined themes will act as a grid transparency, in turn, to highlight outlines of the primal hunt in Huichol data which might otherwise seem random and incoherent.

The Hunt

Once a year small Huichol bands set out from their present homes in the Sierra Madre, and travel three hundred miles northeast down through Jalisco and Zacatecas to the Chihuahuan deserts of San Luis Potosí. Their goal is to gather peyote in what their myths call Wirikuta, a vast desert without roads at the base of two sacred mountains. Since the cactus used throughout the year in religious ceremonies could be purchased conveniently at local markets, clearly the journey itself and the particular Wirikuta cactus have symbolic import. Huichol myths identify Wirikuta as the Middle World where gods and human beings once dwelt together at the beginning of time. Pilgrimage there is a ritual passage back to human origins, a recovery of continuity between the numinous upper world and the human flatlands, between human beings and the magic energy of plants and animals. The exact ethnic lineage and geographical origins of the Huichole are disputed, but anthropologists treasure the slimmest proofs of their relative insulation from Aztec and Spanish influence, and point to the stubborn fidelity with which these people have maintained every detail of their peyote pilgrimage, even through the past eighty years of ethnographic study. The Huichole happen to claim Wirikuta as the site of their actual historical beginnings as a people, and have given Huichol names to clumps of trees, waterholes, and rocks along the route northeast where their ancestors passed during some massive primordial Exodus.

In his sensitive *Way to Rainy Mountain,* Scott Momaday tells of his trip from the Yellowstone Mountains eastward to the Black Hills and down through the plains of Oklahoma to visit his grandmother's grave in the shadow of Rainy Mountain. His own bildungsroman journey reenacts the seventeenth-century migration of his people, the Kiowa, in their descent southward, adapting gradually to use of the horse, to the Plains rituals of worship and warfare, and to the status of a mature, self-confident nation. Each two-page unit in the book is a collage of three methods—mythic, philosophical, and existential-personal. First a Kiowa legend, followed by a paragraph of philological or ethical commentary, then a brief epiphany drawn from the author's early memories. The physical and spiritual odyssey of the Kiowa is juxtaposed with Momaday's personal rite de passage; and Rainy Mountain, a desolate knoll in the Wichita Range, is hallowed by Momaday and his people as the place where Creation began. A journey like Momaday's must be made "with the whole memory, the experience of the mind which is legendary as well as historical, personal as well as cultural. . . . There are on the way to Rainy Mountain many landmarks, many journeys in the one."

We recognize all these dimensions of the Rainy Mountain experience in the Huichol passage to Wirikuta—their communal yet individual return to the Sacred Center, their historical identity reaffirmed as a people. Yet like any Muslim *ḥajjī* or Chaucerian Canterbury pilgrim, each Huichol traveler has a particular motive for pilgrimage. The pilgrim goes to fulfill a vow, to expiate sins, to gain merit or power, to heal disease or beg some other favor, to show respect for familial or ethnic traditions, to enjoy a profound community experience or feel proximity to the gods. Each Huichol aspirant must be screened for pilgrimage, and like the *ḥajjī* will return with a new indelible status, expected now to give evidence of a converted life. It is preferable to make the Wirikuta pilgrimage on foot, chanting prayers and songs the whole rigorous month, fasting, offering sacrifices at daily wayside shrines marked by Huichol names and legendary associations. Today most people cover the distance by car, or zip by the shrines in nonstop buses, spewing offerings in frantic haste from the windows.

The Wirikuta experience can be distinguished from most other world religious pilgrimages by its emphasis on rites of the sacred hunt. Though dependent today mostly on maize farming, the Huichole still linger in imagination on their recent past as a hunting society. In many cultures the hunt is a significant rite de passage, cutting oneself away from the protective and the orderly, wandering into the perilous natural world, and returning in mastery. Some rituals prepare hunters for their separation from society, others produce medicines, spells, and prayers to outwit the adversary, others purify the returning hunter from dangerous contact with the prey's magic powers. As in the spiritual martial art of *t'ai chi,* a familiar and complex relationship develops between hunter and hunted—the quarry proves to be the hunter's own doppelgänger, a numinous presence to be courted, persuaded, appeased before it freely sacrifices its life. The transcendent moment in this relationship is portrayed superbly by "The Bear" and other tales of the initiatory hunting rite in William Faulkner's *Go Down, Moses*: "Suddenly the buck was there, smoke-colored out of nothing, magnificent with speed," as twelve-year-old Ike McCasslin squeezes the trigger. Then he hears the cry of Sam Fathers, his elderly guide, "Olé, Chief, Grandfather," confirming that Sam and the prey possess the same Indian blood in their veins. Sam smears the boy's face with blood from the slain deer. Humble and trembling at this baptism, Ike promises the animal, "I slew you; my bearing must not shame your quitting life. My conduct forever onward must become your death."

By whatever transportation the pilgrims reach Wirikuta, they must cross the last few miles on foot and soon commence the extraordinary ritual of a combined deer and peyote hunt. They have long prepared for this moment by a series of traditional hunting purification rites—a bath before beginning, then during the trip an abstention from sexual relations, bathing, most sleep, most food and drink. Their families at home share vicariously in the pilgrimage by adhering to most of these prescriptions, in the same way that Muslims worldwide celebrate the *'īd al-aḍḥā* festival to coincide with animal sacrifices performed by Mecca pilgrims. Now at Wirikuta the hunters pray even more earnestly than before for many hours, blowing a horn and slapping the hunting bow to soothe the deer at its impending death. They crouch to seek animal tracks, in imitation of their ancestral Ancient Ones, stalking the prey. Once the first peyote plant is spotted, their leader, the Maraakame, takes aim with his bow, sinking one arrow after another around the cactus, and finally cuts it off at the base. "Look there, how sacred and beautiful, the five-pointed deer," the Maraakame says, apologizing and grieving for this death, honoring the deer with gifts. "Take them, Elder Brother, and give us our life." Then "Elder Brother's flesh," the broken segments of this first cactus in the hunt, is placed in a votive gourd and passed around to all the communicants, beginning with veterans of previous pilgrimages. The Maraakame touches a peyote bud to each person's forehead, eyes, throat, and heart, then places it on the tongue, urging each to "chew it well, chew it well, for thus you will see your life."

Later, with the pilgrimage concluded, carrying baskets of peyote —if not intercepted by venturesome Mexican narcotics agents—the *peyoteros* will return home to prepare within five days for an actual deer hunt. A bowl containing some of the first Wirikuta plants is carried like a compass to guide them to the quarry. The sacred deer must be trapped without arrows or bullets, and led gently from the snare back to the sacrificial altar. The victim is honored with its favorite food, and encouraged to surrender its life generously. Portions of its cut heart and blood are sprinkled over the seed corn, for without this medicine of fertility, there could be no maize, rain, or life.

It is a challenge to keep track of so many overlapping symbols. Huichol myths cherish the exploits of Maxakwaxi-Kauyumari, the Sacred Deer Person, their ancestral trickster hero. A tutelary animal in human form, intermediary between gods and the Maraakame, he dwells within each pilgrim group, his deer antlers and tail carried as banners throughout the pilgrimage. To hunt and eat the sacred peyote, then, means to widen ordinary consciousness and feel communion with this tiny band of travelers, with the First Ancestors in their primordial hunting culture, with the totem Kauyumari himself in his kinship with the animal and natural universe, with the sacred life force of the sun god Tayaupa and the fire god Tatewari that pulses through the maize and deer blood. If you desire to become a Maraakame, says Matsuwa, a famous Huichol Maraakame, "Fire Our Grandfather and Sun Our Father will teach you. From peyote comes forth Kauyumari, the Little Deer Spirit ally, . . . emerging like a mirror, and shows you what you must do. . . . When you hear me chanting the sacred songs, it is not I who sing but Kauyumari who is singing into my ear."

The Shaman

The Huichol Maraakame shows many features of the classical *shaman* prototype presented in the writings of Mircea Eliade. This is a figure prominent in inner Asia, and recognizable with some modifications throughout most primal societies. Possessing the gift of controlled ecstatic trance, a shaman's soul leaves the body to visit the domain of clan and nature spirits—sky, underworld, or metaphysical center, depending on the spatial myths assigned by a particular cosmology to the dead and the sacred. The goal of this journey is to guide the recently dead through dangerous roadblocks to their rest, to cure a long-unappeased hungry ghost or a soul threatening to drift loose from its diseased body, to search out clairvoyant spirits for knowledge about the future or for magic remedies. The shamanic insignia are such trance enhancements as music and rhythmical chants and often drugs; psychodrama and leaping dances to mime hazardous adventures of the trip; a costume of bird feathers or reindeer or horse skin for ecstatic flight. Usually the shamanic vocation comes just to those privileged with some unique visionary call in their lives, perhaps a near encounter with death, which familiarizes them with borderlands to the Other World.

Ramón Medina Silva, articulate Maraakame of the Huichol pilgrimages in which anthropologists Myerhoff and Furst were invited to participate, explained to them that the shamanic faith healer must integrate all our fragmented specialties of physician, psychotherapist, priest, poet, and philosopher. From his sixth year, Ramón had recurrent dreams that Tayaupa had elected him a disciple. Then at eight he was bitten by a poisonous snake. His grandfather Maraakame, summoned to cure him, prophesied about the boy's vocation, and after six months of paralysis and meditation, Ramón was set apart for prolonged spiritual apprenticeship. Under a senior Maraakame, he had to learn "how one cures, how one goes to Wirikuta, . . . those stories of ours which are our history. How one makes the sacred things, the offerings." Besides intelligence, spiritual sensitivity, and judgment, a Maraakame should have the talent of singing, storytelling, creating beautiful works of art as offerings, and proficiency in the ways of practical Mexican society in order to protect and counsel his people. Ramón's wife, Lupe, trained in Huichol lore and values, assisted her husband in all his rituals, especially guarding him in moments of vulnerability when his energy was drained and his animal spirit helpers were busy elsewhere. Ramón admitted that each successive peyote pilgrimage proved more taxing to his stamina, for he was taking on "more of the weight of his people."

Ramón's powers bind him closely to his community yet keep him at a mysterious distance from it. Their private dreams and peyote experiences are meant for individual enjoyment and meditation, but his are public revelations of the sacred to the whole community. The mediation of Ramón is needed especially as the pilgrims cross through the Gateway of Clashing Clouds, the critical boundary between everyday life and Wirikuta sacred space. He blindfolds all *primeros,* more vulnerable than the others to numinous glare and whirlwinds barring access. "This walk will be very hard," he warns. "It is a great penance, this journey to Wirikuta, and you will cry very much." These words might be taken at face value, or perhaps mean the opposite, because at this time everyone uses ritual reversal language, which we shall discuss later. Praying and singing, addressing unseen tutelary spirits, sprinkling the pilgrims with holy water, rhythmically beating his bow to accompany their march, Ramón leads the group in single file through a mythical aperture that Kauyumari pries open with his deer horns, before the gates again slam shut.

Frontiersman and mediator between worlds, Ramón is also an accomplished healer. A barren woman from his group prays at various wayside shrines on the journey to conceive a child. The shaman joins his prayer to hers, blows tobacco smoke over her body, makes sucking and spitting sounds to extract obstructions from the vagina, strokes her womb with holy water, a peyote bud, and his magic feather wand to bring fertility. A more spectacular purification rite for everyone occurs at an earlier stage of the pilgrimage. In a penitential service around the campfire, all *peyoteros,* including the Maraakame, are asked to confess publicly every sexual misdeed in their lives. A transgression unconsciously omitted is eagerly brought to memory by one's spouse or neighbors, for a deliberate omission can endanger the ritual purity of every pilgrim present. Departing from confession rituals in most other religious traditions, only sexual transgressions are cited, apparently more to symbolize the violated taboo than moral sinfulness. For the mood of *peyotero* auditors is one of laughter, prowess, and teasing rivalry, characteristic of veteran macho hunting companions. Ramón ties knots in a sacred cord for each act listed, and then, after the others draw as near as possible to the scorching heat of Tatewari, some even touching or leaping over the flames, he rolls the cord into a spiral and throws it into the fire. "Now you see that you are new. Tatewari has burned it all away. . . . Now we can cross over there. The Maraakame has the power to do and undo."

Shamans in other primal societies function much in the same Maraakame pattern—inaugural vision, magic cure, bridging the mystical divide between gods and human beings. Confession by one patient or an entire clan, for example, is often a precondition for the holistic cure. A shaman must often enlist telepathic powers to sort through these sins and ferret out the breach of taboo causing individual illness or a community plague, as in the stricken land of *Oedipus Rex*. Other traditional explanations for the origin of sickness are intrusions by some object or hostile spirit, a soul drifting astray, unrecognized leaks of magic energy, or attacks by an evil sorcerer. Depending on the particular etiological myth of disease, shamans see their healing as a concoction of the right sacred potion, a search for wandering souls, or a combat often aided by guardian animal spirits against alien magic. The ecstatic trance seems indispensable to their healing arts, but whereas some cultures sanction the use of hallucinogens, others restrict themselves to similar mind-altering chemicals triggered in the body by fasting, sleeplessness, intense meditation, and hypnotic rhythms.

Most primal peoples treat the shaman as an unbounded spiritual factotum, whereas a few sharply limit and differentiate the role. Some African traditions usually consult the *nganga* or medicine man for help to pass a driver's test, select a wife or husband, recover lost property, and detect or even prevent a crime. The *nganga* can be a priest, lawyer, policeman, physician, magician. Yet in Chinua Achebe's reconstruction of Ibo village life in his novel *Arrow of God,* the aging priest Ezeulu and his herbalist brother Okeke quarrel because their father split his more comprehensive powers between them. When Ezeulu's family needs medicine, he shows contempt for the profession by sending for some worthless herbalist whose doctoring cannot even support him with three meals a day. Cultures strongly influenced by popular Hindu beliefs about the karma-determined fate of each migratory soul often consult shamans not as protectors of the dead or as warriors against alien spiritis, but as mediums and seers. The Korean Sinkyo tradition sets up an interesting distinction between male and female shamans. The men are *pansoo* exorcists, playing drums and brasses, shouting mantras to summon or banish spirits, whereas *mutang* women mediums dance and entertain the spirits, communicating with them through ecstatic trance.

The shamanic journey to the underworld is usually an act of solitary heroism, bringing wisdom or magic back to one's people. Yet the Huichol shamans confess their transgressions alongside everyone else on the pilgrimage, and all together reach Wirikuta and share peyote communion with the gods. On the other hand, I have asserted that only the shaman's dreams and peyote experiences are believed to contain revelations destined for the Huichol community. An outstanding social vision of this type came during a serious illness to the nine-year-old Black Elk, who years later blamed the massacre of the Sioux at Wounded Knee on his failure to communicate and live out this shamanic vision. The buffalo dream symbol that caused a sacred tree to blossom again meant the power to bring peace and shape his people into a great nation, a responsibility he subsequently tried to evade. I think Jung observes correctly that the average primal society discards little dreams, with contents drawn from an individual's unconscious past, but prizes the big dreams fraught with numinous archetypes, which can occur to anyone in the community, shaman or otherwise, and should be shared communally. It is the custom in many Amerindian societies for a young male to undergo an initiatory vision quest to introduce himself to his lifelong tutelary spirit. He endures a long fast and vigil in some isolated hole or hut, praying to be given this crucial vision.

Shamans are selected in some cultures precisely because of their predisposition to enter and control hypnotic states with facility, to empathize with patients to the extent of replicating their illness by induced hysterical symptoms. Among Tenino Indians near the Oregon Columbia River, for example, the shaman tries to suck an alien spirit out of the patient's body, stiffens, falls into convulsions, and loses consciousness. Then, propped up by two assistants, he spits this captive spirit into his cupped hands and sets it in flight, back to its appropriate place in nature. Lame Deer's shaman ideal is someone who "talks to the plants and they answer him. . . . From all living beings something flows into him all the time, and something flows from him." But most important, he "feels the grief of others." A young woman and her child were killed recently on the highway. "I feel so deeply about them. At sundown I will talk to the Great Spirit for them. I will fill my pipe and offer it on their behalf."

Extraordinary empathy, psychodrama and mime, hypnosis, the placebo-authority and charism of the healer's costume and repute—all these shamanic techniques of cure have their recognizable parallels in psychoanalysis or other current styles of psychotherapy. Over the patient's body the shaman utters an incantation, derived from a social myth believed deeply by the sick woman and her community. Claude Lévi-Strauss's *Structural Anthropology* offers an astute psychological explanation of what happens next. The shaman becomes the myth's present hero, heading a supernatural battalion of spirits, which penetrate endangered organs and release the imprisoned soul. Accepted into the patient's inner life as an object of magic introjection, the healer takes the place of her tormented ego in this boundary conflict between physical and psychic worlds. The shaman might be called a "professional abreactor," in the sense that most shamans relive repeatedly in all its violence and originality the initial situation from which their own neurosis stemmed, before it had been overcome. They reenact this sacred moment of their visionary experience and introduce it as an explanatory myth into the patient's consciousness. The sick woman cannot accept incoherent suffering, but does accept the shaman's efforts to connect her pain with the tutelary and malevolent spirits in which she has never ceased to believe. "The cure would consist, therefore, . . . in rendering acceptable to the mind those pains which the body refuses to tolerate. . . . The shaman provides the sick woman with a *language,* by means of which unexpressed and otherwise inexpressible psychic states can be immediately expressed." And thus, she also abreacts, and perhaps through this experience sparks a self-healing process.

Although most contemporary psychotherapies bank more on listening than on oratory and incantation, I am convinced their cures draw heavily on the secure atmosphere evoked by the social myths behind each therapy. Rollo May's *Love and Will* describes the almost magical reassuring effect of psychological labels—*primal scene, resistance, introvert*—and concludes that the task of psychotherapy is to *name* the unconscious, not as a substitute for transformed behavior, but as an aid to it. "The names are symbols of a certain attitude I must take toward this daimonic situation of illness. . . . The image by which I identify myself can change by its contact with the myth." Jung tells how he would often reach for an old alchemy book from his office shelf to portray a frightened patient's mad fantasy in a slightly more creative form of four hundred years ago. One therapeutic effect of Jung's archetypal unconscious theory is to welcome the isolated psychotic back into the mainstream of human history, experiencing solidarity with great poets and religious visionaries. Out of the terrifying psychotic break, like the shaman's inaugural call and initiatory journey into the underworld unconscious, it is possible to gain the power to heal others. For as Jung insists, "only the wounded physician heals."

The Gift

The human and sacred implications of any gift exchange first occurred to me a few years ago during a museum tour of the celebrated Hideyuki Oka packaging and gift-wrapping collection from traditional Japan. In a range of samples from lacquered candy bags to giant bamboo-lined buckets, materials of wood, straw, and paper were crafted in the most daring and brilliant ways to present a few rice dumplings or pickled eggs handed from one Japanese to another. No item is so prosaic that it cannot be transformed into something of beauty, less to incite the customer's itch to buy than to compliment and delight the person who will receive the gift. The ritual presentation and exchange are more important than the things exchanged. Roland Barthes has a stunning snapshot of two Japanese women in kimonas bowing low before each other, arms and knees resting in a decreed position, with a gift situated halfway between their faces. This is not an encounter between two ego empires, but a flowing ceremonial network of forms, a gift suspended between two vanishing shadows. "The gift is alone," he remarks. "It is touched neither by generosity nor gratitude, the soul does not contaminate it."

Surely the sacred act of self-emptying transcends the mere hunger to give and accept, love and be loved. Yet it is finite, and cannot but be touched by mortality. Gifts betray the unconscious values, needs, and expectations of those giving, and most of all, the image they have formed of the recipient. You might map out a boy's career by the gift of toy soldiers or an erector set, or confirm your possessive claim over him by childish gifts that arrest his maturity. The woman whom Ramón attempted to cure of her infertility shapes a remarkably touching gift to be offered the gods of Wirikuta. It is a small votive gourd, decorated on the inner surface with an angular stick figure of beeswax imprinted with colored beads and bright wool yarn—the image of a baby. Few things could seem of greater value to her at present, perhaps the gods resemble her enough to smile at the sight of a small baby, and besides, busy in governing the universe, they need a memento of her petition. We cannot begin to understand the religious rationale and feelings behind this woman's sacrificial offerings to the gods, until we comprehend her gift-giving attitudes toward human beings within her own community.

I have called the journey to Wirikuta a pilgrimage, a rite de passage that Victor Turner explains in terms of *limen* and *communitas*. The first term means the Wirikuta threshold toward which you climb, a moment in and out of time, when you experience the sacred, either by means of a miraculous cure or an inward spiritual transformation. *Communitas* is the intense comradeship gradually developed along the way, described before as fellowship of the hunt, the sense of closeness, leveled and stripped of antecedent status, long remembered afterward by those suffering together through boot camp or any other critical ordeal. The Huichol pilgrims pray, eat, and sleep many days together, especially if they travel the entire journey by foot. Their mutual confessions around the campfire equalize everyone and establish a bond of shared secrets. On one pilgrimage, for instance, Ramón and the others refused to tolerate a young *peyotera*'s reluctance to confess, and feared for the group's ritual pollution until she could be persuaded to change her mind. Ramón further mentioned the special vulnerability of a Maraakame during the pilgrimage, awake all night to guard the others. Without shared faith and the trust extended by all his companions, Ramón would feel deprived of power, unable to use his gifts.

A few impressive rites reinforce this experience of solidarity. Huichol families assemble special *peyotero* costumes for use exclusively during the pilgrimage, and the insignia of tobacco gourd and squirrel tail worn by veterans as a badge or rebirth long after their return. The Maraakame invests everyone with a new sacred name before setting out, and years later fellow pilgrims still greet each other by these *peyotero* names. At the commencement and finish of the journey, the pilgrims celebrate a special banquet at home, witnessed by those left behind, who share prayerfully in the entire pilgrimage from a distance. Unique among all these ceremonies is the rite of the sacred cord. Before departure from home, a cactus fiber cord is passed around all the pilgrims in a circle, then scorched in the fire, and saved for a more solemn repetition at Wirikuta. There, after two more encirclings of the group, Ramón prays silently and calls each pilgrim to his side one by one. He ties a knot to represent each kneeling person. Describing this umbilicus and chain as a bond "knotting us into unity," he says, "Now we are all of one faith, one affection, one heart." The knots will be undone carefully after the return home, even though Ramón tells of one fervent *peyotero* band that retained the knotted cord and vowed to return on four successive pilgrimages together.

If we measure the *peyoteros*' deep sense of solidarity, we can appreciate what prompts the heartfelt gift exchange during their hours at the sacred Wirikuta threshold. Picking cactus to fill their buckets, many address a plant in terms of endearment, and lay aside what seems the largest, juiciest, or most symmetrical specimen. They chew peyote constantly as they work, eager to bring the finest peyote gifts back to families left behind. *Peyoteros* wander from one person to another, handing over their most cherished buds to others and receiving some in return, blessing a person and placing a piece on the tongue with the words, "Chew well, so that you will see your life." Every communal peyote-eating ceremony during the rest of the pilgrimage emphasizes this ritual exchange.

It is tempting to project this temporary utopian scenario onto primal society in general. Dealings within these communities are seldom just economic transactions, but what Mauss in *The Gift* calls a "total social fact," reciprocal giving for the sake of friendship, magic power, security, status, social and moral influence. We are overwhelmed by the prodigal hospitality shown by most cultures more traditional than our own, the debilitating expense of their festivals to celebrate birth, initiations, marriage, death, and other social rites. At my polite remark about its beauty, a young Saudi neighbor promptly offers to surrender his expensive prayer rug; a Chinese friend throughout our meal together selects with chopsticks the best morsels from his plate and transfers them onto my own. I feel compelled to protest kindly or reciprocate immediately, but hesitate to risk cross-cultural misunderstandings. Just as gifts inappropriately cheap may humiliate some people, so gifts too valuable may impose a crushing obligation. The Marshall Plan, for instance, has built friendships but also some resentful satellites, no doubt, expecting that the price exacted must be endless gratitude and endorsement of unilateral American foreign policy decisions.

The Sun Dance giveaway rite of Canadian Northern Blackfoot Indians fascinated Abraham Maslow as model for a humane socialist economics. Civilizations handle their wealth by either funneling or siphoning. Wealth funneled toward the rich make them richer at the poor's expense; wealth siphoned off the top by philanthropy or a graduated income tax can enrich the whole society. During the giveaway ritual the entire Blackfoot community gathers in a circle around piles of blankets, food, clothes, cases of Pepsi-Cola, which White-Headed Chief has gathered for years. He then stands up to boast of personal achievements and his family's legendary glory, and later, with "a very lordly gesture, a gesture of great pride without being humiliating, he gives this pile of wealth to the widows, to the orphaned children, and to the blind and diseased." Stripped of all material wealth but the clothes he stands in, he has manifested generosity and thus a more profound wealth. In this community, the citizen listed as possessing the most cattle and horses is not even acknowledged wealthy by the group, for "he keeps it." If the latter won a lottery, others would envy or loathe it; if White-Headed Chief won, almost all would take delight.

There is no human value so exalted that the ego cannot twist it to undermine the very conversion in society and self this value demands. The Chinook Indian word *potlatch* is the generic name given to the ceremony just described, prevalent with some variations among Indians of Alaska and the Vancouver region, Melanesians, and Polynesians. Potlatch is a ritual gift-feast, expressing the host's rank and prodigality. It may occasionally achieve the grand beneficence idealized by Maslow, "great pride without being humiliating." More frequently, its goals have proved more prosaic: to announce a group claim to some title or privilege, to celebrate a family change of status, to return with interest those gifts received at a previous potlatch. Often behind the hospitality lies a thinly concealed agenda, according to Lévi-Strauss and others, "to surpass rivals in generosity, to crush them if possible under future obligations which it is hoped they cannot meet, thus taking from them privileges, titles, rank, authority, and prestige."

Masters of the fine art of one-upmanship, coastal Haida Indians used to stage face-saving potlatches to blot out some specified affront to the host's dignity, and vengeance potlatches where two clans would line up competitively, pouring out expensive oil and shredding blankets—sometimes with ferocious joviality—to work out aggression by reciprocal destruction of property. Family members of a potlatch host would subsequently occupy privileged seats at feasts, speak first at public meetings, be quick to threaten a new vengeance potlatch at any infringement of their recently vindicated status. A poor person would be impotent to confront a richer opponent, capable of destroying more property than the poor could possibly amass. In this parody of the exalted reciprocity principle, we have a primal-society version of Veblin's conspicuous consumption, the conscience-money philanthropy of robber barons, or proud lapel buttons that say "I gave."

The same range of attitudes for gift exchange within the community influences the mood of each person's ritual offerings to the gods. There is fealty, ecstatic love, search for glory, or the attempt to bribe and bargain. In Huichol belief, as in most primal traditions, gods and community cannot be separated—the Ancient Ones who made the first pilgrimage are ancestral spirits, Deer-Peyote is Elder Brother, the numinous powers of fire and sun are immanent to homeland. At every Huichol meal, sacred showers of tortilla bits, egg, and melon are scattered up and down and in four directions to feed the gods before people begin eating. At shrines stationed along the pilgrimage route, the *peyoteros* leave coins and lighted votive candles to accompany their prayers. The sacred waterholes of San Luis Potosí are the choice location to open packages of handmade gifts, bless them with holy water, and display them carefully "for our Mothers to see." Some of the arrows, yarn designs, food, or gourds are then placed in the waterholes, offered with prayers for rain, fertility, a successful harvest, and from these maternal cavities, life-giving water is bottled and taken home to be sprinkled on the maize. Ramón later at Wirikuta piles up the remaining gifts in front of holes left by the uprooted peyote, chants and sets them ablaze, and with his feather wand fans the smoke or gift essence toward the sacred mountains of Deer-Peyote. The fire god Tatewari is often the focus of their gifts—families left behind feed a sacred fire throughout pilgrimage time with a wood supply selected earlier by each pilgrim; *peyoteros* at every meal set aside portions to feed the flames, and when they return home, offer to Tatewari whatever tobacco and sacred Wirikuta cactus spines still remain in their pouches. Just as the Huichole must befriend and propitiate the slain deer, or the cut maize, so they must somehow reciprocate toward Deer-Peyote for the cactus taken from Wirikuta, and toward the fire for its generous warmth. Collect more cactus than needed, neglect to leave gifts, and Deer-Peyote on the next pilgrimage might adopt your very attitudes, measure for measure, making the cactus hard to find or withholding crucial gifts from his people.

Primal societies have seemed more aware than most of us about our immersion in debt to invisible spirits, the dead ancestors and tradition, the forces of nature. All that exists "was already a gift," Ernest Becker concludes, "and so to keep things in balance one had to give in return—to one another and, by offerings, to the spirits. . . . Man *needed* to give precisely in order to keep himself immersed in the cosmology of obligation and expiation, . . . to keep the cycle of power moving from the invisible to the visible world. . . . The gods existed in order to receive gifts."

We usually dismiss magic as counterfeit science or as the manipulative travesty of religious worship. Yet magic for primal societies means a sense of kinship and empathy among human beings, animals, plants, and the world of spirits. In Wagner's *Ring of the Nibelung,* Siegfried tastes a drop of dragon blood after slaying Fafnir, and realizes he can now understand the language of birds and the rest of nature, human nature and the cosmos. The world is a "Thou," alive with spiritual power flowing back and forth, and the most worthwhile success implies access to the source of this power. Never to be regarded as a permanent, unconditional possession, power must be balanced and replenished for individuals and the community by the regular performance of ritual. The religious offering and sacrifice—a peyote banquet, for example, or the holocaust of a prized deer to release its gift essence skyward—are a supplicative gesture not only to approach the Sacred Center, but to share the gods' integrative vision of the cosmos and their life-giving magic.

The Mask

We have already noticed distinctive styles of headgear and garb worn during the shamanic journey. Feather caps, cloaks of skin from the slain totem animal, amulets and rattles and bells, the Maraakame's magic feather wand and the ritual drumhead fashioned from the scrotum of a sacred deer. The vestments establish a new identity for the shaman, who in many primal societies will heighten this transformation by the use of body paint and facial or full-body masks. To convey hazards encountered and wisdom retrieved in trance, the shaman paints, composes poetry, dances, sings, and dramatizes journey details. The Paleolithic cave drawings in Lascaux and elsewhere are conjectured samples of such shamanic art. Perhaps the history of drama began, too, in the shaman's visionary mime. Once their tutelary animal guide takes over, shamans howl or snort, and imitate graphic animal movements. They sing to keep up their courage during the descent to the underworld, pant heavily or leap at arduous climbs, balance on imaginary tightropes, shade their eyes when confronted by radiant spirits.

The shaman's incantations and frenzied gestures during a cure may at first seem flashy legerdemain and blind ritual. But besides the obvious intent to dazzle and compel belief, this performance often mimes the mythical travels of an ancient tribal hero, or, as mentioned before, it reenacts the exact prayers and dance that occasioned the inaugural vision in an individual shaman's earlier life. According to the Joycean monomyth pattern of most hero legends, a hero separated from ordinary life, journeying into a realm of numinous wonder, encounters dangers, wins a victory, returns home with magic power and wisdom to share with the community. By dramatizing this visionary quest again, the shaman hopes to entice a sick soul into the dynamics of the myth, and to recover the right healing magic.

More egalitarian than most shamanic adventures, the Huichol pilgrimage plunges both Maraakame and the other travelers into one sacred monomythic quest, and all wear the special clothes and insignia of *peyoteros*. Before they leave home, each is assigned the name of a god by Ramón and a specified offering at Wirikuta to express affinity with that god. At the Wirikuta campfire, Ramón lets the peyote grip him completely, and as he stares at the fire and enjoys intimacy with Tatewari, the ribbons of flame spell out to him new peyote names to be borne by each person until all reach home. The *primeros,* blindfolded because of their special weakness, are again reminded of their initiatory rebirth when fed at times an abbreviated diet as baby food. All the pilgrims are invited to discard their old identity and, especially in receiving peyote communion, to assume the god's identity flowing through their bloodstream. Throughout the pilgrimage, Ramón becomes Tatewari and the others become the deified Ancient Ones who followed Tatewari in the primordial Exodus.

The Huichole have devised a unique dramatic ritual to signal their entrance into the final sacred vicinity of Wirikuta. With playful ingenuity they begin to refer to each action and object by its antonym. Directions to the right mean left, complaints of cold mean heat, women are addressed as men, joy can be expressed only by sadness. Antonyms offered spontaneously as jokes become confusing obligatory game rules from then on. "We shall now begin to pick flowers," one *peyotero* remarks, "under a full moon in Mexico City."

Is there some hidden religious significance to the reversals? "We change the names of things," Ramón explains simply, "because when we cross over there into Wirikuta, things are so sacred that all is reversed." Clearly one effect of a ritual reversal is to diminish the sense of conventional time and space, and your habitual patterns of identity. A recurrent theme in most mystical traditions is the metaphorical eclipse or annihilation of the ego, for "in the depths of this darkness," says Van Ruysbroeck, "in which the loving spirit has died to itself, the revelation of God and eternal life begins." Utopia and Paradise, too, the almost impossible dream, can be represented effectively by a world upside down, by paradoxes of inversion and reversal, by the Taoist Void we shall explore in the next chapter as an apophatic detour to the sacred. The imagination behind Thomas More's *Utopia,* for example, thrives on privitive nouns and name inversions, which deprive us of what they pretend to describe. Utopia is nowhere, the Achoreans are people without a place, Anydus a river without water, Ademus a leader without people to lead.

A showcase for observing the impact of reversals is the carnival rite—generally interpreted as a safety valve for society's repressed deviants—or the archetypes of court fool, clown, and transvestite exhibitionist. They turn our conventional expectations inside out and expose the shallow arbitrariness of many accepted values. The grotesque false face may catalyze the sadism of robbers and Halloween pranksters, the unthreatening psychodrama or "Meeting of Minds" classroom exercise may animate an otherwise reticent group of college students. A mask usually releases you from the ordinary repertoire of defenses, from the everyday face you hide behind. Perhaps because you are now no longer your conventional self, you can risk testing out potential selves. The director Peter Brooke, for example, often asks his cast to perform wearing plain white masks. Liberated for a time from their subjectivity, actors often approach a role with new insight, and by withdrawing attention from the face, gain heightened awareness of their whole body.

The actor par excellence for Brooke is the disciplined Balinese he observed during rehearsals, touching prayerfully a series of sacred traditional masks. Communing with the first mask until actor and role became almost identical reflections of each other, and then the next piece in succession, this actor modified his breathing slightly for each mask. A definite tension and tempo in the body could be discerned for each specific role, even before the actor donned a single mask. Balinese usually dip a frangipani petal in holy water and sprinkle it on the mask, and then on their own face. Actors have been known to take a mask home to study its traits and story, revere the mask at the family altar, sleep next to it, hoping to evoke dreams associated with its image. The role or mask might contain forces within itself greater than the forces at an actor's conscious disposal, and sometimes almost by magic can transform the good actor into a truly inspired one.

Comprehensive mask traditions in primal cultures include not only the carved face mask but full African and Polynesian costumes of cloth and raffia and leaves, ornamentation in the form of tattoos and body mutilation, paint and cosmetics, stilts or any other device to alter one's ordinary identity. The mask hanging on a museum wall seems lifeless, but it is usually a long-established script to be interpreted by the dancer in a trance-like performance before an audience chanting and clapping to music. A mask may protect its wearer from the evil eye and predatory spirits, enhance the warrior's image of terrifying invincibility, change a shaman into the uncanny totem animal, bold and unpredictable. Eyeholes are sometimes omitted intentionally to enclose the wearer's field of vision within an inner cell of contemplation. Although explanations vary, the ancestor or god is believed to be present somehow within each sacred mask. Thus mask carvers do not so much dominate their materials as search meditatively for a presence there and bring it to new life. When the sacred power in a deteriorated mask needs new embodiment, the old mask remnants must be interred with reverence. It is interesting to discover a Shinto temple in Tokyo that annually cremates old dolls and *bunraku* puppets at a special liturgy.

Masks not in present use are usually concealed and guarded, encircled by severe taboos. To destroy the dramatic illusion by peeking at performers behind their masks violates taboo and threatens to dispel the sacred power concentrated there. Achebe's novel *Things Fall Apart* pictures the desecration of an Ibo masked ancestral spirit by the swaggering Christian convert Enoch. Enoch has already tested the impotent taboos of his former religion by killing and eating a sacred python revered by the entire village. During the annual earth-goddess ceremony, with bands of masked spirits abroad, women and all the uninitiated are forbidden to gaze on them. When some wandering spirits cane Enoch for his taunting blasphemy, he catches one of them and rips off his mask. The others immediately surround their exposed companion to shield him from the profane glance of women and children, and pledge to revenge the ancestor's murder by burning down the local Christian chapel.

In his virtuoso analysis of children riding the wooden horses on a carousel, Erving Goffman has observed younger children terrified or mesmerized by the role of heroic rider, older children developing sophisticated ploys to mock or tamper with a role they can no longer take seriously. There are techniques to play a role or play at it; to get into a role, or be taken in by it, or get beyond it. When the Huichol *peyotero* is invested with the name and identity of a god, when the Kono dancer of West Africa receives instructions on how to serve the needs of a sacred mask or of the spirit dwelling within this mask, each individual responds with attitudes that range from ecstatic immersion to partial or even ironic detachment. For the committed believer, the ritual of donning the mask is a sacrament. One prays for self-abandonment, for openness toward the mask's magic power, for the rapt experience of possession by the gods. Only the shallow actor playing a saint's role night after night can remain untouched by the horizon and heart shaped through this new identity. The *peyotero*'s goal, as for the follower of any spiritual tradition, is to sustain the experience and expression of sacred fellowship and worship after the return from Wirikuta.

FURTHER READING

1. **Huichol Culture.** Sound methodology and a literate style characterize Barbara Myerhoff, *Peyote Hunt: The Sacred Journey of the Huichol Indians* (Cornell University Press, 1974), and Peter Furst, "To Find Our Life: Peyote among the Huichol Indians of Mexico," in Furst, ed., *Flesh of the Gods: The Ritual Use of Hallucinogens* (Praeger, 1972), pp. 136–84. Fernando Benitez's *In the Magic Land of Peyote,* tr. John Upton (University of Texas Press, 1975), gives many Huichol myths but is flawed by intrusive editorializing, worried that a civilization will have died before it can be appreciated. Additional essays by Myerhoff, Furst, and other scholars can be sampled in Kathleen Berrin, ed., *Art of the Huichol Indians* (Fine Arts Museums of San Francisco/Abrams, 1978). See also "Matsua" in Joan Halifax, ed., *Shamanic Voices: A Survey of Visionary Narratives* (Dutton, 1979), pp. 249–52, and other excellent case studies collected there.

2. **Primal Path.** For primary Amerindian materials, N. Scott Momaday's *The Names: A Memoir* (Harper and Row, 1976) is a helpful companion to *The Way to Rainy Mountain* (University of New Mexico Press, 1969). *Lame Deer: Seeker of Visions* by John Fire or Lame Deer, as told to Richard Erdoes (Simon and Schuster, 1972), offers a lively picaresque narrative. As a commentary on John Neihardt, *Black Elk Speaks* (William Morrow, 1932), and Joseph Epes Brown's *The Sacred Pipe* (Penguin, 1971), see the discussion of Black Elk's Christian beliefs in Thomas Overholt, "Short Bull, Black Elk, Sword, and the 'Meaning' of the Ghost Dance," *Religion* 8:2 (Autumn 1978), pp. 171–95. Although most of the Castaneda books prove an interesting read, I prefer *The Teachings of Don Juan: A Yaqui Way of Knowledge* (Ballantine, 1969), and *A Separate Reality: Further Conversations with Don Juan* (Simon and Schuster, 1971).

For an overview on primal societies, see Mircea Eliade's many books, but especially *The Myth of the Eternal Return,* tr. Willard Trask (Pantheon, 1954), and "The Yearning for Paradise in Primitive Tradition" in Henry Murray, ed., *Myth and Mythmaking* (Beacon, 1960). Victor Turner's essay on pilgrimages originally appears as "The Center Out There: Pilgrim's Goal," *History of Religions* 12 (1973), pp. 191–230. A development of the African Triangle theory can be found in E. W. Smith, ed., *African Ideas of God,* revised by E. G. Parrinder (Lutterworth, 1962). See E. E. Evans-Pritchard, "The Nuer Concept of Spirit in Its Relation to the Social Order," in John Middleton, ed., *Myth and Cosmos* (Natural History Press, 1967); and Miguel Leon-Portilla, *Aztec Thought and Culture: A Study of the Ancient Nahuatl Mind* (University of Oklahoma Press, 1963).

3. **The Shaman and the Hunt.** Eliade's *Shamanism: Archaic Techniques of Ecstasy,* tr. Willard Trask (Routledge, 1964), is the comprehensive work on this subject, later distilled by Eliade in his entry "Shaman" in Richard Cavendish, ed., *Man, Myth, and Magic* XIX (BPC, 1970), pp. 2546–9. Andreas

Lommel's *Shamanism: The Beginnings of Art,* tr. Michael Bullock (McGraw-Hill, 1967), is conjectural and evocative. The *History of Religions* journal has presented a series of specific studies on Shamanism: Rex Jones, "Shamanism in South Asia: A Preliminary Survey," 7(1967–8), pp. 330–47; John Hitchcock, "A Nepalese Shamanism and the Classic Inner Asian Tradition," 7(1967–8), pp. 149–58; and Jung Jung Lee, "The Seasonal Rituals of Korean Shamanism," 12(1973), pp. 271–87, Michael Gelfand in *Witch Doctor: Traditional Medicine Man of Rhodesia* (Praeger, 1965) presents what seems to me a flimsy argument for distinguishing the nganga from the shaman because of the former's physical and mental "normalcy." Two superior essays by Claude Lévi-Strauss on the psychotherapeutic implications of shamanic cure are "The Sorcerer and His Magic" and "The Effectiveness of Symbols," two chapters of *Structural Anthropology,* tr. Claire Jacobson et al. (Basic Books, 1963). Comparisons stretch to the breaking point in Robert Beck's "Some Proto-Psychotherapeutic Elements in the Practice of the Shaman," *History of Religions* 6 (1966–67), pp. 303–27. George Murdock's "Tenino Shamanism" in his *Culture and Society* (University of Pittsburgh Press, 1965), pp. 251–60, recounts a detailed cure. In addition to Rollo May's analysis of the daimonic in chapters 5 and 6 of *Love and Will* (Dell, 1969), see Joseph Campbell, "Schizophrenia—The Inward Journey" in *Myths to Live By* (Viking, 1973), pp. 201–32, where Campbell detects monomythic patterns in a psychotic break. An insightful apologia for magic is presented by Rosalie and Murray Wax in "The Magical World View," *Journal for the Scientific Study of Religion* 1 (1961–62), pp. 179–88; and Terence Turner, "Hunting Magic" in Cavendish, *Op. Cit.* X, pp. 1370–75.

4. **The Gift.** Most presentations on this topic begin with Marcel Mauss, *The Gift: Forms and Functions of Exchange in Archaic Societies,* tr. I. Cunnison (Free Press, 1954); but I would suggest the more lively treatment of this subject in Barry Schwartz, "The Social Psychology of the Gift," from Arnold Birenbaum and Edward Sagarin, eds., *People in Places: The Sociology of the Familiar* (Praeger, 1973), pp. 175–90. Also Ernest Becker's "The Primitive World: Economics as Expiation and Power" in *Escape from Evil* (Free Press, 1975), pp. 26–37; and Paul Tournier, *The Meaning of Gifts,* tr. John Gilmour (John Knox, 1968). The concept of gift exchange is applied to alliances between nations in Wilton Dillon, *Gifts and Nations: The Obligation to Give, Receive, and Repay* (Moulton, 1968); and to religious offerings in Marcel Mauss and Henri Hubert, *Sacrifice: Its Nature and Function,* tr. W. D. Halls (University of Chicago Press, 1964). There are magnificant photographs of the Hideyuki Oka collection in *How to Wrap Five Eggs: Japanese Design in Traditional Packaging,* photographed by Michikazu Sakai (Harper and Row, 1967); Roland Barthes's *Empire of Signs,* tr. Richard Howard (Hill and Wang, 1982), contains a few chapters on ritual Japanese bows and packages.

Abraham Maslow's idealistic description of the potlatch occurs in "Synergy in the Society and in the Individual," from *The Farther Reaches of Human Nature* (Penguin, 1978), pp. 191–202. Claude Lévi-Strauss's more balanced appraisal can be sampled in "The Principle of Reciprocity," tr. Rose

Coser and Grace Frazer, in Lewis Coser and Bernard Rosenberg, eds., *Sociological Theory,* 3rd ed., (Macmillan, 1969), pp. 77–86. Murdock gives vivid evidence of potlatch abuse in "Rank and Potlatch among the Haida," *Op. Cit.,* pp. 262–89; however, Sally Snyder in "Quest for the Sacred in Northern Puget Sound: An Interpretation of Potlatch," *Ethnology* 14:2 (April 1975), pp. 149–62, insists that rivalry potlatches in these cultures were rare.

5. **The Mask.** Trace the broad context of G. H. Meade's and John Dewey's transactional social psychology behind study of the mask and persona, and then examine Erving Goffman's popular *Presentation of Self in Everyday Life* (Doubleday, 1959). His essay on "Role Distance" in *Encounters* (Bobbs-Merrill, 1961), pp. 85–152, is most pertinent to our discussion. There are similar approaches in Ronald Grimes, "Masking: Toward a Phenomenology of Exteriorization," *American Academy of Religion Journal* 43 (1975), pp. 508–16; and the entire 1981 Summer issue of *Parabola* 6:3, devoted to the theme of Mask and Metaphor, especially the interview with Peter Brooke. Roger Abrahams and Richard Bauman, "Ranges of Festival Behavior," in Barbara Babcock, ed., *The Reversible World: Symbolic Inversion in Art and Society* (Cornell University Press, 1968), pp. 193–208, surveys divergent explanations for carnival behavior. Diane Wolkstein's "The Master of the Shadow Play," *Parabola* 4:4 (1979), pp. 46–53, interviews an articulate Wayang puppet master in Bali. Excellent plates and text on religious masks can be found in C. Von Fürer-Haimendorf, "Masks" in Cavendish, *Op. Cit.* XIII, pp. 1756–65; and especially Ladislaus Segy, *Masks of Black Africa* (Dover, 1976).

2

Chinese-Japanese Tao

Each of the three great indigenous Chinese and Japanese spiritualities is often underestimated as mere ethic, incomplete religious creed, museum vestige of folklore and costume exhumed just for holiday pageants. Where are the deceptively clear dichotomies of creator-creature, sacred-secular, spirit-matter that most of us smuggle into debates about God's existence? When atheists and theists both endorse these two-storied terms in discourse, atheists define their identity by easy denial of a distinct creator-spirit-sacred reality their opponents affirm. Yet both positions would be stripped of tidy clarity if transposed into the fluid, holistic world view of traditional China and Japan.

The spiritual center in this cosmology is no separable, astral Prime Mover, but the balanced symbiotic cosmos itself: an electromagnetic field of *yin* and *yang*, people interacting with their natural environment, physical with spiritual forces, dead ancestors with the living, microcosm with macrocosm. Hungry ghosts or cycles of stars might tamper with one's destiny, a single moral choice today could temporarily disrupt or reconfirm the evolving harmony of the universe. This ordered process and the plan regulating it are what is meant by Tao, a sacred principle too pervasive and formless for the average theist to distill, or the atheist peremptorily to disavow.

Three Faces of Tao

The term *Tao,* essentially untranslatable, has been idealized for its mystifying flexibility. Someone once computed that Lao-tzu uses the term seventy-six times and never with exactly the same connotations. The noun means path, channel, roadway; the verb, to tell or guide. Thus, the many schools contemporary with Confucius and Lao-tzu taught their own Taos, their doctrine, code of moral guidance, or spiritual Way. Tao at a more metaphysical level means the dynamic cosmic equilibrium described in the preceding paragraph, but Taoist, Shintō, and Confucian traditions each contribute distinctive coloration to the term. Their approaches might be summarized in the Taoist *tao-te,* Shintō *shen-tao,* and Confucian *jen-tao* concepts. Try to view these three Taos as complementary, not contradictory, despite the customary polemics by some adherents. In one resourceful blend, for example, you might prefer Confucian social ethics, Taoist meditation, a Shintō wedding, a Buddhist funeral. Moreover, all three Taos will be abstracted for a moment from their ragged evolution in time. We shall freeze these three traditions at a relatively late peak of synthesis, an era when their own scholars feel ready to give shape to the zigzags and sinkholes of developing theory. Even Confucius of the *Analects,* Lao-tzu of the *Tao-te ching,* and Chuang-tzu cannot be approached as fundamentalist scriptures, but multilayered compilations by later schools.

The Taoist classic *Tao-te ching*'s first line reads: "A Tao that can be told of [or, "tao-ed"] is not the ultimate Tao (*ch'ang-tao*)." This latter Tao, called the Absolute, or Incommensurable (*ta*) later in the text, is the sacred mystery underlying all reality. It is primordial Chaos emerging in a *yin-yang* dialectic, the supreme germinative power of letting-be. Meditate on it, worship and live it, but you cannot philosophize very far about the ineffable.

The wisdom taught by all human Taos is just a secondary refraction from this *ch'ang-tao*. Tuned to the presence of *ch'ang-tao* in nature, each person can soon uncover a derivative imprint of *ch'ang-tao* inside, the distinctive *te* within each life. *Te* is the hidden power in something, the vital energy and ruling force to which all life must conform for the sake of integrative cosmos. This internalized *tao-te* is the only echo of *ch'ang-tao* that Taoists feel competent to expound. Unlike the medley of competing spiritualities, therapies, and creeds introduced from outside, this Tao is *the* Way, endemic to each individual, the forces within one's very nature viewed as potentially directive. *Tao-te* resembles Bergson's *élan vital,* the immanent *natura naturans* of

Spinoza and later Idealists—an uncoiling spring within human nature and the material universe, causative and numinous.

If the Taoist tradition concentrates its attention on the essence of Tao-ness itself, Japanese Shintō luxuriates in a plurality of Taos. The elevator operator in white gloves, the wrestler, a grandfather in his family—the most commonplace duty or role can be cultivated into a genuine art, an individual's own rigorous spiritual Way. The sacred lies hidden in interior attitudes of serenity and care—shown, for example, in the disciplined gracious manner of acknowledging a gift or receiving a visitor. What matters here is not substance but form, style, training. Not the Tao as religious doctrine, but as code and cultus. The arts of self-defense *(judō),* fencing *(kendō),* flower arrangement *(kadō),* calligraphy (*shodō*), and the tea ceremony (*chadō*) bring to mind a line of traditional techniques and rituals, most of them with *dō* or *tō* suffix, the Japanese for Tao.

Shintō or *Kami no michi,* the name adopted by Japanese scholars to distinguish their native faith from Buddhist imports, emphasizes both the pervasiveness of religious awe and Japan's rich proliferation of Taos. In this Tao of the *Kami, Kami* means the numinous source, symbolized either as an emanating ubiquitous *Kami* force, or as personified *Kami* spirit(s). Any physical object, energy, moral attribute, dead hero, living person, felt to be somehow "above" and "superior" (*Kami*), awesome and mysterious (the particle *ka*), can be reverenced as *Kami.* Filtered through anyone's enlightened affectivity, all reality, then, is potentially numinous, just as every committed pursuit is a virtual Tao.

Less impersonal and diffuse than Taoist *ch'ang-tao,* the *t'ien-tao* of Confucius offers an explicit moral revelation, which the paradoxes of *tao-te* and training rituals of *shen-tao* merely intimate. The Will of Heaven (*t'ien-ming*) is inscribed on every human heart. Legendary sages of the Golden Age came closest to embodying this ideal, so their example and teachings give us a human Tao virtually replicating the *t'ien-tao* itself. Wisdom of the revered past must be scrutinized and interpreted by each individual, but followed only when it matches the dictates of one's interior Tao—*jen-tao,* a mature human conscience. "*Jen* is the distinguishing characteristic of a human being," states the *Book of Mencius.* "As embodied in human conduct, it is called Tao."

The Chinese ideograph for *jen* places alongside the word "human being" the numeral two. Whereas Aristotle isolates the marks of reason and animal-continuity to define human life, the Chinese traditions define humanity indisputably as relational. In yourself alone, you are not a complete human being; you exist as the developing center of relationships within a community. It is necessary to live compatibly, to learn empathy and civilized compromise. *Jen-tao* is your own humanity as guide and source of moral energy (*te* in the Confucian sense). It prompts you to mature in *jen,* which can be translated as human-relatedness, implying love, generosity, sympathy, but in an explicitly widening social perimeter. When Confucius is questioned in the *Analects* about his lofty *chün-tzu* ideal, he uses *jen* first in the sense just explained, but also as the summation of all goodness, almost the transcendental Good possessed alone by Heaven and the mythical past sages.

To sense the range of implications in *jen-tao, shen-tao,* and *tao-te,* we shall now develop the Confucian concept of *li,* then Shintō *chūgi,* and finally Taoist *wu-wei.*

The Li Option

The *chün-tzu* is Confucius' sage and gentleman prince model, with a nobility not of pedigree but moral achievement. And the crucial means by which the *chün-tzu* might channel personal *jen-tao,* and by which the entire body politic could reach a stable peace, is through a life of *li,* or ritual propriety. History has situated Confucius alongside Lao-tzu and Chuang-tzu in China, Zoroaster in Persia, Gautama Buddha and Mahavira and the Upaniṣads in India, Plato and Aristotle in Greece, and the major Hebrew Prophets in that era of extraordinary spiritual and moral insight from 800 to 300 B.C.E., which Jaspers has called the Axial Period. In all five centers of civilization a protest erupts almost in unison against patterns of dying symbol and ceremony no longer integrated with the rest of life. It is necessary to reinterpret religious myth, revitalize, establish a balanced dialectic between ritual sacrifice and ethical responsibility. Compare Jeremiah in Israel and Confucius in their outrage against abused religious formulas: "You keep saying, 'This place is the temple of the Lord, the temple of the Lord, the temple of the Lord!' This catchword of yours is a lie. . . . You steal, you murder, you commit adultery and perjury. . . . Do you think that this house, this house that bears my name, is a robbers' cave?" (7:4–11). In the *Analects* Confucius complains, "'It is *li,*' they say. 'It is *li,*' they say. 'It is according to the rules of propriety,' they say. Are presents of gems and silk all that is meant by *li*? Music, music! Does it mean no more than bells and drums?" (17:11).

Confucius in the fifth century witnessed a China in chaos. The centralized Chou dynasty had been atomized into squabbling feudal enclaves, the gentry displaced by merchants and entrepreneurs, the wisdom tradition and every chivalric code of warfare forgotten in a rage of slaughter and venality. What remained of value from the past seemed only tatters of *li*: rubrics of sacrifice, gestures of courtesy, proverbs that no longer made sense, all a heritage from the three dynasties of Hsia, Shang, and Chou. A famous Hasidic tale recounts the progressive distancing of successive generations from their central religious ritual. A rabbi of the first generation would carry the burden of his people to God by lighting a fire and saying a prayer at a definite place in the woods. In the final era, after the erosion of detail through history, a rabbi sits in his chair and realizes he does not know the prayer, the spot in the woods, nor how to light the fire, but at least can tell the story about how it was once accomplished. Confucius, too, remained hopeful because he could at least reconstruct his people's sacred vestiges of *li*. Master of pragmatic compromise, he attracted conservatives by canonizing the forgotten past, and gradually enlisted progressives by reshaping the legendary past as an innovative criterion against which to measure both present disorder and a past recently repudiated.

The Chinese ideograph for *li* portrays a sacrificial vessel with two pieces of jade raised above it, in the manner of a consecrated chalice elevated for worship during the traditional Catholic Mass, perhaps to symbolize the unutterable threshold between heaven and earth. The connotations of *li* bear the stamp of a wide encapsulated history: liturgy of wine and food offerings to ancestor spirits, then the courtly feudal codes upholding privilege and stability, then thinned out along a spectrum of everyday courtesies, rites of interaction, familial obligations. Perusal of the *Li chi,* "Records of Ritual and Practice," introduces the reader to exact times, gestures, and music required in each specific sacrifice, the hierarchical placement of carriages in a cortege, the customary period of bereavement regulated differently for each surviving family member, a manual of correct dress, bows, honorifics, even ways to cut and serve a melon depending on rank at table. *Li,* then, means appropriate behavior, what the French suggest by words like *politesse, courtoisie, urbanité, les formes, savoir-vivre. Li* suggests images of the charted, predictable life, with the aesthetic balance and elegance of a gavotte, each detail fitting into its proper place.

The Confucian reform insisted first on a recovered fidelity to the rubrics of traditional State and family liturgies of sacrifice. The ritual deed must be matched by a devout state of mind. "I cannot bear to see . . . ritual performed without reverence," says Confucius, and "If someone is not genuinely 'present' at the sacrifice, it is as though there were no sacrifice" (*Analects* 3:12, 26). The second intent of Confucius was to enlarge the scope of reverence and religious seriousness from the specific sacrificial cultus to the realm of every human activity. He reminds the ruling classes, "Deal with the common people as though you were officiating at an important sacrifice; do not do to others what you would not like done to yourself" (12:2). The Golden Rule of ethics is reconnected back to its vital religious roots, so that all of life becomes ceremonial, harmonious, charged with the numinous. There must be one caution, however. "What can someone without *jen* have to do with *li*?" (3:3). In other words, the mere external dance of *li* will hopefully penetrate inside and lead to a conversion of attitude, so that *jen-tao* will animate ritual, and the person straining to act out the father's role, for example, will become eventually a true father. "Let the prince *be* a prince, the minister a minister, the father a father, and the son a son" (12:11). This is what Confucius means by "rectifying names" in the basic husband-wife, parents-children, elder-younger, ruler-subject relationships: the achievement of profound consistency between *li* and *jen,* appearance and actuality.

Widespread counterfeits of *li* today, and a few tendentious emphases in what might be called textbook Confucianism, deserve careful scrutiny. Otherwise, we shall not get beyond these obstacles to appreciate the mature life shaped authentically by *li.* We can observe at least four major distortions.

1. Domination of youth by dead and living elders. Much of Chinese folk piety is centered on befriending clan and nature spirits, tapping their secret knowledge through arts of astrology, geomancy, and augury. Some think this tendency reinforced excessively by Confucius' reinstatement of ancestral rites. Clan gatherings to invoke and feed the ancestors symbolically at gravesites or home altars strengthen not only ties between living and dead members, of course, but also among the living clan. *Hsaio,* originally the term for piety toward dead ancestors, in the Confucian glossary means filial piety toward living parents and elders first of all—then, as a corollary, sustained reverence for their presence after death. "Till you have learned to serve human beings, how can you serve ghosts?" Confucius remarks. "Till you know about the living, how are you to know about the dead?" (11:11).

The mad reversal of Confucian priorities is parodied in Maxine Hong Kingston's memoirs *China Men.* Her cousin Sao in America gets desperate letters for years from his mother in China, complaining of starvation and neglect, begging for a fraction of the cash spent on his television set, refrigerator, and other luxuries. Her ghost finally lashes Sao into a frenzied trip home, where he heaps up extravagant offerings on her grave—gifts of food, shoes, clothes, and paper money. He pours wine on the earth and explodes firecrackers, neglecting not a single Chinese funeral custom. "Rest, Mother, rest," he weeps in guilt, craving to get her ghost off his back.

Among living people, those of age and experience get obvious deference from Confucius. A deserving old age, however, is no mere accumulation of years. Yuan Jang, whom most commentators identify not as some young disciple but as an unmannerly old colleague, sat waiting for Confucius in a sprawling position. "The Master told him, 'In youth, not humble as a junior should be; in manhood, doing nothing worthy to be handed down. And merely to live on, getting older and older, is to be a useless pest.' . . . With this he hit him across the shins with his stick" (13:21; 14:46).

2. Displacement of the religious cultus by a humanistic ethic. Seventeenth-century Jesuits were consistent in their deemphasis on specifically religious features in the Confucian phenomenon, when they interpreted their Chinese missionary experiences back in Europe. The Confucian Tao lacked any of the recognizable European signs of a developed religious creed. To the so-called Chinese Rites Controversy about the compatibility between a convert's new Catholic faith and the old Confucian ancestral rites, one opportune solution was to neutralize the religious Tao into an adaptable Natural Law ethics. Later apologists of the Enlightenment claimed Confucius as an Oriental Voltaire or Sam Johnson, his pert aphorisms a deist argument for the universality of innate human common sense. However, this by no means is the Master Kung portayed at devout worship in our popular Confucian bible, the *Analects*. He performs the rites of ancestors faithfully, offers sacrifices to exorcise illness or purify an army before military expeditions, and repeatedly prays to Heaven and Heaven's Will. This is more than unctuous window-dressing.

Confucius praises the ruler who "by respect for the spiritual forces keeps them at a distance" (6:20). Appropriate exorcism rituals keep away harmful spiritual forces that cause sickness and insanity. Yet this encouragement of ritual has been widely misinterpreted as flippant distancing of it. Perhaps anyone trying to widen the scope of religious experience beyond rites enacted in a specified sacred time and space must expect to be accused of underrating the rites. Locating the numinous everywhere looks suspiciously like locating it nowhere. When Ben Franklin was thanked by the flamboyant Methodist revivalist Whitfield because of hospitality done for Christ's sake, he replied wittily that it was done not for Christ but for Whitfield. Though saints, Franklin reasoned, had the custom "when they received any favor to shift the burden of the obligation from off their own shoulders and place it in Heaven, I had contrived to fix it on earth." I think Franklin and Confucius would treat this situation in an identical hard-nosed way, but Confucius would not risk religious irreverence. The *t'ien-tao* and *jen-tao* must be translated into down-to-earth behavior that balances all the everyday human obligations of *li*.

3. Enshrinement of conservative political traditions from the distant past. Some anecdotes and apothegms collated in the *Analects* reveal a flawed Confucius, insenstive to the dogmatic bias of his own era and caste: "Women and people of low birth are very hard to deal with." Or his disciple Yü upholds training in family piety as the cornerstone of a whole people's obedience to state authority, for "no instance has ever occurred in which such men would start a revolution" (17:25; 1:2). Later Christian theologians strain to disentangle the basic Christian Tao from biblical passages that take for granted a milieu of anti-Judaic polemics, with tacit assumptions about slavery and patriarchal dominance. Similarly, reactionary and reformed Confucians at the end of the last Chinese dynasty in 1911 dredged up quotes from the Master to vindicate both sides to their controversy with each other. Confucian saints now most eulogized were those who because of their integrity had once chosen official banishment. The sacred concept of venerable age had by now become a form of insult. Violent Red Guards of the 1960s pounced on four "olds" as their enemies—old customs, habits, culture, social thought—and tried to root out every vestige of traditional China, a crusade sustained by Mao Tse-tung in his Criticize Confucius Campaign of the early seventies.

The final verses of his poem "Snow" in 1936 express the keynote of Mao's quarrel with Confucius. After paging through a few great historical names, he underscores their deficiencies, and concludes: "Now they are all past and gone./To find heroes in the grand manner/We must look rather in the present." "Past" means the human viciousness that still persists despite all Mao's cultural revolutions—such as family narcissism, the itching for privileged status and money, esteem for mandarin professors rather than workers and peasants, women's enslavement to men. In other words, the loss of genuine *jen*. We are tempted to dismiss this revolutionary cry of pain as the mere pique of a child whipped into grammar-school memorization of Confucian classics. Yet the cry will no doubt be accepted as a strident but relevant half of any future *yin-yang* balanced polity—which also has need for the traditional *chün-tzu* endowments of compromise, moderation, civility, and flexible relatedness.

It is a mistake to view Confucius' Golden Age, the exemplary reign of sage-emperors like Yao, Shun, and Yü, or the more recent Duke of Chou, as nostalgia for an actual historical past. All these figures are simply the transcendent *chün-tzu* moral ideal, etched in the vaguest narrative detail, which could have been projected as a myth of future apocalypse as readily as retrojected back to a mythical genesis. For example, Confucius and many of his contemporaries conjectured with excitement about an expected messiah king (Wang), who would govern purely by force of his own *jen,* and in whose reign "within a single generation *jen* would prevail" (13:12). A later Confucian-Taoist description of the Golden Age of Yao and Shun, or the future Wang-Utopia, occurs in the *Li chi* classic. *Jen*-saints would be chosen to rule, all would treat others' parents as their own, others' children as their own. Widows, orphans, and the childless would be fed by the community. All would have steady work, a stable home. The *jen* and *li* model are the criterion against which every era must be measured.

In 1925 Kuo Mo-jo, Mao's close friend, wrote a short satirical dialogue, "Marx Visits the Ancestral Temple of Confucius." Marx arrives in a red lacquered sedan chair, initially bristling and apprehensive that Confucius and his school will reject Marx's irreligious materialism. His explanation of a classless society proves so idealistic that Confucius approves it with matching quotations from his own utopian dreams, but doubts if Marx has calculated the human cost of its radical implementation. Both thinkers diverge, of course, on one serious issue. Confucius is driven to tolerate inequality for the sake of public harmony; Marx can only demolish any spurious peace that condones injustice.

4. Artificiality and artifice. Castiglione's Renaissance model Courtier depended mostly on the trait of *grazia* to integrate all the other courtly talents. Since ambition and the manipulation of other people backfire by calling attention to themselves, these endowments need the polish of a casual sense of proportion, art that conceals art. Europe's Age of Elegance supplements Castiglione with two cynical yet characteristic definitions of politeness. Sam Johnson calls it fictitious benevolence, and Rousseau a mask of dishonest irony that assumes the appearance of every virtue without the reality of any. For many non-Orientals, the drive to preserve *li* at all costs, the anxiety about gaining, keeping, and losing *mien-tzu,* or "face," promote stereotypes of the inscrutable diplomat, a fawning smile pasted over sinister machinations. Many of us prefer a frank informal relationship that penetrates the social cocoon imprisoning a naked person inside. We assume that the "outside" is evasive facade, and that the person preoccupied with correct social surfaces probably signals distance and indifference to any warm "inside" overtures of friendship.

No facile defense of *li* could make it more accessible to people of the mind-set just sketched, except to discriminate genuine *li* from its distortions, and show how cross-cultural misconceptions often arise from divergent values and social psychologies. We need an expanded imagination of possibilities, which can be stimulated by representative popular fiction like Robert Daley's *Year of the Dragon,* published in 1981. Let me summarize the book in some detail, to show how it explores the vocabulary of face and *li* behind one criminal mask, and tries to usher the reader one notch beyond the poisonous stereotypes of Fu Manchu and Charlie Chan. The character Koy, Cho-kun of the major New York Tong, first appears as a furtive murderer and extortionist, taxing every legitimate business and vice on his Chinatown turf. He is multilingual, urbane, intelligent. The narrative plays cautiously on our empathy, delaying the introduction of his gentle family relationship with young daughters and his second wife. Then it moves backward in time to his plight as a refugee from mainland China, scrounging for work in Hong Kong, his poignant first marriage, to which he still remains somehow faithful. The New York cop, with whom we are initially asked to identify in his pursuit of Koy, proves less scrupulous perhaps than Koy in resolving his own wife-mistress dilemma and his indirect responsibility for others' deaths. Koy takes remarkable steps to preserve face, switching from sweaty hiking clothes and boots, for example, to appear at the Thailand opium king's headquarters in silk suit, Dior tie, combed hair.

The secret behind Koy's daring, his loyalty to friends and wife, is *li,* the word he uses to explain the rigid rules of conduct that have made him prosperous. Returning to his Hong Kong home after fifteen years abroad, he feels alienated from the walls covered with red and gold tablets commemorating the dead and pictures of the gods. Only the aftertaste of *li* remains from all this faded religious tradition. What is not *li* must never be done, even by the criminal. You stipulate the amount of money to be extorted from everyone equally, without preying on just a few, never exceed these demands, and give clients exactly the protection against street marauders and police they paid for. If violence becomes necessary, you order it reluctantly a few removes from yourself, only at the hands of those with a talent for it. Koy is caught finally, not on the murder charge, but ironically because his sense of *li* demands he try to smuggle his first wife and son from Hong Kong into

America. He kills himself, rather than bear the public disgrace of jail or deportation.

I have defined *jen* as the capacity for human-relatedness. Prompted by *jen,* you search instinctively for ways to give others the *li* due them in their assigned high or low, close or distant position, because the group itself, the harmonious system of power relationships, deserves at least as much respect as the individual, if not more. So you bow in deference or dismissal, compliment your dullard son-in-law, attend an unwelcome party. By observing the forms, each person guarantees minimal conditions of security for the others. The possibility of a better relationship at least remains dormant, never lopped off definitively. To be kind implies responding not to the prompting of subjective moods, but to the "outside" situation and conjectured needs of other people. Yet the disciplined Confucian golden mean, as always, lies between extremes of a solipsistic individualism wallowing in sincerity, and a sterile repression of honest feelings. Fidelity to *li* ritual achieved in even one balanced human relationship mirrors and helps consummate Confucius' harmonious cosmology. It also renews the broken continuity between the present community and its past source of religious meaning, portrayed in the myth of divine sages and a Golden Age paradise.

The Chūgi Option

Two images suggest the paradox of *Bushidō*, often called the core of the Japanese national ethos. The first is the bewildered face of Sergeant Shoichi Yokoi, convinced that World War II had never ceased, discovered at last, hiding in a Guam cave twenty-eight years after the Japanese defeat. Military orders had to be obeyed with rigorous literalness; rather a ritual *seppuku* or a solitary burial alive than shameful surrender. The second image captures a *sumi-e* artist leaving a deft casual track of ink over a fibrous piece of rice paper. White space combines with squibbles and blots to suggest a branch of plum blossoms, fragile and evanescent. The Bushidō code somehow animates figures as disparate as the soldier and the artist, a dichotomy that will seem less mystifying the more we investigate it. Yet many of us will still experience disquiet at the eerie, jarring blend of militarism and aesthetics in Kurosawa's film *Kagemusha*. The incredible beauty of armies on horseback in huge symmetrical masses, a rich ocean of blood, silver and bluish glint of steel in the moonlight, multicolored banners flapping in the wind.

From the constellation of Bushidō values, I have chosen *chūgi* as their logical center. *Chū*, the first figure in the ideograph, means humanity, human-heartedness. *Gi* stands for trustworthiness, fidelity, gratitude. For example, the traditional interpretation of a *girigatai* person is someone who fulfills reciprocal social obligations incurred because of generous favor (*on*) from others, but in recent decades means someone of moral responsiveness, alert to the presence of *li* and *jen* in human relationships. *Chūgi* would thus characterize only a human relationship, not the obedience of a dog to its master, for example, and only a bond lifelong and totally committed. Unlike *chūjitsu*, connoting a broad spectrum of loyalties, *chūgi* loyalty means most of all the ritual subjection of vassal to lord or emperor, the fealty common to Christian knighthood and other feudal eras throughout the world.

Attitudes prevalent in Japan since the earliest Shintō legend take classical shape in the seventeenth-century Tokugawa Shogunate as *Bushidō*, code of the samurai warrior class. An early eighteenth-century Bushidō handbook, the *Hagakure*, widely distributed during the decade of ultranationalism before World War II, spells out the truly heroic vows of *chūgi*: "We have sworn to do four things—to be second to none in performing our duty, to make ourselves useful to our lord, to be dutiful to our parents, to do great deeds of benevolence." What distinguishes the samurai's military obedience from that of his European contemporaries—citizens toward their king reigning by divine right, or monks toward their religious superior mediating God's will—is a note of fierce tragic expendability, almost an eagerness to court death as the crown of loyalty. Here are a few sentences from the *Hagakure* that have had the deepest impact: "Bushido consists in dying—that is the conclusion I have reached. . . . Never in my life have I placed my own thoughts above those of my lord and master. . . . Every morning, prepare your mind to get ready to die. . . . When your mind is always set on death, your way through life will always be straight and simple."

Bushidō *chūgi* for most contemporary Japanese smacks of the formal literary past—a militarism officially discredited, the chain reactions of compulsive *on* and *giri* interchanges of favor. It is fashionable for the cinema to mock samurai aggressiveness in the swaggering rogues played by Toshiro Mifune or the sly antiheroic buffoonery of Zatoichi, the blind swordsman. Akiyuki Nosaka's novelette *American Hijiki* implies a more subtle critique of this tradition. The Higgins couple, elderly Americans who once befriended Toshio's wife, Kyoko, in Hawaii, are feted extravagantly on their visit to Japan, at first puzzling and gradually enraging their hosts because they take all this *giri* for granted. Toshio's sense of wounded samurai pride has been unable to forgive his emperor's surrender to that giant MacArthur, or the conquerors' chewing gum and thick muscular hips under glossy gabardine. Now an aging American male casually outdrinks and outmans Toshio, who keeps trying to intimidate Higgins by guiding him through a gauntlet of hilarious sexual athletic events with prostitutes and pornographers. Too late Toshio recognizes the macho malice behind his whimpers to Kyoko about their unrequited rituals of hospitality: "I want to turn this grinning, maddeningly self-possessed son of a bitch on to something—anything—Japanese and . . . bring him to his knees."

The Bushidō military spirit in this century, however, has shown itself remarkably durable. Martial arts and epic samurai "easterns" in the Clavell *Shogun* style flourish worldwide as never before. Even the stylized *chūgi* vocabulary has allegedly been adopted within some Japanese mafia and ultraright political groups. A discipline and esprit almost military, the fealty and fixed hierarchy distinctive to Japanese corporations today date clearly from the rise of the samurai class to *zaibatsu* leadership during the Meiji restoration. Cameras recorded the vivid exit of novelist Yukio Mishima, who penned the manifesto introduction to a new 1967 textual edition of the *Hagakure* that passed through sixteen editions in forty days. He committed his publicized *seppuku* for a nest of conjectured motives, including rage at a disarmed, impotent Japan. It is fascinating to examine today the one book banned by name from governmental circulation, listed in MacArthur's historic 1945 directive to abolish State Shintō. My own 1949 edition of the *Kokutai No Hongi: Cardinal Principles of the National Entity of Japan,* written in 1937, includes a cautionary introduction to what the editor calls blatant official propaganda, garbled by logical inconsistencies he guesses are probably traceable to Buddhist and Shintō mysticism.

The *Kokutai No Hongi* is a teacher's manual for ethics courses to be taught students from grammar school through university. Three of its theses, garnished with quotes from Shintō scholars, are reiterated sharply enough to stand as an outline for our own analysis of *chūgi.* First, the Japanese emperors are divine offspring of two primordial heavenly *Kami,* and therefore must be accepted as fathers of the national family and obeyed with religious fealty. "Reverence for the deities and for the ancestors and the Way of Loyalty are . . . essentially inseparable." This organic harmony among godhead, emperor, people, and land is explicitly distinguished from parliamentary or people's democracies based on Western ideologies of individualism and communism. Second, the book tries to identify family piety and patriotic loyalty. Nominal filial piety, extended beyond personal parents and ancestors to the present emperor, at that moment completes itself as true filial piety. Unquestionably, obedience to the emperor's divine will takes priority in any apparent conflict of loyalties. The third thesis encourages poetry, calligraphy, the tea ceremony, and all the arts to preserve Shintō traditions but with creative originality. The marks of this idealized art are significant: harmonizing with nature; restrained (*wabi*) and self-effacing; elegant, tasteful, serene, reverent. Despite its jingoistic platform, the *Kokutai* syllabus hints at a more comprehensive religiocultural Bushidō heritage which we have not yet examined.

The *Hagakure* vows cited before could be summarized as pledges of *chūgi* loyalty, *ko* (Chinese *hsaio*) filial piety, and *jin* (Chinese *jen*) human-relatedness or concern for others. *Chūgi* isolated from the other two can easily be stripped of its human and numinous overtones. During the Tokugawa period, Confucian scholars like Razan Hayashi and Sokō Yamaga labored to civilize and Confucianize the manners of the warrior caste. They did this by constructing bridges between the rough samurai fighter and Confucius' *chün-tzu* gentleman scholar. A genuine samurai must excel in the arts both of war and peace. "A person who is dedicated and has a mission to perform is called a samurai," says Hayashi; "someone of inner worth and upright conduct, who has moral principles and mastery of the arts." The samurai's only business in society, according to one official Tokugawa directive is "to preserve *giri*," for a land without *giri* lacks justice and a sense of shame. Sokō Yamaga must be recognized as the first great apologist for Bushidō. He synthesized this new ethic in a book called *Shidō* or *Way of the Samurai,* and numbered among his disciples the future leader of the forty-seven Ronin, immortalized in so many legends, especially Chikamatsu's *Chushingura,* the story of a long-patient conspiracy to avenge the death of their lord. Besides fidelity to the five Confucian relationships of lord–subject, friend–friend, husband–wife, father–son, older–younger brother, Yamaga demands that each samurai aspirant try explicitly to reconcile martial arts with civil virtue. "Within his heart," the *Shidō* says, "he keeps to the ways of peace, but outside his heart he keeps his weapons ready for use."

Alongside this Confucian component in Bushidō, Buddhism contributes a strain of monastic austerity and abandonment of the ego, whereas Shintō transforms the entire ethic into something potentially numinous. By this Tao you unite yourself with the heavenly *Kami,* become their child, or emulate great past deeds that transformed heroes and heroines into *Kami*. *Chūgi* is directed first of all toward the *kuni-hito,* a term coined to suggest the *Kami*-animated combined nation and individual person, all in fluid interaction, and toward the emperor or anyone else who symbolizes this *kuni-hito* reality. Loyal response can be described further as *kenshin,* close to the uncompromising surrender implied in the very word *Islām* and the fervor of Hindu *bhakti. Kenshin,* which some world religious traditions render only toward the godhead—such restrictions would seem intolerant according to Shintō belief—is extended also to your family living and dead, your birthplace, nation, and the entire world.

Bushidō loyalty leads at best to the selfless heroism cherished by differing names in most spiritualities of the world. This is embodied in the figure of a wandering lone samurai, ready to protect the poor and exploited, perhaps some of the ugliest human faces representing the sublime *kuni-hito* abstraction. The character Kambei comes to mind in Kurosawa's *Seven Samurai,* leaderless and displaced, struggling to live out his values, organizing a small samurai force to defend a village long pillaged by bandits. In an early scene from the film, he shaves off his topknot, last remnant of his samurai identity, to soothe the suspicions of a thief with whom he must bargain to save a kidnapped baby. The peasants for whom he risks his life show hesitation to organize under his leadership because most cannot imagine protecting any more than their individual homes.

I have mentioned as a second theme in the *Kokutai* the effort to reconcile family loyalty and State loyalty, two of four vows emphasized in the *Hagakure*. This dilemma has always been a nightmare for the conscientious Confucian, forced to sift through the frequently colliding obligations of *li.* A Communist party booklet on "The Correct Handling of Love, Marriage, and Family Problems," published in 1964 by the People's Republic of China for the use of rural cadres, tries to reinforce traditional parental authority against what it interprets as Western bourgeois erosions of the family structure. Yet parents are forbidden to view their offspring as personal property or to encourage children in the grab for selfish careers and money. "To determine whether or not parents' love is true or false," it concludes, "we must see if their opinions accord with the Party's demands upon us." Taijun Takeda in his Japanese retelling of an old Chinese tale, "To Build a Bridge," also attacks myopic versions of Confucian family loyalty. The younger must defer to the elder son's judgment, agreeing to abet his mother's illicit affair with a priest. Torn by loyalty to the home and his dead father's memory, and by obedience to his mother, the elder faces his younger brother's scorn: "Was filial piety a matter of such twists? If his brother was following the teachings of venerable Confucius, then was not Confucius in effect a pimp?"

One searches vainly through Bushidō literature for approval of the rare heroic dissenter, daring to place family before country, *ko* before *chūgi,* or religious conscience before emperor. An unusual anecdote tells of a retainer's decision to die rather than renounce belief in Buddha at his lord's whim. The lord surprises everyone by praising the man's fidelity to his spiritual teacher, surely the best presage of deepest loyalty to his feudal lord. More prevalent seems to have been the exacting model of unquestioning military obedience, remembered especially in "Kirishitan" martyrdoms under the Tokugawa shoguns. In a post-World War II setting, the dying Watanabe of Kurosawa's *I kiru* defies his senior bureaucrats and even the mayor himself to leave behind a playground for deprived urban children, one courageous gesture of worth in what seems an otherwise useless life. The final ironic third of this film uncovers the impenetrable dodges used by his colleagues to diminish the impact of his valor.

It has often been said that pre-Communist China ranked kinship and filial piety above patriotism and, like Japan, seldom allowed room for dissent in the name of some more universal principle. Yet I am convinced that Confucius of the *Analects,* though upholding consistent deference to parents, recognizes nothing higher than loyalty to the Tao itself: "How can someone be said to be truly loyal, who refrains from admonishing the object of one's loyalty?" In another context he says, "What I call a great minister is one who will only serve his prince while he can do so without infringement of the Tao, and as soon as this is impossible, resigns" (14:8; 11:23). The notion of *chung* in Confucian ethics should not be understood simply as personal loyalty toward parents and rulers. It reaches beyond the person exercising authority to the symbolic office itself, and beyond this to all humanity. It is self-devotion, the duty of conscience dictated by the *jen* within oneself.

Loyalty to the comprehensive Japanese *kuni-hito* may displace and redefine the role of family piety, but the filial motif apparently never recedes. Takeo Doi's best-seller *The Anatomy of Dependence* threads together random attitudes unique to contemporary Japan and makes occasional sense of them according to his social psychology of *amae.* The verb *amaeru* connotes a need to be protected, loved, indulged, to feel at home in one's surroundings, to snuggle up to someone, to hanker for the lost symbiotic mother-child envelopment. Doi takes note of Japan's indulgent child-rearing system, tendencies in adult society to differentiate an inner circle of warm *amae*-friends from an outer cold periphery of strangers, and especially the spiritual and social alienation felt by a nation left "fatherless" with the emperor's humiliating defeat in World War II. Emperor, ancestors, and *Kami,* Doi concludes, exist "in a realm beyond the anguish of unsatisfied amae—which is where . . . the essence of the Japanese concept of divinity lies." Recall Freud's reduction of immature religious faith to the projection of a provident Father-God image in order to recover a primordial "oceanic feeling" of symbiosis with the mother, or to compensate for Oedipal hostility toward the father rival. According to the logic of *amae,* then, Shintō and specific patterns of culture and history mutually fortify each other, nurturing in many Japanese what Freud would label an intense positive transference, unsatisfied with *ko* or *chūgi* until the object of their loyalty proves somehow numinous.

The last of the three theses drawn from the *Kokutai* booklet advocates a national art that is disciplined, austere, serene. If we appreciate the samurai as a *chün-tzu* knight, and Bushidō as mastery of arts both of peace and war, then Sergeant Shoichi's refusal to surrender in Guam and the blossoms painted by a *sumi-e* artist are prompted by a single comprehensive vision. Haiku, song, and painting arrest our attention on favorite images of twilight, the fluid pastels of fading seasons, the fall of blossoms, brevity of love and human life. This mood is caught best in the tea ceremony, described in the Shintō tradition as *ichigo ichie,* a ritual encounter "once in a lifetime," where friends must endow the fleeting instant with spiritual intensity, for it might be their last moment together. The *Hagakure* concludes, "Bushido consists in dying," and encourages daily meditation on death to keep life "straight and simple." Constant meditation on death can plunge you into the cherished now, the simple beauty of everyday impermanent things, stripped of all pretense.

Samurai *chūgi* connotes mostly the soldier's life, mobile and expendable in service—an obvious analogue to the aesthetics of fragile impermanence. Habits of military preparedness may condition people to prefer a frugal, disciplined style in art. An emphasis on devoted achievement for one's lord had in postfeudal times led to a spartan achievement-oriented economy, and now disposes many to view their career, family role, sports, arts as a Tao discipline demanding constant improvement.

Ignazo Nitobe, whose *Bushido: The Soul of Japan* in 1899 introduced the West to Bushidō, spent his later days explaining America and Japan to each other, trying to preserve his Bushidō ideal from Japanese militarists who borrowed many passages from his books. A fervent Quaker, active in the League of Nations, Nitobe tried, despite a developing conviction of failure, to force a synthesis between Bushidō, Quaker spirituality, nationalism, and internationalism. His final books, mirroring Japan's historical transition beyond feudalism, turned from Bushidō to self-discipline and the art of living. Persons shape their own deeper personality, not merely conform to some external ethic or guide. Nitobe challenges samurai loyalty to mature into a more authentic Shintō *chūgi,* which he identifies with the Inner Light of Quakerism: "The samurai standard of right and goodness was too often decided by outward human relations rather than by the inward voice of the Spirit."

The Wu-wei Option

Sokō Yamaga, introduced above as the earliest Bushidō apologist, in his *Autobiography in Exile* recounts how books by sages such as Lao-tzu and Chuang-tzu corrected inadequacies from his own Confucian background. The Taoist masters gave him "more life and freedom. The identification of human mental activity with the mystic activity of nature produced deep insight. From that point on I followed the impulses of my own nature; all was spontaneous." It is hard to improve on this summary of Taoist spirituality. Taoist traditions of painting transformed stock river and mountain backdrops in portraits into an independent landscape genre. Tiny pilgrims, hermits, poets, dot huge boulders and mountain forests, and meditate away from the crowded towns. The Taoist master Wang Wei once explained his theory of artistic creativity: "The wind rises from the green forest, and foaming water rushes in the stream. Such paintings cannot be achieved by physical movements of finger and hand, but only by the spirit entering into them."

An enthusiasm for the intuitive rather than the studied mannerly deed, a romanticist identification with nature uncontaminated by civilization, a respect for the simplified contemplative life. Each time anywhere an era seems to neglect these values, prophetic voices in society call for a healing return to beginnings and basics. The label *Taoist* will be used here to identify the elusive declarations of Lao-tzu's *Tao te ching* and the parables and dialogues of the *Chuang-tzu*. Each work, of course, has its own emphases, each has been claimed to antedate the other, but tradition readily combines them both into one Lao-Chuang scripture. Moreover, *Taoist* will not refer to the later Taoist church of history but to the widespread counterculture movement inspired by the Lao-Chuang, in relentless counterpoint to the Confucian establishment. Protest rallies and experimental life-styles of the 1960s come to mind, the greening of America, the same zest for yoga, handicrafts, organic foods, natural medicines, and the criticism of most conventional verities.

Like the Confucian Golden Age of Yao and Shun, the Taoist ideal society was retrojected back to a mythical utopic when the mountains had no trails, the rivers no bridges, and people and nature all lived at peace together. Rousseau, sickening of his century's verbal squabbles and ultracivilized glitter, went so far as to approve the burning of Alexandria's library. He yearned to recover a simple pastoral Eden, forfeited once the viper of private property intruded with its cry, "This is mine!" Chuang-tzu has his own version of the Fall. Once upon a time, you find human beings loving, trustworthy, just, not knowing that they are following the path of righteousness and *jen.* "In the simplicity of an uncarved block they attain this true nature. Then along comes the sage, huffing and puffing after benevolence, reaching on tiptoe for righteousness, . . . snipping and stitching away at his rites. . . .Then for the first time people learned to stand on tiptoe and covet knowledge, to fight to the death over profit, and there was no stopping them" (9A).

A corollary to this insight is Lao-tzu's ironic observation, "The more laws that get promulgated/The more thieves and bandits there will be" (57). I think the argument from both books moves in the following direction. Excessive statutes are more likely to prove oppressive and unenforceable, and thus elicit contempt for even the few creditable laws. Likewise, excessive Confucian preaching about *jen* and *li* could talk the authentic Tao to death, lead people to trivialize it or mistake *jen* appearance for *jen* actuality. With the emergence of self-consciousness and the anxiety to preserve social appearances, the decline from self-preservation to the divisive self-aggrandizement of *coveting* undercuts the original harmony existing between people. Paul's Epistle to the Romans pieces together some psychological conjectures on almost the same dilemma. The Mosaic Torah allegedly piled a moral burden on people without giving the inner power to master this burden. Without the spiritual strength which Christians interpret as the gift of Christ, a person can only despair. "I should never have known what it was to covet if the Law had not said, 'Thou shalt not covet'; . . . but when the commandment came, sin sprang to life and I died" (7:7–11). As Chuang-tzu expresses it, you forget your feet and waist when shoes and belt are comfortable, you forget worries about right and wrong when the heart is comfortable.

The Taoist frame of mind I have chosen to analyze is *wu-wei,* usually translated as not-doing, actionless action, creative inaction, effortless effort. *Wei* means action, and *wu* means no-thing, an absence of perceptible features, or with overtones of mystery and wonder, the Void. As explained earlier in this chapter, *ch'ang-tao,* the Absolute, resists conceptualization, whereas *tao-te* can be broached dimly through analogies (nature, watercourse, valley, mother, energy) or without them (void). This latter apophatic or *via negativa* approach, common throughout world mystical traditions, thinks the numinous sufficiently remote from our ordinary sense categories that we converge on it best by a series of negations separating it from all it cannot be—the In-finite, Im-mutable, In-comprehensible. Chuang-tzu enjoys the playful use of denials in order to back into positive assertions: "I can conceive of the existence of nonexistence, but not of the nonexistence of nonexistence. . . . How could I ever reach such perfection?" (22H).

One brief line from the *Tao-te ching* sums up the full paradoxical impact of *wu-wei*: *"Wu wei erh wu pu wei"* or "No-action yet not no-action" (37). What may appear to be inaction is in reality action, or Tao does not look active but through it everything gets done. From this root insight evolve a multitude of further paradoxes, the axioms for almost every world spirituality. Die in order to live, no self-completion without self-emptying, the soft overcomes the hard and the weak the strong, glory cannot be won except by letting it go, one who know does not speak and one who speaks does not know. Lao-tzu says the Tao is slight and almost without savor. "If one looks for Tao, there is nothing solid to see./ If one listens for it, there is nothing loud enough to hear./ Yet if one uses it, it is inexhaustible" (35). Some aspects of truth are so momentous or so fragile that they can be grasped only through the poetic indirection of parable, myth, and paradox.

The subtle ironic texture of this thinking makes it ripe for conflicts in interpretation, no less by disciple than adversary. To commend simple life-styles, Chuang-tzu tells of a gardener's refusal to use a labor-saving device because "where there are machine worries, there are bound to be machine hearts. With a machine heart in your breast, you've spoiled what was pure and simple" (12 I). Passages like this prompt some to disdain technology, or withdraw as confirmed mountain ascetics, or just live an austere, detached inner life while actively involved in society. There are Taoists in an ecstasy of spirit almost indifferent to the threat of physical death, and others intent to prolong youth and sexual potency through ritual diet, yoga, and various alchemical elixirs of immortality. Nowhere do Taoist interpretations contrast more dramatically than in the arena of practical politics. Does the *wu-wei* attitude promote a stable responsible government or anarchy?

Chuang-tzu devotes his entire twenty-eighth chapter to a parable series in which various kings offer their throne to one scholar and simpleton after another, all of whom wisely turn down the offer. Chaung-tzu refuses political office, too, reluctant to give up his fishing pole, preferring to remain a live tortoise dragging its tail in the mud rather than become a sacred tortoise mummified, boxed, and venerated. Most citizens obey kings and stand ready to die for them, says Chuang; "Then how much more should one be willing to do for the Truth!" (6C). Once he upbraids a minor dignitary for boasting about the huge retinue given him because of court preferment. Physicians get higher payment, the more distasteful their speciality. "From the number of carriages you've got, I take it you must have been treating his piles. Get out!" (32C). A robber seems to offer the most trenchant estimate of China's corrupt political order: "The petty thief is imprisoned but the big thief becomes a feudal lord" (29B).

An apparent contempt for political office and for Confucian clichés of public morality, panegyrics on the contemplative recluse, and the insistence by both Lao and Chuang that nations meet hard aggression by reluctant counterforce, or better, by soft pacifist nonresistance—all this seems grist for dissent, revolution, anarchy. As the slippery old opportunist in Joseph Heller's *Catch-22* explained in Rome to Nately, his patriotic moribund American conqueror, "It's not 'better to die on your feet than live on your knees,' but 'better to *live* on you feet than die on your knees.'" Yet I think every Taoist argument urged thus far can be turned upside down to vindicate the existence of an honest, compassionate government. Much of the *Chuang-tzu* and at least one-third of the *Tao-te ching* yearn for a model ruler who lives the Tao. The attitude of *wu-wei,* prized in common citizens, becomes precisely their best qualification for office. "Only one who has no use for empire is fit to be entrusted with it," says Chuang-tzu, who then explains why the state of Yueh smoked the uncooperative Prince Sou out of his cave and dragged him back to run the government (28A). Those too eager for power are prone to abuse their position in order to gratify compulsive inner needs. The wise, permissive leader, ruling serenely without seeming to rule, must be a balanced, low-profile human king, disposed to rule others only as the leader would expect to be ruled, diffident to rank and glory. We presume here a citizenry of utopian maturity, of course, governed by the inner Tao and able to appreciate such leadership. This empathy and responsibility of the leader toward an entire people is exemplified in Po Chu's amazing reverence for the corpse of an executed criminal. Chuang-tzu describes him wrapping the body in his own royal robes and crying, "The world is in dire misfortune, and you have been quicker than the rest of us to encounter it. . . . They pile on responsibilities and then penalize people for not being able to fulfill them" (25H). And Lao-tzu says, "Only one who takes upon oneself the evils of the country can become a king" (78).

I have developed the theme of Taoist political theory expansively to suggest a pattern for appreciating most Taoist polemics against Confucian orthodoxy. From an abstract history-of-ideas viewpoint, Confucian and Taoist approaches ought to have been capable of rapprochement and mutual adjustment to most of each other's criticisms, since both profess the same ethic of a golden mean and a constantly renegotiated balancing. In the actual record of history, though ideological animosity and debate raged for centuries, assimilation and experimental montage rapidly swept throughout common practice. The parodies of Confucius as stilted, doddering, aloof, effete, hypocritical, the mischievous touches by Chuang-tzu to represent Confucius as groping Taoist convert or even Taoist saint—few critiques seem so explosive that they cannot be turned around to enhance Confucius' *chün-tzu* prototype. The *Analects* had affirmed, "What can someone without *jen* have to do with *li?*" Lao-tzu scrutinized his own society and found too often only the husks of *li*. Confucius and the two Taoist masters agree on the centrality of *jen,* but differ significantly in their estimate of *li*. The Confucian human ceremonial dance of *li* is acceptable to Lao-tzu and Chuang-tzu only to the degree it conforms to the more comprehensive natural rhythms of *wu-wei.*

A spirituality based on *wu-wei* implies two fundamental stages. The first I shall call a negative propaedeutic. Some of Chuang-tzu's most eloquent pages explain this process: "People have to understand the useless before you can talk to them about the useful./. . . You must fast and practice austerities, cleanse and purge your inner mind, destroy and do away with your knowledge" (26G, 22E). Another name for this discipline is listening not with physical ears but with the spirit. For "spirit is empty and waits on things. The Tao gathers in emptiness alone. Emptiness is the fasting of the mind" (4A). The detritus of truly useless habit and cliché must be cleared away, and what has previously been disparaged as useless must be given a new spiritual reappraisal. In the Christian Pauline sense, those thinking themselves wise according to the standards of this passing age must become fools to gain true wisdom. You begin to respect the uselessness of a tree spared by woodcutters because of its age and rot; or of the hunchback Shu, pitied and given the largest dole of grain, waving goodbye to others his own age, who are forced into military service.

The negative features of this propaedeutic have been celebrated in Plato's Socratic dialectic. Socrates cannot begin the search for knowledge until he demolishes the pretentions to knowledge, every shred of false confidence. Teacher and disciple must admit their mutual ignorance before proceeding further together to learn. Socrates' attack can be stinging, and few pages in Plato are more memorable than the plight of some unwary expert tripping over a series of self-contradictions, with the master professing ignorance, the mask of wise Socratic irony. Like disturbing Taoist paradoxes, the dialectical shock tactics of Socrates could be misunderstood by literal minds, quick to bring charges against a teacher for "corrupting youth," encouraging questions irreverent enough to threaten Greece's political and religious authority.

Chuang-tzu calls this first stage "thawing and freeing the ice-bound," stripping oneself down to the condition of an unconscious infant, "its body like the limb of a tree, its mind like dead ashes" (23A). We are warned not to mistake this for the highest stage. You may recall Thoreau's exasperation at those visiting his Walden hermitage, expecting only to find a rebel and reformer forever singing, "This is the house that I built;/ This is the man that lives in the house that I built." Thoreau abandoned noisy Jacksonian politics, machines, cities built on ruins of older cities, taxes and institutions with their dirty, rapacious paws, professors inexperienced in the art of life, philanthropists intrusively doing good without being good. His renunciation of all these things was indeed a criticism of them in the best Taoist tradition. But more important, he intended to simplify life of all this clutter, so that "the laws of the universe will appear less complex, and solitude will not be solitude, nor poverty poverty, nor weakness weakness." He says again, "Not till we have lost the world, do we begin to find ourselves." The log cabin of *Walden* or the jail of *Civil Disobedience* is a sanctuary where one retreats to penetrate appearances, discover real priorities, and then return to the world.

The final stage of *wu-wei* is *tzu-jan,* naturalness and spontaneity, the Natural Way. Not quietism, but action that is relaxed, intuitive, attuned to the *yin-yang* cyclical pattern of seasons and stars, letting the world go, letting others be. This process can be described, too, as a return to original simplicity and harmony, to the Tao that Lao-tzu calls root, quiet, "the always-so"(16). It is not surprising to meet so many fishermen, farmers, and recluses in Taoist literature, or to track most similes back to worlds far removed from civilized human life—baby and savage, silence, wild horses, wood and stone and water. No matter how comprehensive the Natural Way may appear, it clearly excludes attributes like artificiality and artifice, and the will to manipulate, possess, or intrude.

All the reverence Confucians hoped to find animating an authentic life of *li* is expected by Lao-tzu and Chuang-tzu to be channeled into *wu-wei,* and this demands a stunning control and sensitivity. The photographer Eliot Porter, for example, in preparing to capture a flight of birds on film, scrutinizes carefully the habits of a particular bird so that he can anticipate the ideal instant for an exposure. Or he knows a grove of aspens so well that he can plan the time of day and season to capture specific variations in tone and color. His theory is to discover rather than invent—not impose a pattern on nature, but try to compose a picture in such a way that it reveals a design not usually perceived because of distractions. One observes this same receptive creativity in the sculptor who tries to carve with the grain, the poet whose meaning springs uncharted out of half-conscious wordplay, the ballerina whose body dances almost by itself.

Chuang-tzu presents a shrewd psychological sketch of the truly receptive teacher, whose approach to things is "to go along with them and be merry. . . . So there may be many times when, without saying a word, one induces harmony in others; just standing alongside others, one can cause them to change, until the proper relationship between father and son has found its way into every house" (25A). Again, the tutor of a pampered prince is advised: "If he wants to be a child, be a child with him. If he wants to follow erratic ways, follow erratic ways with him. If he wants to be reckless, be reckless with him. Understand him thoroughly, and lead him to the point where he is without fault" (4C). A mother or father, neither controlling nor surrendering control, recognizes the risky balance *wu-wei* implies. No less does the client-centered therapist alert to the art of interpreting without manipulating. Jerzy Kosinski's *Being There,* despite its heavy satire, demonstrates brilliantly the power of this receptivity in the character of Chance the Gardener. Smiling and unthreatening, a retarded recluse, he wanders naively among leaders of American politics and finance. His ignorant silence is misunderstood as deep compliance with any questioner's viewpoint, his literal comments on gardening are inflated into oracular metaphors by the press. As a pliable confidant, he summons the worst but mostly the best out of those befriending him.

The spontaneous rhythms of *wu-wei* are best symbolized in the sacred dance of *t'ai chi.* It allegedly originated in the experience of a thirteenth-century monk, Chang San-feng, who one day noticed a shrike and snake in combat. The bird would swoop down and attack, while the snake in casual sinuous movements managed to escape the line of attack and turn the hunter's force back upon itself. The shrike eventually collided against a rock and broke its neck. One principle behind most of the Chinese and Japanese martial arts is to sidestep your opponents' offensive momentum and reverse it to hoist them by their own petard. In the spiritual martial art of *t'ai chi,* you are both hunter and quarry, the quiet watchful protagonist and, at the same time, the inner resistence to be healed and reintegrated. The graceful movements of *t'ai chi,* numbering about forty basic postures, circling and converging on the body's spinal center of gravity, alternate in a steady cosmic rhythm. Now the gentle receptivity of *yin,* now the assertive creative power of *yang*—a solitary microcosm reenacting the origin of the macrocosm out of Chaos. You dance out expressively the pulse of *tao-te* within, body and spirit, nature and the human person.

FURTHER READING

1. **Texts.** I prefer the Arthur Waley translation of both the *Analects* (Allen-Unwin, 1938) and the *Tao-te ching,* which he calls *The Way and Its Power* (Allen-Unwin, 1934). His annotations and introduction are thorough. Burton Watson's translation of *The Complete Works of Chuang-Tzu* (Columbia University Press, 1968) is lively and accessible. James Legge's translation of the *Li Ki,* vols. 27–28 of F. Max Muller, ed., *Sacred Books of the East* (Oxford University Press, 1885), gives a useful synopsis of the *li* concept in his introduction. See the cautionary introduction in the *Kokutai No Hongi: Cardinal Principles of the National Entity of Japan,* tr. J. O. Gauntlett, ed. R. K. Hall (Harvard University Press, 1949).

2. **Chinese Religions.** D. Howard Smith, *Chinese Religions* (Holt-Rinehart, 1968), and Laurence Thompson, *Chinese Religion: An Introduction,* 3rd ed. (Wadsworth, 1979), chart the growth of Confucian and Taoist movements through Chinese history, with important sections on Buddhist and also Communist China. The single most resourceful work on the evolving history of our *li* concept is Noah Fehl, *Li: Rites and Propriety in Literature and Life* (Hong Kong Chinese University Press, 1971). Max Kaltenmark, *Lao Tzu and Taoism,* tr. Roger Graves (Stanford University Press, 1969), and Holmes Welch, *Taoism: The Parting of the Way,* rev. ed. (Beacon, 1966), summarize basic Taoist teaching and suggest contemporary applications. William Prensky, "Tai Chi: Spiritual Martial Art," *Parabola* 4:2(1979), pp. 68–73, gives a concise appreciation of the discipline.

3. **Chinese Cultural Background.** An indispensable history of cultural transitions is Joseph Kitagawa, *Understanding Modern China* (Quadrangle, 1969). Wolfgang Bauer's *China and the Search for Happiness,* tr. Michael Shaw (Seabury, 1976), traces utopia themes through four thousand years of history; it gives major sections of Kuo Mo-jo's Dialogue between Marx and Confucius, otherwise omitted from his collected works. Two outstanding essays on the

implications of *jen* in constructing a social psychology occur in Wei-ming Tu, "The Confucian Perception of Adulthood," in Erik Erikson, ed., *Adulthood* (Norton, 1978), pp. 113–20; and Yu-wei Hsieh, "The Status of the Individual in Chinese Ethics," in Charles Moore, ed., *The Status of the Individual in East and West* (University of Hawaii Press, 1968), pp. 271–84. A droll essay on "face" is the chapter "Games Chinese Play," in Leon Stover's *The Cultural Ecology of Chinese Civilization* (Pice, 1974), pp. 242–66. Exerpts from current diaries, newspapers, government manuals, useful in assessing how institutions affect different sectors of the Chinese people, are collated in Patricia Ebrey, ed., *Chinese Civilization and Society: A Sourcebook* (Free Press, 1981).

4. **Japanese Religions.** Instructive overviews occur in Masaharu Anesaki's *Religious Life of the Japanese People,* 4th rev. ed. (Japanese Cultural Society, 1970); Fernando Basabe et al., *Religious Attitudes of Japanese Men: A Sociological Survey* (Sophia University Press, 1968); and Joseph Kitagawa, *Religion in Japanese History* (Columbia University Press, 1966). Clear exposition of Shintō and Buddhist concepts and excellent bibliography can be found in Joseph Spae, *Japanese Religiosity* (Oriens Institute for Religious Research, 1971). Jean Herbert's *Shinto: At the Fountain-head of Japan* (Stein and Day, 1967) overwhelms readers with its detail, but the encyclopedic breadth is useful. The socioeconomic impact of Bushidō ethics is explored in Robert Bellah's *Tokugawa Religion: The Values of Pre-Industrial Japan* (Free Press, 1957). Exerpts from Yamaga and other Bushidō writers are collected in Ryusaku Tsunoda et al., eds., *Sources of Japanese Tradition* (Columbia University Press, 1958).

5. **Japanese Cultural Background.** Roland Barthes's *Empire of Signs,* tr. Richard Howard (Hill and Wang, 1982), is a delightful impressionistic glimpse at food, language, faces in Japan. Another popular anthology is T. S. Lebra and W. P. Lebra, eds., *Japanese Culture and Behavior: Selected Readings* (University of Hawaii Press, 1974). The entire collection of articles is valuable, of which Sharlie Ushioda's article is a part—"Man of Two Worlds: An Inquiry into the Value System of Ignazo Nitobe," in F. H. Conroy and T. S. Miyakawa, eds., *East across the Pacific: Historical and Sociological Studies of Japanese Immigration and Assimilation* (Clio, 1972), pp. 187–210. Exceptionally insightful into the Tao of ordinary roles and careers is Thomas Rohlen's "The Promise of Adulthood in Japan," in Erik Erikson, ed., *Adulthood* (Norton, 1978), pp. 129–47. In addition to his *Anatomy of Dependence,* tr. John Baster (Kodansha, 1973), Takeo Doi has managed to apply the concept of *amae* to various situations in other essays.

3

Hindu Dharma

Fielding, the British Humanist in E. M. Forster's *A Passage to India,* elicits a coy, daring remark from elderly Brāhmin Professor Godbole, whose scrupulous sense of caste integrity forces him to dine separately from his colleagues. Godbole learns about the unjust imprisonment of their Muslim friend Aziz for his alleged rape of Miss Quested in the Marabar Caves. Reacting with apparent detachment from Aziz's suffering, he proceeds to distribute guilt indiscriminately to Aziz, himself, Fielding, and anyone else, because "when evil occurs, it expresses the whole of the universe. Similarly when good occurs. . . . Good and evil are different, as their names imply. But in my humble opinion, they are both of them aspects of my Lord." Fielding comments irritably on this aloof, amoral speculation, "And everything is anything, and nothing something."

For many of us, elementary concepts like the *trimūrti, Brahman-Ātman* equation, *saguṇa-nirguṇa Brahman,* presented by textbooks to pin down that abstraction called Hinduism, seem after a short time to blur and dissolve. The Hindu phenomenon caves into Professor Godbole's undifferentiated sinkhole—nothing exists but the Absolute in its whimsical *māyā* disguises. Or at the other extreme, the Hindu tradition is incomprehensibly multiple, an ancient sprawling banyan tree, with myriads of unrelated animals seeking fixed or temporary shelter in its shade. In the United States today, news articles on the cults surrounding exotic swamis, and our repeated contact in air terminals with bouncing saffron-clad Krishna Consciousness acolytes, succeed in expanding our awareness of Hindu spirituality beyond an image of sedate Vedanta Society seminars and bookshops. Until this recent reassessment, Śaṅkara's philosophy of Advaita Vedānta seemed to reign with unquestioned authority, interpreted by Vivekananda and his familiar neo-Vedānta Ramakrishna Mission as the sole Hindu orthodoxy. Many of us knew only the Hindu Dharma outlined in *Bhagavad Gītā* commentaries, and the few Upaniṣadic classics quoted by Thoreau, Schopenhauer, and T. S. Eliot.

I suggest we try to view the kaleidoscopic Hindu phenomenon as comprehensively as possible—neglecting neither its esoteric tradition of a progressively intensive God-consciousness (*samādhi*), nor its numerically more dominant exoteric traditions of myth, dance, moral duty, and worship in home or temple. Since Hindus lack formal creed and an institutionalized religious authority, the brilliant Śaṅkara can act as their limited spokesman, but so can Rāmānuja, Mādhava, and other medieval scholastics, the *bhakti* poet Kabīr or the activist Gandhi, and a few contemporary swamis. Hindu pluralism is too diffuse and complex to be sized up under the single lens of Advaita Pantheism (world and godhead identical) or Dvaita Panentheism (world and godhead distinct but inseparable). Centered, of course, on the great Vedic and Upaniṣadic scriptures, we must not underestimate the spiritual authority of the *Bhagavad Gītā,* the *bhakti* heritage of later Purāṇas, and the ancient widespread tantric oral traditions.

In any dialectic of the One and the Many, it seems wisest to begin by acknowledging the empirical Many, and then painstakingly to search for some plausible framework of unity. Surely from the beginning, one cannot but be overwhelmed by floods of Hindu divinities, separate religious sects, revered *gurus* and *sādhus.* I shall try to organize this abundance under four categories—many *Dharmas, sādhanas, mārgas,* and *pūjās.*

Many Dharmas

The diverse religious groups flourishing in their land for centuries are summed up loosely by Indians themselves under a single protean family name, the Dharma, which they prefer to the term *Hinduism.* From the root *dhṛ,* meaning to uphold or hold together, this word bears the historical tidemarks of two millennia in its wide usage. Roughly parallel to the Sino-Japanese concept of Tao, which the Dharma notion, mediated by Buddhist missionaries, helped to deepen and enrich, *Dharma* can be defined today as dynamic cosmic order, mirrored in the driving force of conscience within each individual. Aurobindo's Advaita system describes it as the law of the Absolute within us, the ideal pattern of social relations enabling each being to realize its divine capacity.

In the earliest centuries, Dharma meant most of all the Hindu common-law tradition or *varṇāśrama-dharma,* based on the Laws of Manu and other sacred Dharma Śāstras, which apportion moral responsibilities, depending on each person's specific caste (*varṇa*) and developmental stage of life (*āśrama*). According to Manu, one can reconstruct true Dharma in any era by discerning the behavior "followed by those learned in the Vedas, and what is approved by the conscience of the virtuous who are exempt from hatred and inordinate affection" (2:1). *Varṇāśrama-dharma,* like the Mosaic Torah and Muslim Sharī'ah, has generated its own historical line of fundamentalist interpreters crystallizing custom, and of developmentalists searching for emergent pattern and value behind custom.

Largely through influence of the Buddhist reform, later Hindu scholasticism introduced the concept of *sanātana-dharma,* eternal and transcendent Law—similar to Aquinas' *lex aeterna–lex naturalis* correlation. *Sanātana-dharma,* then, achieves hallowed but only provisional embodiment in human *varṇāśrama-dharma.* To render sacred *varṇāśrama-dharma* more malleable, some interesting ploys had been adopted by earlier legalists, groping toward an implicit *sanātana-dharma.* Employing a developmental theory of four successively declining eras (*yugas*) of history, some scholars conjecture the *yuga-dharma* levied on mankind during the Golden Age must be different from the more compassionate *yuga-dharma* operative in this present *Kali-yuga* era, so depraved that it could undermine moral defenses of an even more heroic era. Our first impression of this *yuga* theory might contradict facile generalizations about Eastern cyclical time versus Western linear time, until we encounter the guess that *Kali-yuga* lasts 432,000 years.

A second way to modify strict *varṇāśrama-dharma* is called *āpad-dharma,* equivalent to the *epikeia* principle in Roman canon law. In times of serious adversity, we are released from ordinary legal obligations, for it can be argued that sacred law never intends the morally impossible. Satyajit Ray's film *Distant Thunder,* for example, tests the relaxation of caste law during the critical 1943 Bengali famine. A pampered, fastidious, caste-insulated Brāhmin priest-doctor begins to discover his repressed humanity. His traditional sanctuary and privileges no longer tenable, Ganga and his wife gradually submit, welcoming into their pure Brāhmin home an endless march of famine victims. A third device of flexibility is *svadharma,* meaning one's own innate destiny and duty. Each individual soul, of course, bears a *karma* residue accumulated by previous rebirths. We meet a cognate notion to *svadharma* in Gandhi's famous *svarāj,* or self-rule, the right of individuals and nations to govern themselves. In this present life one should uncover one's own unique *svadharma,* the criterion by which all extrinsic obligations must be finally measured, for what may be right for one person is not always right for another. This insistence on intrinsic identity—and its implied program of situation ethics—evolved probably to counterbalance influential Hindu theologies that seemed to engulf each individual soul within the cosmic *Brahman.*

The Hindu tradition is usually extolled for its pacificism and inclusiveness, its prodigal toleration of religious differences. Yet Hindu critics themselves call attention to the blind disdain and repression enshrined in caste distinctions, even today, and the outrage of modern hostilities among Muslims, Sikhs, and Hindus that match our cruelest religious wars in the West. Still, we can register these harsh impediments to toleration and learn more admiration for the efforts of contemporary Indian courts to reconcile the colliding demands of inherited *varṇāśrama-dharma,* the *svadharma* of individual conscience, and the ethics imposed by thousands of divergent religious sects. In the *Kijab* v. *Sanji* case (1965), for example, the courts ruled against Muslims killing a sacred cow in full view of protesting Hindus. Even though cow slaughter was legal in Assam, the deed seemed intended to wound religious feelings and disturb public order. Yet judges dismissed the case of *Ahmad* v. *the King* (1949), in which an accused Muslim claimed Allah in a vision urged an Abrahamic sacrifice of his five-year-old son in a mosque. One day the courts decide an ancient dowry obligation must be fulfilled, even in contemporary India; another day an Untouchable can no longer be excluded from worship in a Brāhmin temple.

Given these complex circumstances, the measure of compromise and tolerance commonly achieved seems commendable. The way has no doubt been smoothed, more by some particular Hindu mind-sets than by others. First, the *svadharma* theory accepts harmonious juxtaposition of separate monads, each governed by its own laws, and demands only that rights of the wolf do not infringe upon rights of the sheep. Second, Vaiṣṇavas are especially open to endorse saints from any other religious tradition as possible *avatāras* of their god Viṣṇu. Third, various schools of Advaita Vedānta tend to interpret apparent religious differences as an illusion, or at least a provisional limit that will disappear as we all converge toward higher *samādhi.* "Wherever I look, I see people quarreling in the name of religion," says Ramakrishna. "But they never reflect that he who is Kṛṣṇa is also called Śiva, and bears the name of Primitive Energy, Jesus, and Allah as well—the same Rāma with a thousand names." Since the *Brahman* of the Upaniṣads transcends all of its *iṣṭa*s, or god-manifestations, every revelation and image necessarily falls short. No *iṣṭa* deserves preferred or exclusive public dominion.

Guru Authenticity

A superb formulation of *sanātana-dharma* occurs in the lengthy *Bṛhadāraṇyaka Upaniṣad.* This myth gives the finale of T. S. Eliot's *The Waste Land* three onomatopoeic Sanskrit words to suggest sounds of thunder, and three possible avenues of release from spiritual sterility. At the end of their first *āśrama* period as *brahmacārin* disciples, the gods and devils and human beings ask the Creator-Guru for a sacred *mantra.* The syllable assigned them for meditation is *da,* which each group interprets variously as *damyata* (discipline), *dayādham* (mercy), and *datta* (giving). The parable concludes, "The divine voice of thunder repeats the same. Da, da, da . . . Therefore let that triad be taught—discipline, giving, and mercy" (5:1). It is significant that Dharma in this Upaniṣad as in most of the others emerges from living dialogue between *guru* and *dvija* (twice-born disciple). To appreciate this relationship, so crucial to Hindu spiritual practice, we shall analyze its demands, first within the conventional Brāhmin *āśrama* structure, and then more variably within the *āśrama*-communities of contemporary *sādhus,* those aspiring toward *samādhi.*

Early Hindu tradition divides each life cycle into two phases, the first devoted to gradual involvement in the world, the second to gradual detachment from it. World involvement requires a twelve-year apprenticeship period for the *brahmacārin* (celibate student) to study the Vedas, develop a mature moral identity, and train for a profession. Next follows the *gṛhasthya* (householder) stage, a time to marry, become a productive citizen and parent, and support generously those in the other three *āśramas.* Stages three and four of world detachment are far less institutionalized. The *vanaprastha* (forest-retiree), a solitary individual or married couple pledged hereafter to celibacy, cedes career and family responsibilities to the next generation, withdraws to cultivate the contemplative life, diminish bodily needs, and expand caste and kin hospitality to include all living things. The *saṁnyāsin* (*saṁnyāsa,* complete renunciation) gives up home, possessions, caste, religious ritual duties, and even personal name to pray alone or within some religious community, awaiting death and *mokṣa* (liberation from *saṁsāra* rebirth cycle).

Until a male from the top three castes receives initiation into the *brahmacārin āśrama,* his birth status is only biological, like that of the lowest caste. If he were to remain uninitiated beyond requisite age limits, the Laws of Manu would treat him as an outcaste. The celebrated *upanayana* or Sacred Thread ceremony transforms him into an acknowledged *dvija,* formally ready to begin Vedic studies, born into a life of new social and spiritual duties. Among the steps in this elaborate ritual, a few symbols seem especially meaningful. The boy is dressed only in a loincloth when introduced by his father to the *guru.* Calling him by name and commending him to the care of various gods, the *guru* touches the boy's head and breast to signify his full acceptance of the student. In the same way that wives in their marriage rite mount a stone to promise fidelity to their husbands, so the student takes a pledge on stone to his *guru.* If a putative Brāhmin, he is then invested with the sacred thread over his left shoulder—this is both a magic charm for protection, a chain binding him to his new caste identity, and a badge which must be stripped off before performing any future actions that might endanger caste purity. As directed by the *Paraskara Gṛhya Sūtra,* his *guru* touches the *dvija*'s heart, saying, "May your pure heart ever hold me dear. . . . Under my direction I place your heart. Your mind will follow my mind. In my words you will rejoice with all your spirit. May the godhead unite you with me" (2:4,1).

During their long *brahmacārya* together, spent usually in the *guru's* home, the *dvija* studies and meditates, tends the sacred fire, and helps the *guru*'s family with housework. One can piece together an idealized scenario of these years by paging through the Laws of Manu, representative of society about 200 B.C.E. and after, with its quaint directives on proper gifts for the teacher, methods of Vedic study, and cautions against seductive women, masturbation, and standard frivolities. A true disciple even anticipates the commands of his teacher, obeying him as "the image of Brahman, . . . as his father and mother" (2:266,144). He should never dress more fashionably than his teacher, nor rise later and go to bed earlier than he. "Controlling his body, speech, senses, and mind, let him stand with joined hands, gazing at the face of his teacher." There are amusing warnings against nicknames behind the *guru*'s back or parodies of his walk and speech. Even when the disciple hears proper criticism spoken against the *guru,* "he must cover his ears or depart to another place. By censuring him, even justly, he will in his next incarnation become an ass; by falsely defaming him, a dog; . . . by envying his merit, an insect." The next two wise injunctions seem to stretch the tradition beyond narrow boundaries of caste and fixed authority. "One who possesses faith may receive pure learning even from a person of lower caste; . . . even from a child, good advice; even from a foe, lessons in good conduct." And the disciple's profound docility itself might prompt him someday to outdistance the conscious mind of his master: "As one digging into ground with a spade obtains water, so an obedient student obtains knowledge which lies hidden in his teacher" (2:192,200,238,218).

Another possible interpretation of the hidden knowledge mentioned above emerges when the reader finds a Veda teacher cautioned to adopt a facade of ignorance, and "rather die with his knowledge than sow it in barren soil. . . . Unless asked, one must not explain anything to anybody, nor answer someone who asks improperly" (2:113,110). Sacred wisdom, in other words, must not be profaned by indiscriminate dissemination. Or, as Freud observes, wise therapists, like the Socratic teacher, do not show off, overwhelm, or threaten by their knowledge, but time their interventions to coincide with the client's independent verging on insight, groping for an appropriate concept or myth. The *guru* must try to teach with "sweet and gentle words" and "without giving his student pain." Most important, how the *guru* lives, as well as what he teaches, must be exemplary to students. He merits their reverence only for his wisdom and holiness, not for white hair, wealth, and status.

It is difficult to determine how strictly a present-day Hindu follows this *brahmacārya* model and the entire *āśrama* sequence. We cannot differentiate in texts like the Laws of Manu between utopic blueprint and common practice. At any rate, the *āśrama-dharma* tradition has focused mostly on males, and exclusively on the top three castes. Today this tradition still survives in many rural joint family systems, and in orthodox Brāhmin families almost everywhere, but with less frequency in urban settings. Most students enroll routinely in large State institutions, and the ritual *āśrama* progression often shrinks to the predictable routine decisions about when to marry or retire.

Yet even this fading tradition has left its imprint. In most contemporary Hindu society, stages in the Eriksonian life cycle tend at least to be separated by recognizable rites of passage, celebrated and sacramentalized by custom. Other styles of life are plausible options alongside those of wealth and workaholism. And the homeless ascetic, adolescent student, or retired grandparents living at home are less often required in this society to justify their distinct identities. The widower Jagan in R. K. Narayan's *Vendor of Sweets,* for example, after days of meditating on the *Gītā* and sitting at his Gandhian spinning wheel, decides finally to bequeath candy shop and house to his irresponsible son, and join his swami-sculptor friend in a deserted park. This resolution is greeted in the village of Malgudi as something consistent, sanctioned, and not particularly eccentric: "I will seek a new interest—different from the set of repetitions performed for sixty years. I am going somewhere, not carrying more than what my shoulder can bear. . . . I am a free man. . . . Everything can go on with or without me."

The *āśrama* system, too, can introduce order into the juxtaposed laughter and tears, and ongoing rites of death, puberty, marriage, and childbirth occurring almost simultaneously within the extended family structure. This collage of differing rhythms in life is presented with mastery in the *Apu Trilogy* of Satyajit Ray, which follows a boy's climb toward adulthood, with each gain along the way accompanied by loss, including the deaths of the five people closest to him. A characteristic scene in the first film centers on the expanding consciousness of young Apu, surrounded by three generations of women—his mother scrounging for meals, his sister eager to marry, and his parasitic grand aunt. Here are four destinies at differing levels of growth, separate but somehow entwined.

What today largely replaces the relationship between *brahmacārin* and Brāhmin Veda teacher, and to a certain extent the formal *āśrama* stages, is a bond stemming from another ancient tradition, which cuts across *varṇa* and *āśrama* distinctions. This is the relationship between an adult *chela* (novice) and the *sādhu* selected as spiritual guide. The *sādguru* may have initiated a unique emergent fellowship, or may represent explicit ordained authority in some long-established sect. *Brahmacārya* and *saṁnyāsa āśramas* can be combined into lifelong service under a chosen *sādguru,* and also into renunciation of the world to live in a quasi-monastic setting. The *gṛhasthya* option can be preserved, too, which implies partial commitment to the *guru*—a life of active family and professional duties, with peridoic *āśrama* retreats and conferences to retain contact with the *saṁnyāsin* mystique. The *dīkṣā,* or rite of initiation into a *guru*'s fellowship, often borrows rebirth symbolism from the ancient *upanayana* rite. *Gurus* may invest disciples with the sacred thread, or garlands and prayer beads. They may assign an ocher garment and a *daṇḍa,* the robe and staff associated historically with *śaṁnyāsin* hermits. They may give a secret *mantra,* or merely a significant touch or glance, somehow transmitting the presence of God-consciousness. In fact, many disciples speak of a miraculous *śaktipat,* the experience of an electric shock of power radiating from the *guru* at this instant in the ceremony.

My description of the *sādhana* relationship between *chela* and *sādhu* thus far touches only the commonplaces of most world spiritual traditions. There are the lay retreats, spiritual director, monastic fellowship and obedience, even the twice-born rite of solemn religious vows. What is distinctive about the Hindu *sādhana* relationship—and especially controversial in the Western World today, after the Jonestown slaughter and countless investigations into exploitative cults—is an aura of exclusive attachment, even slavish worship, surrounding the person of a *guru*. Many *bhaktas* in their daily *pūjā,* removing a Kṛṣṇa statue from the tabernacle for bathing, feeding, and worship, unfold a white cloth containing the mark of their *guru*'s footprints, and bow in adoration. Some rapt *chelas* delight in hyperbole: "Our *guru* is greater than god [i.e., the *iṣṭa* or theophany] because he leads us to God [*Brahman*]." Yet, on reflection, this Hindu rhetoric seems open to no more abuse than the clichés of Christian monasticism—obey blindly, submit like a dead body or a walking stick, bow to God's will in the superior's command. Devout Advaitins, convinced of their own identification with the cosmos and godhead, show consistency by extending this sacrality to include their *guru*. Claims like "God sent me," "I am God," and "God is my *guru*" can function in any culture as a pseudo-Nietzschean criminal alibi, a megalomanic lament, or a plausible affirmation of faith.

Few indictments of *guru* cults reach the savagery of Ruth Prawer Jhabvala's *A New Dominion,* an Anglo-Indian novel with characters so rapacious or gullible that they at times strain belief. Banubai, renowned female *guru*, after welcoming an Indian college student into her *āśrama* promptly falls in love with him as a Kṛṣṇa image and reincarnation of her own son. Popping candy into his mouth, fondling him on her lap, she makes him her regressive prisoner. Nearby, Swamiji, a rival male *guru,* reduces three alienated American women to serfdom, the first a mechanical white mouse, the second dying of hepatitis but unwilling to seek medical help without her master's permission, the third repelled but masochistically enthralled by his efforts to tame her will and rape her. The author's ironic raisonneur is Raymond, an unassertive British visitor, who registers only the flat empirical details of Swamiji's manipulation, the girl's illness, and Banubai's jealous infatuation. The novel's most effective satire is the Indians' naive complaint that Raymond sees only the outer person, but cannot grasp by Western conceptual categories the intuited spiritual explanations they offer for their deluded behavior. While Raymond dines in public with Swamiji, for instance, we pick up Raymond's hawk-eyed appraisal of the *guru*'s voluptuous eating habits, eyes roving, the obvious preening as various admirers glance over. Raymond listens patiently to plans about setting up *āśramas* in America, and feels alarmed at the insensitive way Swamiji plays with the question how *gurus* can tell when someone should be broken and remade. "New dominion" in the title underscores this tyranny by Hindu religious frauds, unconscious like Banubai, malevolent like Swamiji, over both India and the West, supplanting the earlier overt British dominion over India.

It seems to me that authentic *gurus,* like true prophets, are not easy to distinguish from their counterfeits. Perhaps the ideal *guru* is reluctant to accept the role, both its glory and its oppressive responsibility. Swami Rajnishji of Bombay once remarked that there must be disciples who own up frankly to their ignorance, reaching always toward further self-realization. But India today has deteriorated into a land of almost no disciples, only *gurus.* Convinced they have attained the goal, *gurus* itch to commercialize their secret. Too many demand that *chelas* love them exclusively as spouse or mother. However, when only the disciples' good has been at the center of the *sādhana* relationship, "they come to you and learn and feel reverence, then go to someone else and learn and feel reverence, . . . then the whole life becomes a guru, . . . and everything becomes a point of reverence. . . . When the guru has been at the center, the guru has failed the disciple." A model *guru,* in the tradition of classical psychotherapy, should not want disciples to cling or merge, but to uncover their own inner *guru,* and resolve the intense positive transference relationship. This deference toward the *chela's* integrity has been expressed in some *dīkṣā* ceremonies by the master's prostration in front of a trained candidate before bestowing the final *mantra*: "Now you have become a god, and now I am worshipping you." Sustained reverence for the *chela* has no place in its dictionary for manipulative arrogance, or a prying violation of the human heart.

"Do you think it is easy to be someone's guru?" is the self-serving question Swamiji raises with Raymond. "To take over this responsibility so that the other person need do nothing but have trust and faith, . . . and say 'now I am yours, take me, do what you like with me . . .'?" Swami Jyoti of Pune believes an outer *guru* is needed only by some of us, and then perhaps just temporarily, in order to animate the inner *guru* dwelling in us all. He prefers the modest attitude his own teacher adopted: "If anybody has the feeling that I am his guru, then, yes, I am. But I am nobody's guru. I am of service." What begins here as his teacher's apparent assertion of professional diffidence ends up a deep redefinition of role. It seems you form an implicit pact to leave the everyday *saṁsāra* world and enter a *guru*'s visionary world to reach *samādhi.* Yet you and the *guru* both must be responsible partners in a relationship that could prove harmful because either or both might have chosen unsuitably. The wise *chela* must resist projections from those with the neurotic need to dominate; the wise *guru* must resist even more subtle projections from those with the neurotic need to submit.

It may be helpful to distinguish between transcendental guruhood and its manifestation in some particular teacher. "The guru is a power," says Swami Ānanda of New Delhi. "The Guru-Śakti lives in the particular person who, himself at some time, was a disciple of a guru, so that he knows the psychology of a disciple." While yet a *chela,* Ānanda always used to challenge his own master, accepting him as friend and *guru,* but not as God. Now he expects the independent *chela* to follow his own example, scrutinizing all *gurus'* claims of succession from an accredited *samādhi* tradition and demanding coherence between their words and their life. And one should not rush to apply spiritual labels onto *sādhana* behavior before it is analyzed with some psychological sophistication. "The false *guru* market is growing because the false disciple market is growing," Swami Muktananda shrewdly cautioned. People want a *guru* no different from themselves, to give them instant *samādhi* without discipline and prayer, to dance and drink and take drugs with them, to practice therapy on them. "It is very good to be mistrustful of *gurus,* because in this way we exercise our discrimination and learn how to choose a real *guru.*"

The ideal teacher has been defined perennially as someone able to catalyze the self-teaching process in students, and also one who never gets in their way. Similarly, a famous *sādhu,* celebrating his *guru*'s feast day, once explained to his colleagues, "Because this man refused to be my *guru,* I began to learn. And now I venerate him." Gandhi in his autobiography tells of a Jain jewel merchant who befriended him on his return from England to India. Gandhi felt attracted to him as a spiritual guide, but "in spite of my regard for him I could not enthrone him in my heart as guru. The throne has remained vacant and my search still continues. . . ."

Comprehensive Mārga

The average Hindu home often contains portraits of *gurus* and other prominent human figures called *deśikas,* a term used in Hindu iconography to distinguish concrete historical people from *iṣṭa* god images. Some few stereotypes recur, reflecting the three classical pathways of Hindu religious life: the contemplative (*jñānin*), seated in solitary yogic trance; the activist (*karma-yogin*), with busy gestures animated by liturgical, family, civic, career duties of the second *āśrama*; and the rapt enthusiast (*bhakta*) beyond caste or sex distinctions, a carefree Indian troubador chanting and dancing for the gods. Before we trace the convergence of these three streams—called *mārgas, yogas, vādas,* or *yānas*—in the complex personalities of Ramakrishna and Gandhi, we must first clarify each type in its more heightened embodiment.

A favorite *deśika* contemplative is Śaṅkara, systematic theologian of Advaita Vedānta in the early ninth century, often pictured meditating in the lotus position, one hand raised in teaching, the other holding a book. The trident marks on his forehead identify him as a disciple of Śiva, patron god of ascetics; his staff, water bowl, and mendicant garb are those of a *saṁnyāsin.* The lack of a sacred thread on this Brāhmin confirms his *saṁnyāsin* transcendence of all former *varṇāśrama* privileges and responsibilities. In popular legend, Śaṅkara is an *avatāra* of Śiva, who sought human form so he could discredit theologically the errors of Gautama Buddha, whom many Hindu syncretists had astutely reclaimed as a reformer *avatāra* of the rival god Viṣṇu. Thus, Śaṅkara is usually seated on Śiva's distinctive sacred tiger skin. Śaṅkara's mother represents conventional Viṣṇu worship, the desire for a married son and worldly *gṛhasthya* values. Her son chooses to leave home as a celibate Śaiva *saṁnyāsin,* returning only to bury her. Śaṅkara confuses her with deathbed lectures about Advaita theology, and sings hymns to Śiva. But as heavenly spirits identified by Śiva's trident mark swoop down to guide her spirit, she remains stubbornly inconsolable until her son complies with a dutiful hymn to Viṣṇu. Despite Śaṅkara's teaching on the acosmic identity of everything with *Brahman,* and the superiority of *jñāna-mārga,* he still respects each person's preference for Viṣṇu, Śiva, or other *iṣṭas*; but these remain only a propaedeutic to higher *samādhi* and world renunciation.

Our second type, the *bhakta* ecstatic par excellence, is Kṛṣṇa Caitanya, sixteenth-century founder of the Bengali sect that indirectly inspired the contemporary Krishna Consciousness Movement. As a young man, after his first wife's death, he experienced a religious conversion that left him intoxicated ever after with the name of Kṛṣṇa. In street parades with roaring crowds that unnerved their Muslm rulers, he would dance and sing to the music, chanting "Hare Kṛṣṇa, Hare Kṛṣṇa, Hare Hare!" again and again in a crescendo of sound and speed, until many could feel an explosion of religious frenzy. This experience of Kṛṣṇa-Śakti pulsing through the blood meant salvation by the healing power of his love. Many Vaiṣṇavas worshiped a reincarnated Kṛṣṇa in Caitanya or saw in his frequent swoons, tears, and laughter a lovesick Rādhā yearning for the presence of her Lord Kṛṣṇa. Although Caitanya lived into his late forties as a tonsured *saṁnyāsin,* his *deśika* image usually catches him at the moment of conversion as a young white-skinned Brāhmin husband with sacred thread, shoulder-length hair, his feet in a gentle dance step, eyes uplifted, arms flailing, hands holding wooden clappers to beat a tempo to the march. Contrasting this blissful Kṛṣṇa-consciousness with Śaṅkara's palid *jñāna* union with *Brahman,* one Caitanya-Caritāmṛta passage derides the latter as stale water puddles gathering in the hoofprints of a sacred cow.

The third idealized figure in our typology is the *karma-yogin,* best represented by the anonymous Brāhmin who bathes and offers sacrifice in early-morning *pūjā* before leaving home for work. Yet standard Hindu iconography seems more fascinated by the paradox of the reluctant activist, a *saṁnyāsin* like Vinoba Bhave, torn away from *samādhi* trance to become the Walking Messiah, with his picture on a 1952 cover of *Time* magazine. To offer a traditionalist alternative to both capitalism and communism, Vinoba led massive marches from one village to another to collect voluntary grants of four million acres for land redistribution and to call for a decentralized India of loosely federated units, each with its own cottage industries and village assembly. There are popular snapshots of Vinoba in glasses, *dhotī*, and white beard, raking an *āśrama* vegetable garden, or marching briskly with hordes of the poor, or seated at his spinning wheel. We find all the familiar Gandhian gestures of fast, nonviolent march, public prayer, sit-in—but, in my opinion, without the shrewd political touch and flexibility of Vinoba's master. Like Śaṅkara and Caitanya, Vinoba has become an *avatāra* to many of his followers, and permits them to call him Vāmana, the fifth incarnation of Viṣṇu, a symbol remarkably evocative of Vinoba's redistribution campaign for the dispossessed. In one myth, the dwarf Vāmana requested three paces of land from a king, whose outrageous ambition had driven him to annex even the home of the gods. Once his wish was granted, Vāmana sprouted into the enormous proportions of Viṣṇu, took two paces that covered the whole earth and heavens, and reclaimed all misappropriated land again for the gods. Declining to take his third pace, Vāmana gave the king dominion over hell, the only space remaining.

With *mokṣa* as the principal aim, which of these three *mārgas* is the most certain and direct means? This question arises with ceremonial regularity in Hindu spirituality, just like the active-contemplative conundrum in traditions of the West. The resourceful ways of handling this question interest us as much as the question itself. The *svadharma* response is that our question as posed is specious, for each person has a unique destiny, and therefore a unique *mārga* to achieve that destiny. Assess your own temperament and needs, experiment seriously with *jñāna, karma,* and *bhakti* approaches, adopt what seems most suitable now, and perhaps modify it at some later reappraisal.

A second answer has already been implied in the established *varṇāśrama-dharma* sequence, followed with or without *bhakti* fervor—two *āśramas* of *karma-mārga* world involvement, followed by the final two *āśramas* of *jñāna* world withdrawal. Socialized within this framework, the average twice-born male hopes to pass through all four *āśramas* to savor a complete human destiny. Not without some ambivalence, many Hindus honor the celibate *chela* for following the more perfect *mārga,* heroically foreshortening a normal *āśrama* progression to anticipate the renunciation that lies ahead for everyone. For example, the great *sādhu* Ramana Maharshi of South India once, as an adolescent, held his breath, foresaw the details of his final cremation, and decided to renounce the body and reach God-consciousness now, since only his soul could survive the inevitable pyre.

Another answer to this question is to insist on the primacy of *jñāna,* by which you pierce the world's veil of *māyā,* repudiate ignorance and ego-attachment, and rediscover your total identity with *Brahman.* This viewpoint has its renowned pedigree in Śaṅkara's Advaita Vedānta, among other schools. Strictly conforming to the traditional *varṇa* system, Śaṅkara expected all Untouchables (*śūdras*) and women, forbidden by law to study and meditate on the Vedas and Upaniṣads, to follow the less perfect *mārgas.* Later Advaitins like Vivekananda argue that most of us in the present *Kali-yuga* can cope only with the scaled-down demands of *karma-mārga.* For Vivekananda, an activist monk of the Ramakrishna Order, engaged work in a *māyā*-bound world does not mean joyful creativity and freedom so much as frustration, suffering, and duty.

The *mārgas,* according to a fourth approach, can be perceived as three aspects of a single *samuccaya mārga.* I have borrowed this term from Kalidas Bhattacharyya's recent efforts to identify widespread generic adversaries against his own conviction that "the further one proceeds along the cognitive, the actional, or the emotional path, the further these three diverge: cognition, seeking to discover the self, looks more and more inward; action proceeds more and more outward; and emotion, unable to be at peace with either, alternates between the two." He objects to a contrived *mārga* synthesis that distorts and slurs over disparities. Yet I confess to an awareness of worse distortions in the exaggerated clarity of my typology above, trimming and boxing the complex figures of Śaṅkara, Caitanya, and Vinoba. The *mārgas* come down to us as a triad mostly because three different historical traditions flourished separately, beginning to merge by the time of the *Bhagavad Gītā*. The *bhakti* stream, flowing outside caste boundaries, stems from popular devotional cults, myths, early tantric literature. Emphasizing first the ritual deed, and then later in the Axial Period, a more explicit ritual-moral deed, the *karma-mārga* stream comes from the Vedas and Upaniṣads. *Jñāna* derives from earliest yoga ascetical traditions, the Jain and Buddhist reforms, but especially the Upaniṣads. The further that Bhattacharyya's three *mārgas* diverge, the more authentic they seem to become. On the contrary, my own conception of the *mārga* synthesis predicts self-parody in the one-sided pursuit of any *mārga*. But *mārgas* merging centripetally are more likely to draw creative influence from one another. In the trifaceted *samuccaya mārga,* once you select one aspect as your principal aim, the other two become essential means. For the highest *karma* and *jñāna* are actually permeated by *bhakti,* and *bhakti* and *karma* are the fruition of a most unwavering *jñāna*.

The fifth and most authoritative attempt to reconcile the three *mārgas*—a position, I believe, that approximates my own solution above—occurs in the *Bhagavad Gītā,* the central text on which almost all major Hindu thinkers, especially Śaṅkara and Gandhi, have written their own partisan commentaries. Without amassing elaborate textual evidence, I shall try to summarize my own interpretation of the god-charioteer Kṛṣṇa's answer to his cousin Arjuna's dilemma: "If your thought is that vision (*jñāna*) is greater than action (*karma*), why do you enjoin on me the terrible action of war?" (3:1). The following is Kṛṣṇa's fourfold argument: first, *jñāna* or yogic concentration is an excellent way, but only for those capable of following it profoundly (12:3–5,9–10). Second, not just by *karma* alone, but by *niṣkāma-karma*—action detached from the selfish desire for results and reward, somewhat similar to the Taoist concept of *wu-wei*—you can reach all the aims of *jñāna* (3:7,18–19,30–31;5:7–14). Third, *jñāna* can be distorted by pursuing it in too negative or one-sided a manner: "Not by refraining from action do people attain freedom from action; not by mere renunciation do they attain supreme perfection" (3:4). Fourth, the dilemma as initially stated, stressing only your own efforts at *jñāna* and *karma,* sidesteps a more crucial issue, the need for God's grace to prompt and sustain any initiative you take. In the spirit of Mahāyāna Buddhists and Augustinian Christians Kṛṣṇa demands the "yoga of union," a *bhakti* loving surrender to God, as the basis for knowledge and action. "Those who set their hearts on me and ever in love worship me with unshakable faith, these I hold the best yogis. . . . If you are not able to practice yoga concentration, . . . then take refuge in devotion to me, and surrender to me the fruit of all your work . . ."(12:2,10–11).

To exemplify the *samuccaya mārga* or the *Gītā*'s yoga of union, we shall examine the lives of two multifaceted Hindu saints, the nineteenth-century mystic Ramakrishna and the modern activist Gandhi—a stunning convergence of *jñāna-bhakti* in the first, of *karma-jñāna* in the second. In most neo-Vedānta hagiography, Śambhu Chadra or Ramakrishna is presented as the ideal Śaṅkara-Advaitin, realizing at last his complete identity with undifferentiated *Brahman,* after an apprenticeship of many years through various tantric and *bhakti* practices that evoked in him unsatisified cravings for the highest *jñāna.* Careful reading of the Boswell-like Mahendranath Diary in the *Gospel of Shri Ramakrishna,* prefaced by Nikhilananda's thorough biography, I think, provides a richer, more accurate portrait. His tantric identification with the *Śakti* life-force of Kālī, his recurring *bhakti* "mad" periods of thirst for Kālī, Kṛṣṇa, and Rāma—these are not mere overtures to Advaita Vedānta conversion, but the continuous basis for his realization that "the whole world is filled with God alone."

As a paradigm of his mature vision, notice the context of Ramakrishna's trance in the presence of Anglo-Indian friends on December 6, 1884, two years before his death. He had just been acknowledging errors in all spiritual paths. "Everyone thinks his watch is right, but as a matter of fact no watch is absolutely right." Then he plunged into the God-intoxicated state of *samādhi,* to the amazement of his listeners. After a few moments, he regained partial consciousness and began an ecstatic dance, concluding with his forehead bowed to the ground, and said, "Salutations to the *jñānīs, yogīs,* and *bhaktas!* Salutations to all!" Repeated passages confirm his eagerness to reconcile all the *mārgas,* and, resisting Śaṅkara's oversimplifications, to integrate *samādhi* trance with the loving service of Śakti-Kālī. Addressing the mother goddess, he says, "Mere knowledge of Advaita! I spit on it!" And again, "Mother, don't make me unconscious through the knowledge of *Brahman.* . . . A million salutations to the knowledge of *Brahman!* Give it to those who want it. . . . Let me remain in contact with men. Don't make me a dried-up ascetic. I want to enjoy your sport [*līlā*] in the world." To the *jñānin,* the world is a "framework of illusion." Yet the *bhakta* sees it as a "mansion of mirth. . . . He has realized both aspects of God, personal and impersonal. . . . It is a joy to merge the mind in the undiversified *Brahman* through contemplation. And it is also a joy to keep the mind on *līlā,* the relative, without dissolving it in the Absolute." In Ramakrishna's thought, *līlā, māyā, Śakti, Kālī,* and *Brahman* are all identified.

The *guru* Totapuri is often viewed as the Advaita culmination in a progessively important sequence of mentors moulding Ramakrishna's spirituality. The Master thinks otherwise: "Once I fell into the clutches of a *jñānī,* who made me listen to Vedānta for eleven months. But he couldn't destroy the seed of *bhakti* in me. No matter where my mind wandered, it would come back to the Divine Mother." It is deceptive, by the way, to translate these habitual Bengali references to "Divine Mother" into the English "God," as some of Ramakrishna's Western apologists have done, especially when we read of his final dying words, "Kālī, Kālī, Kālī!"

One repeated Ramakrishna image is the flowing ocean of *Brahman,* solidified by influence of the *bhakti* moon into ice-block individual *iṣṭas,* more manageable for common worship. When asked if renunciation is the best way to *mokṣa,* he compares world involvement to the Indian game of Nax, in which you cannot remain a player unless you score below seventeen points. "Why should you renounce everything? You are all right as you are, following the middle path—like molasses partly solid and partly liquid. Do you know the game of Nax? Having scored the maximum number of points, I am out of the game. I can't enjoy it. But you are very clever. Some of you have scored 10 points, some 6, and some 5. . . . The game can go on. Why, that's fine!" The *karma-yogin* involved in the world must still try to attain God-consciousness by habitual prayer, even occasional solitary retreats: "With one hand hold to the lotus feet of the Lord, and with the other do your work." Elsewhere he says, "If you but realize God, you won't see the world as insubstantial. One who has realized God knows that God himself has become the world and all living beings. When you feed your child, you should feel that you are feeding God. You should look on your father and mother as veritable manifestations of God and the Divine Mother, and serve them as such." His biographer, Nikhilananda, remarks that Kālī asked Ramakrishna not to be lost in featureless *Brahman* but, like a Bodhisattva, to remain on the threshold of ordinary consciousness for the sake of mankind.

In other words, Ramakrishna brings to his own pantheistic or panentheistic position a distinctive *bhakti* and tantric emphasis, so world-affirming that it cannot be reduced to Śaṅkara's style of *advaita-jñāna.* Furthermore, if you follow him day by day from private *samādhi* to some spiritual conversation at the theater to enjoyment of a circus or birthday party, you sense a person relaxed with the world. The later Ramakrishna Mission hospitals and soup kitchens are often explained as Vivekananda's Americanized organizing innovations, a sort of Pauline adaptation of the original charismatic impulse, or as neo-Hindu Christian imports. But I have suggested more obvious Hindu roots to his compassion and activism, both in Ramakrishna's personal life and in his teaching. The details of his *bhakti* and tantric devotions will be presented later in this chapter.

The unique synthesis of political activism and religious discipline in Gandhi, too, is usually traced beyond an endemic Hindu context to his British legal education, and the influence of Ruskin, Tolstoy, and Thoreau, sources he acknowledged in his autobiography. The surprising triumph of Attenborough's film *Gandhi* has recently occasioned a few reviews quick to argue how unfeasible such a synthesis looks to the American pragmatist. Gandhi's tactics of nonviolence, perhaps too polite to deter Hitler or a nuclear apocalypse, are assessed independently of what seem quaint, cranky Hindu obsessions about cows, vegetarian diet, celibate *kuṇḍalinī* strength, clean toilets, and utopian agricultural communes. Yet it seems perverse to dismantle a coherent political theology based so obviously on Gandhi's ruling axiom, that "politics bereft of religion is absolute dirt." He saw the moral life as essentially integral. You cannot do right in one area of life while doing wrong in another; you cannot use hateful violent means to achieve a loving nonviolent goal. National *svarāj*, or self-government, is attained precisely the same way required for each individual's *svarāj*. For this reason, Gandhi suspended his nonviolent *satyāgraha* campaign after the Rowlatt Bill riots in 1919 because he judged his followers were not sufficiently trained in prayer and renunciation: "I had called on the people to launch upon civil disobedience before they had thus qualified themselves for it. . . . It would be necessary to create a band of well-tried, pure-hearted volunteers who thoroughly understood the strict conditions of Satyagraha."

Any authentic Gandhi disciple is challenged to live out the unsettling paradox of an activist *saṁnyāsin,* as we observed before in the career of Vinoba Bhave. In *Gandhi's Truth,* Erik Erikson gives some attention to Gandhi's inadequacies as a father and husband, the vow of celibacy between Gandhi and Kasturbai as an effort at wider communal intimacy, and his lifelong suspension between second and third developmental *āśramas*. Gandhi's autobiography gives his own rationale for celibacy: "If I wanted to devote myself to the service of the community in this manner, I must relinquish the desire for children and wealth and live the life of a Vānaprastha—of one retired from household cares."

To prepare for the prospect of beatings, imprisonment, the mobility and flexibility demanded of freedom fighters, Gandhi urges his *gṛhasthya* volunteers to follow his own example, detaching themselves from family, possessions, and career: "First, an aspirant after a life devoted exclusively to service must lead a life of celibacy. Secondly, he must accept poverty as a constant companion through life. He may not take up any occupation which would prevent him or make him shrink from undertaking the lowliest of duties or largest risks." One must expect to suffer, but with heroic spiritual resignation, not bitterness. "I want you to feel like loving your opponents, and the way to do it is to give them the same credit for honesty of purpose which you claim for yourself. . . . I know this requires a detached state of mind, and it is a state very difficult to reach."

Frequently, Gandhi appeals to the *karma-yogin* ideal, especially its *niṣkāma karma* attribute, from his favorite Hindu scripture, the *Bhagavad Gītā*. Criticized for the apparent liberties taken in his *Gītā* commentary, he defends his attempt to breathe new life into the Hindu tradition, which itself is an evolving divine revelation. "I have endeavored, in the light of a prayerful study of the other faiths of the world, and what is more, in the light of my own experiences in trying to live the teaching of Hinduism as interpreted in the *Gītā*, to give an extended but in no way strained meaning to Hinduism, not as buried in its ample Scriptures, but as a living faith. . . ." The words *God* and *truth* are convertible terms in Gandhi's theology, and for the sake of what he calls "the Religion which transcends Hinduism, . . . which binds one indissolubly to the truth," he is ready to dismiss or radically reinterpret stock Hindu practices like animal sacrifice, erotic temple rituals, the taboo of Untouchability.

According to this same hermeneutic, the nonviolent Gandhi scales down the *Gītā*'s civil warfare, approved by Kṛṣṇa, to a mere allegorical spiritual combat. Although Gandhi's public use of the nonpartisan term *God* implies a shared Hindu-Muslim-Sikh religious heritage, yet he seems unaware that his Hindu sectarian *bhakta* preferences might alienate many Muslims. For example, his favorite *Rāma-Nāma* prayer becomes his last spoken word; *Rāma-Rāj* is a royal title from the Purāṇas he applies to the future Indian millennium; *Vaiṣṇava dharma* is the term he uses to describe his own faith. "The popular notion of bhakti is soft-heartedness," his *Gītā* commentary states, "telling beads and the like, and disdaining to do even a loving service, lest the telling of beads . . . might be interrupted." But Kṛṣṇa says, "If even I were lazily to cease working, the world would perish. How much more necessary, then, for the people at large to engage in action!" Gandhi thinks the *Gītā* has transformed earlier Vedic connotations surrounding words like *sacrifice* and *saṁnyāsa*. Now the noblest sacrifice is "body-labor for service. . . . The *saṁnyāsa* of the *Gītā* will not tolerate complete cessation of all activity. The *saṁnyāsa* of the *Gītā* is all work and yet no work. . . . The most excellent way to attain self-realization . . . is renunciation of the fruits of action."

In perhaps a conscious imitation of the Pauline hymn on charity, Gandhi defines a *niṣkāma* activist as the self-realized dispossessed person "without selfish desire," someone versed in action yet "unaffected by it, who renounces all fruit, good or bad, who treats friend and foe alike, who is untouched by respect or disrespect, . . . who does not go under when people speak ill of him, who loves silence and solitude, who has a disciplined reason. . . . He who is ever brooding over results often loses nerve in the performance of duty." The Gandhian Vinoba recounts a myth about the Goddess of Prosperity Lakṣmī's offer to her prospective wedding partner: "I shall garland only the man who has no desire for me!" No one could qualify except Viṣṇu, lying peacefully on his serpent, before whom Lakṣmī now sits, stroking the feet of the only man who does not hanker after her. This Hindu paradox of renunciatory world involvement is the axis of Gandhi's spirituality. "I have felt that the *Gītā* teaches us that what cannot be followed out in day-to-day practice cannot be called religion," Gandhi concludes. There must be "no line of demarcation between salvation and worldly pursuits."

Pūjā Mosaic

The hard-nosed test of Hindu tolerance is its ability to manage with relative serenity the motley traffic of festivals, pilgrimages, parades, and temple liturgies that center on an astounding 300 million gods selected from one of the richest mythologies in the world. The Advaitin, as indicated before, views this cloud of *iṣṭas* simply as the resourceful predicates of one *Brahman,* not as distinct substantives. *Brahman* is *nirguṇa* (beyond attributes), but tolerates both the need and preference of an average worshipper to address the more recognizable face of *saguṇa Brahman* (with attributes). In his most famous prayer, Śaṅkara apologizes for visualizing in contemplation the formless *Brahman,* praising in hymns the ineffable *Brahman,* visting in shrines the omnipresent *Brahman*.

Hindu theologians have devised other formulas to harmonize apparent disparities in worship. The *trimūrti* triad looks like a strategy by Brāhmin apologists to reconcile their Vedic Brahmā cult with popular extracaste movements surrounding the non-Vedic gods Viṣṇu and

Śiva. *Brahman,* "the Lord God," states the *Viṣṇu Purāṇa,* "though one without a second, assumes the three forms respectively of Brahmā, Viṣṇu, and Śiva for creation, preservation, and dissolution of the world." Each god has his female counterpart, his personified *śakti.* However, the *trimūrti,* and especially the Brahmā-*iṣṭa,* have left just negligible imprints on Hindu art and worship, and though defensible theologically, do not reflect the three dominant public traditions in worship and devotion—Vaiṣṇava, Śaiva, and Śākta. A more unsuccessful, and patronizing, ecumenical effort by Brāhmin theologians has been called *pañcāyatana pūjā* or the Fivefold Pūjā, introduced for the five most widespread religious sects, each with its different *iṣṭa.* Assigning a god's name to each of five stones on a metal tray, you place your sect's god-stone at the center, and arrange the others at cruciform points of the compass. Sharing in common worship, each sect in turn rearranges the stones to symbolize its relative priorites.

The broad term *pūjā* spans the common forms of worship available to all Hindus at home or temple, including meditation, dance and communal hymns, and especially *mantras* and petitions directed to physical or mental images of a god. No dramatic dichotomy need be drawn between the *pūjārin*'s devotion or ritual on one hand, and an activist moral life on the other. Many *bhakti* theologians denounce the *karma-yogin*'s preoccupation with good works and *karma*-merit. However, as already noticed, Gandhi stressed an activism stripped of hankering, and Ramakrishna, in rapt surrender to Kālī's grace, tried at the same time to detect and serve her image in others. Again, the ancient Vedic Brāhmin sacrifices of *soma* and fire, as caricatured by later Buddhist and Vedānta reformers, often seem decadent ritual transactions. Yet the *Śatapatha Brāhmaṇa,* for example, gives a touching expansion of the sacrificial rite into a pervasive code of life, just as Confucius revitalized the *li* ceremonies. In a vivid myth, the one godhead is broken into many pieces by the act of creation, and can regain power and unity only as these human pieces offer gifts, sacrificing their separate existences. "The sacrifice to Brahman consists of sacred study. . . . Man *is* the sacrifice. . . . As soon as Man is born, his whole person is to be regarded as a debt owed to death. When he performs sacrifice he is purchasing himself back from death" (III-6-2:16;I-3-2:1).

The most popular *pūjā* tradition is simple veneration of a *pratīka* or *iṣṭa*-image, but often this leads to effusive iconophyllic rites of welcoming, invoking, bathing, clothing, and feeding it. The *pratīka* deserves only the most passionate human response—gestures and attitudes of a devoted child or mother, servant, lover. It is interesting to recognize similar rituals of obeisant hospitality and *darśana* (awesome encounter) accorded both *pratīka* and *guru,* for both figures mediate the divine presence. When discussing masks and mime in the first chapter, we noticed the performer's extraordinary suggestibility, an openness to ecstatic possession by the identity and numinous power represented in each mask. Hindu *pūjā* demands the same resources of dramatic identification. You bathe the feet of a Kṛṣṇa statue to remove dust from his long journey to your home; a retinue of temple priests garland a Kālī statue and wheel her carriage to hold royal *darśana* and enjoy an outing. Tantric masters wisely recommend adopting not just the role of Arjuna or Rādhā who love Kṛṣṇa, but of the conniving Śiśupāla who despises Kṛṣṇa, in order to face and perhaps exorcise our inner rage and rebellion against the godhead. One familiar rite preparatory to *pūjā* is called *nyāsa,* in which you touch parts of the *pratīka* with fingertips or palms, and then recite a *mantra* while touching corresponding points in your own body—a graphic technique to internalize the divine *Śakti* pervading the *pratīka.*

Most of Ramakrishna's Victorian apologists dismiss as temporary madness, or suppress the embarrassing details of, his eccentric *pūjārin* identifications during the years of *bhakti* and tantric training. In early adolescence he had formed a troop of actors and played famous Purāṇic roles, so after his conversion, as a priest in Kālī's temple, it is not surprising to find him imitating the monkey Hanuman, ideal servant of the god Rāma. To immerse himself in the selfless role of Hanuman, Ramakrishna spent months perching in the trees, eating only roots and fruit, and with part of his loincloth dragging like a tail, hopping instead of walking. In a later phase, after receiving a metal *pratīka* of the child Rāma from a wandering Vaiṣṇava monk, he became absorbed in nursing and playing with it. Visions soon occurred of Rāmlāla dancing, plucking flowers, begging to ride piggyback, and so Ramakrishna began to view Rāmlāla and the whole universe with a mother's tenderness. Just as the ecstatic Caitanya would at times adopt the dress and womanly gestures of yearning Rādhā, so Ramakrishna during this period assumed the feminine identity of Kālī's handmaid.

In his eight years of Tantra initiation, Ramakrishna trained strenuously to reach an even more heightened identification with Kālī. Here the goal is to shatter conventional barriers between sacred and profane, and to realize that one's entire body, even those experiences viewed by orthodox Hindus as most repulsive and defiling, is nothing but divine Māyā-Śakti. "In that state I sometimes ate the leavings from a jackal's meal, food that had been exposed the whole night . . . ," Ramakrishna told his disciples. "Sometimes I rode on a dog and fed him with luchi, also eating part of the bread myself. I realized that the whole world was filled with God alone."

These florid mimetic forms of *pūjā* are a nightmare to the aniconic temperament throughout the West, but also within the Hindu tradition itself. Statues in popular Roman Catholic piety that shed purportedly real blood or tears, plaster Madonnas to be kissed and stroked, the crowned Infant of Prague vested in a changing wardrobe of costly silks—these prepare our imagination somewhat for the extravagances of Hindu *bhakti*. Yet some of us can never appreciate the affectionate care lavished on a *pratīka,* until we first measure the same *pūjārin*'s care extended toward *gurus,* impoverished strangers, and the whole numinous world. Besides this pragmatic touchstone of coherence between inner and outer life, a few traditional safeguards have been endorsed by many Hindu reformers. They first recommend simple aniconic stone forms, such as Viṣṇu footprints or the Śiva phallus. Or if more vivid anthropomorphic forms are desired, then some expressive many-armed collage might be suitable, or a highly stylized human torso. Or the *pratīka,* like many African masks, can be carved from or painted on material of planned obsolescence, so that each *pūjārin* can be conditioned to distinguish *Śakti* from its replaceable embodiment. R. K. Narayan in his short story "Such Perfection" retells the iconophobic legend of a sculptor laboring five years to carve a lifelike *pratīka* of Śiva Naṭarāja (Lord of the Dance). Horrified at a glimpse of the completed work, a Brāhmin priest warns him, "This perfection, this God, is not for mortal eyes. He will blind us. At the first chant of prayer before him, he will dance, and we shall be wiped out. Take your chisel and break a little toe or some other part of the image, and it will be safe." But the sculptor refuses to comply. Whirlwinds, lightning, and floods pummel the village, and there is no peace until the providential crash of a tree, uprooted by the storm, happens to snap off a toe of the sculpture. By this time, even the sculptor has concurred, "The image is too perfect."

Another spiritual deterrent is the rite of *prānapratiṣṭhā,* by which the vital breath (*prāṇa*) or soul of an *iṣṭa* is invoked and infused into the *pratīka* to be consecrated. Reciting *mantras,* the priest touches all senses and limbs of the *pratīka,* blessing them and asking that each part become a dwelling for the sense life and *Śakti* of the god. Similarly, an obsolescent *pratīka* can be deconsecrated by the rite of *visarjana* before the materials are destroyed. In addition to these public rituals, the eminent Indologist Ananda Coomaraswamy cautions the individual *pūjārin* to say prayers of invocation (*āvāhana*) and dismissal (*visar-*

jana) in order to bracket every sacred *pūjā* occasion from ordinary time and space. The godhead does not come and go, but our projections do; outside formal *pūjā* times, the *pratīka* is best treated as just a devotional utility, no more sacred than any other object. "By invocation he announces to himself his intention of using the image as a means of communication . . . ; by dismissal he announces that his service has been completed, and that he no longer regards the image as a link between himself and the deity." In contemplating the form of Śiva Nāṭarāja, for instance, the cosmic dance and songs and tinkling bells must eventually be discovered within one's own heart. *Nādevo devam yajet* is an old Hindu aphorism—only by inner identification with a god can one worship a god.

Hindu *pūjā* remains vulnerable to abuse and misrepresentation, then, for its graphic identifications, but also for its polytheistic dispersal of focus. The clutter of *pratīkas* in many Hindu temples presents some outsiders a showcase of divine chaos. Yet rumors of chaos have been known to enhance the mature religious vision. First, they may testify to the existence of a distinct *svadharma* for each person, and also a *sva-pūjā* and *sva-iṣṭa,* for the godhead manifests no more of its reality than the limited grammar of each person's imagination and conceptual system can handle. A second advantage is suggested by William James in *Varieties of Religious Experience*. James affirms the possibility of many gods, mostly because he takes seriously his multiverse theory of personal monads, each of us experiencing a unique religious revelation. An orderly monistic and monotheistic system, he fears, might succumb to a craving for logical coherence, and trim away some of the mystery, rich indeterminacy, and tragic ambiguity in a complete numinous experience. For some temperaments, the ambivalent gentleness and savagery of fate can be imagined effectively in a godhead split into personified attributes, sometimes at war, sometimes in shifting alliance.

Perhaps *henotheist* describes better than *polytheist* the Hindu tendency to adopt a single traditional *iṣṭa* without excluding the existence of alternate *iṣṭas*. Scarcely any interest is shown in constructing an orderly pantheon of gods. For centuries the followers of Viṣṇu, Śiva, and Kālī have so expanded their gods' attributes to match claims of rival gods, that now perhaps most of them worship a single functional godhead under a few favorite names. This syncretistic accumulation of attributes, a measure of religious tolerance, and the Hindu passion for completeness combine to produce a truly exuberant art and mythology. No doubt the average *pratīka,* created by artists unwilling to temper their completeness of vision, can end up grotesque, disjointed, and garrulous. Yet it often has enough tension and imaginative power to assert a bold *coincidentia oppositorum.*

Mythmakers of the world strain to capture the vital dialectic in Otto's description of the sacred as *mysterium tremendum et fascinosum*—simultaneously an object of shuddering awe and loving ecstasy. The recurrence of mad, stunning events is the ususal way the *mysterium* proves it can never be contained within the framework of one-dimensional normal human kindness. In Judaic religious experience, God's loving fidelity guarantees his covenants, but his wrath, irrational and terrifying, sometimes erupts to make him regret and smash all guarantees. The Book of Job dramatic dialogue, for instance, portrays a benign trusting Creator, confronted by a doubting, manipulative Satan doppelgänger, both combining to form one complete godhead, which imposes suffering that we think humanly undeserved. In his *coincidentia oppositorum* notion, Nicholas of Cusa perceives God as absolute completeness, the principle of reconciliation that transcends and enfold all opposites in perfect balance—like the Tao underlying an emergent *yin-yang* duality. By immersion in these tragic antinomies that pervade God's interactions with the world, the mind, in a trusting leap beyond them, may intuit the God described by Scotus Erigena as "opposition of oppositions, the contrary of contraries."

At any rate, Hindu iconography and myth handle this religious dialectic with casual brilliance. Kālī, for example, may be the gentle Mother cherished by Ramakrishna, but she is also the dark lady with four arms, two raised to bless worshippers, two holding weapons and the severed head of a giant. With a necklace of skulls and earrings of infant corpses, she dances out of control, threatening to destroy the cosmos. The benign Viṣṇu beckons with a conch shell in one hand to welcome devotees, a flaming discus in the other to demolish those who turn away. Even affectionate young Kṛṣṇa is first a darling but mischievous child, then a trickster adolescent teasing his lovers and disrupting marriages.

Vaiṣṇavas are said to dwell mostly on the *fascinosum,* Śāktas on the *tremendum* aspect of the *mysterium.* Śaivas focus on the colliding synthesis itself, either in a riot of images or in bare aniconic design. Śiva, the paradoxical god of both fertility and *saṁnyāsin* celibacy, savior and destroyer of the cosmos, haunts cremation grounds, dresses in wild animal skins, smears himself with ashes. The *Śiva Purāṇa* tells how he once destroyed demons with fire from his third eye, the eye of *samādhi* vision. But this healing fire soon takes on a life of its own, raging out of control in the villainous guise of Jaladhara, which returns as a destructive force to threaten the existence of Śiva's redeeming force.

Jung has said that the multiplicity of gods and the multiplicity within each god corresponds to multiplicity within the human Self. "The ambivalent god-image plays a crucial part in the *Book of Job*," he says. "Job expects that god will, in a sense, stand by him against god. . . . The unavoidable internal contradictions in the image of a creator-god can be reconciled in the unity and wholeness of the Self as the *Conjunctio Oppositorum* of the alchemists or an *Unio Mystica*. . . ." Jung's concept of polycentric wholeness is a psychological description of the *mokṣa* sought by Vaiṣṇavas, Śāktas, Śaivas, and also by Advaitins. Advaitins remind us of the *Brahman-Ātman* that is undifferentiated, whereas *bhaktas* by their graphic *pūjās* and *pratīkas* remind us of the *Brahman-Ātman* that is polycentric.

FURTHER READING

1. **Overview.** The best descriptive bibliography is David Dell et al., *Guide to Hindu Religion* (Hall, 1981); and specifically on the topic of *bhakti,* Eleanor Zelliot, "The Medieval Bhakti Movement in History," in Bardwell Smith, ed., *Hinduism: New Essays in the History of Religions* (Brill, 1976), pp. 143–68.

The short encyclopedia entries on rites and themes are an indispensable guide in Benjamin Walker, *The Hindu World,* 2 vols. (Praeger, 1968); Margaret and James Stutley, *Harper's Dictionary of Hinduism* (Harper and Row, 1977); and the more popular Edward Rice, *Eastern Definitions* (Doubleday, 1978), though flawed by Rice's incessant diatribe against Western missionaries.

Robert McDermott and V. S. Naravane, eds., *The Spirit of Modern India: Writings in Philosophy, Religion, and Culture* (Crowell, 1974), gives a first-class selection from recent thinkers on major themes such as *dharma, karma-yoga,* aesthetics. John Koller, *The Indian Way* (Macmillan, 1982), has three fine chapters on the *Gītā* and devotional Hindu forms; David Kinsley, *Hinduism: A Cultural Perspective* (Prentice-Hall, 1982), illustrates his material by biographical sketches of Caitanya, Ramana Maharshi, Śaṅkara, and Gandhi.

2. **Reassessment of the Esoteric Hindu Tradition.** Begin with Huston Smith's explanation of his predilection for the esoteric rather than exoteric traditions in his influential writings, as recorded in John Loudon, "The Meaning of Tradition: A Conversation with Huston Smith," *Parabola* (Winter 1976), pp. 80–91. A landmark essay is Walter Neevel, Jr., "The Transformation of Shri Ramakrishna," in B. Smith, op. cit., pp. 53–97, which distinguishes the *bhakta* and tantric influences from the Advaitin reconstructions by biographers. Robert Minor, "Shri Aurobindo's Integral View of Other Religions," *Religious Studies* 15 (September 1979), pp. 365–77, shows how Aurobindo's limited Advaitin view of Hindu and other faiths undermines his attempt to syn-

thesize all religious traditions. See the discussion following Kalidas Bhattacharyya, "The Status of the Individual in Indian Metaphysics," in Charles Moore, *The Status of the Individual in East and West* (University of Hawaii Press, 1968), pp. 47–63, where Bhattacharyya criticizes non-Hindu apologists' equation of Advaita Vedānta with Hindu orthodoxy. Arvind Sharma, "Some Misunderstandings of the Hindu Approach to Religious Plurality," *Religion* 8:2 (Autumn 1978), pp. 133–54, searches for non-Advaitin formulas to account for Hindu tolerance. The conflict between *jñāna* and *karma mārgas,* and the evolving attitudes toward labor, receive interesting development in Ursula King, "Who Is the Ideal Karmayogin? The Meaning of a Hindu Religious Symbol," *Religion* 10 (Spring 1980), pp. 41–59.

3. **The Dharma.** A massive, outstanding work is Raymundo Pannikar's *The Vedic Experience: An Anthology of the Vedas for Modern Man and Contemporary Celebration* (University of California Press, 1977), giving lucid translations and commentaries on Vedic and Upaniṣadic texts. See G. Buhler's translation of *The Laws of Manu* in Max Müller, ed., *Sacred Books of the East* 25 (Motilal Banarsidass, 1886). In Peter Brent, *Godmen of India* (Quadrangle, 1972), famous swamis give a creative range of responses to the interviewer's questions about their profession; you can follow up the teaching of Swami Muktananda in more detail by reading *Where Are You Going? A Guide to the Spiritual Journey* (G. S. Peeth, 1981). *Dikṣa* rituals of various types are outlined in Walter Kaelber, "The 'Dramatic' Element in Brahmanic Initiation: Symbols of Death, Danger, and Difficult Passage," *History of Religions* 18 (1979), pp. 54–76. Bangalore Kuppuswamy's *Dharma and Society: A Study in Social Values* (South Asia Books, 1977) is excellent on the current practice of *varṇāśrama-dharma.* Various religious-legal decisions can be sampled in J. D. M. Derrett, *Religion, Law, and the State in India* (Free Press, 1968).

4. **Mārgas and Deśikas.** An introduction with helpful illustrations to the iconography of saints occurs in Daniel Smith, "Hindu Deśika-Figures: Some Notes on a Minor Iconographic Tradition," *Religion* 8 (Spring 1978), pp. 40–67. A particular cultus is explored in Charles White, "The Sai Baba Movement: Approaches to the Study of Indian Saints," *Journal of Asian Studies* (August 1972), pp. 863–78. David Lorenzen, "The Life of Shankaracarya," in Frank Reynolds and Donald Capps, eds., *The Biographical Process: Studies in the History and Psychology of Religion* (Mouton, 1976), pp. 87–108, traces the Śaiva elements in myths surrounding Śaṅkara. Vaiṣṇava themes in Caitanya's life are developed in Norvin Hein, "Caitanya's Ecstasies and the Theology of the Name," in Smith, op. cit., pp. 15–32. See the uncritical Shriman Narayan, *Vinoba: His Life and Work* (Popular Prakashan, 1970); and the literate ridicule of Vinoba in V. S. Naipaul, *India: A Wounded Civilization* (Knopf, 1977).

I prefer the Juan Mascaro translation of the *Bhagavad Gītā* (Penguin, 1962). Louis Fischer, ed., *The Essential Gandhi: His Life, Work, and Ideas* (Vintage, 1962), uses Gandhi's *Story of My Experiments with Truth* autobiography as a framework, to which many valuable selections are added in a balanced narrative. Gandhi's *Gītā* commentary is represented by large excerpts in Ronald Duncan, ed., *Gandhi: Selected Writings* (Harper, 1971). See the provocative critique of Gandhi as idealized in Attenborough's film, by Elie Kedourie, "The Rush to Make a Saint: False Gandhi," *New Republic* (March 21, 1983), pp. 9–11; and a less partisan reconstruction by Ralph Buultzens, "Another Side of Gandhi," *America* (April 9, 1983), pp. 274–8. I cannot commend too highly the discussions of theology and spirituality that emerge from the Nikhilananda translation of *The Gospel of Shri Ramakrishna* (Ramakrishna-Vivekananda Center, 1942).

5. **Pūjās and Iṣṭas.** Plates, sketches, and other aids needed to study Hindu iconography are presented in Veronica Ions, *Indian Mythology* (Hamlyn, 1967), and Albert Moore, *Iconography of Religions: An Introduction* (Fortress, 1977). Also, see the fine introductions and selected texts on each major *iṣṭa* in Cornelia Dimmitt and J. A. B. van Buitenen, eds., *Classical Hindu Mythology: A Reader in the Sanskrit Puranas* (Temple University Press, 1978). Jan Gonda's *Vishnuism and Shivaism: A Comparison* (Athlone, 1970) is a dense but helpful introduction to the *bhakti* movements. See David Kinsley's two articles on Hindu portrayals of the irrational and demonic: "'Through the Looking Glass': Divine Madness in the Hindu Religious Tradition," *History of Religions* 13 (1973–74), pp. 270–305; and "Freedom from Death in the Worship of Kali," *Numen* 22 (1975), pp. 182–206. Correlations between Greek polytheism and the polycentric Self as interpreted by James Hillman are developed enthusiastically by David Miller's *The New Polytheism: Rebirth of the Gods and Goddesses* (Harper and Row, 1974). Robert Ellwood, Jr., "Polytheism: Establishment or Liberation Religion?" *JAAR* 42 (June 1974), shows that Japanese polytheistic trends do not verify Miller's idealized private subjectivity. Ananda Coomaraswamy builds an interesting aesthetic on his theology of the image, as expounded in *The Transformation of Nature in Art* (Dover, 1934), and *The Dance of Shiva: Fourteen Indian Essays* (Asia Publishing House, 1948).

4

Buddhist Dhamma

Few facts are certain about Siddhartha Gautama, historical founder who later became the Buddha of sacred myth. With characteristic differing emphases, his Theravāda disciples in Southeast Asia, Mahāyāna in China and Japan, and Tantrayāna or Vajrayāna in Tibet revere his conversion and apotheosis as a paradigm of the ideal human life. Born in the sixth century B.C.E., of a ruling *Kṣatriya* caste in northern India, Gautama abandoned wife and possessions, achieved a profound *samādhi* awakening *(bodhi)* after years of prayer and harsh asceticism, gathered a *saṁnyāsin* fellowship (the *saṃgha*) to share the spiritual discipline derived from his own enlightenment experience, and at death reached *mokṣa* or final extinction *(parinirvāṇa)* of all selfish craving and exploitation.

Dispossession, the progressive deepening of *bodhi,* the hovering between self-liberation and a compassionate decision to save others—this heroic life pattern is reenacted today in the popular Theravāda *shin byu* rite. Sinhalese youths, for example, are tonsured, given saffron robes, parasols, and begging bowls, and thus identify sacramentally with Gautama's renunciation for a brief or sustained period in the monastic *saṃgha.* This pattern is present, too, in the austere silent self-abandonment of a Zen disciple at *zazen,* or in the shocking bonfire self-immolation of activist Vietnamese monks two decades ago during the crumbling Diem regime. The Dalai Lama in 1956 on his first pilgrimage to the Indian Buddhist shrine at Buddh Gaya, praying for insight whether to seek political asylum in India or return to Chinese

Communist guardians in Tibet, sought his own distinctive participation in Gautama's transfiguration: "Now I stood in the presence of the Holy Spirit who had attained *mahāparinirvāṇa,* the highest *nirvāṇa,* in this sacred place, and had found for all mankind the path to salvation. As I stood there, a feeling of religious fervor filled my heart, and left me bewildered with the knowledge and impact of the divine power which is in all of us. . . . So after a few more days, I had to drag myself back to the world of politics, hostility, and mistrust."

The Dalai Lama in his act of Buddha-*pūjā* at Buddh Gaya is the first of two corrective images that should not escape attention as we expose ourselves to the stock esoteric-exoteric, *jñāna-bhakti,* Theravāda-Mahāyāna dichotomies of Buddhist spirituality. One finds a balanced, comprehensive tradition represented by his long training, described in *My Land and My People,* as an immersion in the moral guidance of Theravadists, and the more esoteric meditation methods of both Mahayanists and Tantrayanists. "For Tibetan Buddhists do not separate these teachings, but pay equal respect to them all."

Our second image is a huge Chinese cliff carving at Longmen that portrays Gautama, old and serene, flanked by the passionate *bhakta* Ānanda on his right, and the severe, detached *jñānin* Kaśyapa on his left, each disciple embodying a single facet of the master's plenitude. Embracing all three traditions, especially the Theravāda, we shall now study the metamorphosis of Buddha's role after his death, the rudiments of a contemporary lay spirituality, and the elusive influence of the Bodhisattva ideal.

Dhamma Wheel and Stupa

In the *Mahaparinibbana-sutta* of the Pali *Dīgha-nikāya,* we encounter some touching legends of Gautama's last seven months on earth. Recognizing the recurrent portents of death, Ānanda presses him for explicit instructions about the *saṃgha*'s future leadership. "Enough, Ānanda! Do not be troubled, do not weep! Have I not already on former occasions told you it is in the very nature of all things dearest to us that we must leave and sever ourselves from them? . . . Everything contains within itself the inherent necessity of dissolution. . . . " In a dialogue with Māra, his personified doppelgänger tempter, Gautama declares himself ready to die, now that the *saṃgha* has so matured that it no longer depends on his person or detailed directives. He thus insists with Ānanda, "Be lamps to yourselves, a refuge to yourselves. . . . Look not for refuge to anyone besides yourselves"

(5:34–5;2:32–3). Centuries of an evolving cultus and routinized charisma intervene between this alleged stance of Gautama, and our later profuse Vinaya monastic codebooks in the Pali Canon, or the *triratna* formula of popular *bhakti:* "We take the Buddha, the Dhamma, the Saṃgha as our refuge!"

This so-called *Book of the Great Decease* records a plausible spectrum of reactions to Buddha's death. Some "not yet free from passions" moan that he died too soon, that the world has lost its only light. Another extreme is encountered in the elderly Subhadda: "Stop weeping! We are rid of the great *samaṇa,* who annoyed us by saying, 'This beseems you, this beseems you not.' But now we shall be able to do whatever we like. . . ." Kaśyapa and most others respond with sad finality, "Impermanent are all component things. How could they possibly not be dissolved!" (6:39–41). In Buddhist scriptures the easy Buddha-*vācana* style of attributing any later sectarian opinion to Gautama's own lips appears most ingenuous in some of the injunctions antedating his death. He promises "rebirth after death in the happy realms of heaven" to those dying while on pilgrimage to the sites of his birth, enlightenment, first preaching, and death. The same reward is extended to those venerating Gautama's relics, or building a stupa to his memory. Whoever should place "garlands, perfumes, or paint there, express a greeting, or in its presence experience serenity in heart—such an act shall bring them profit and joy" (5:16–26).

After Buddha's *nirvāṇa* dissolution, the most tangible evidence of his actual historical existence and renunciatory life pattern were his relics and a pilgrimage map indicating concretely where "the Lord was born," "received enlightenment," "turned the wheel of Dhamma," and "passed away." In the first centuries, artists were asked to summon every aniconic resource that could evoke Buddha's egoless glory, sustained somehow paradoxically after his death. "There is more atmosphere of prayer in a Pagoda than in most churches," says Graham Greene in *Ways of Escape*. "The features of Buddha cannot be sentimentalized like the features of Christ, there are no hideous pictures on the wall, no stations of the Cross, no straining after unfelt agonies." If Greene's assessment at least of the best Buddhist art is tenable, one reason for later iconic restraint must be the early tradition's prolonged aniconic apprenticeship.

Buddha's birth has been symbolized by the lotus—viewed laterally, pure beauty rising from slime, or phallic diamond in the womb; viewed from above, a petaled *maṇḍala*. The bo tree, tree of life, stands for the tree under which his unfathomable *bodhi* experience occurred. The many-spoked *dhammacakka* signifies the eight precepts of Buddha's teaching, a cosmic wheel reversing the relentless wheel of *saṃsāra*. Royal burial mound, phallus, or cosmic mountain, the stupa memorializes his death and achievement of *parinirvāṇa*. By the time that Hellenized personal images of Buddha first appear at Gandhara, the religious imagination seems to have exhausted most aniconic possibilities. In stupa marginal carvings at Sanchi and Barhut, for example, elegantly rendered human groupings cluster around a dramatic void—the empty throne, riderless horse, the royal parasol spread over blank space, gigantic footprints left by an absent wandering preacher. Many of the pictures are surrounded by a nimbus embroidery of awestruck animals and demigods, distancing the scene beyond ordinary experience. In Buddhist art elsewhere, a few aniconic symbols are sometimes juxtaposed to form the crude outlines of a personal body, such as footprints below a bo tree topped by a *dhammacakka,* or a stupa spiraling up through its various levels to suggest a triangular seated body, head, and Buddha's *uṣṇīsa* topknot.

This Unseen Buddha convention, like the faceless blank or blinding flame representing Muhammad's presence in Persian miniatures, apparently intends to comply with the early Theravāda insistence that Gautama remain just a dead teacher and superman, not another Indian *avatāra,* the focus of one more *bhakti* cultus. But this strained artistic reticence had no doubt the opposite effect. We have traced in other chapters the powerful apophatic symbolism in Taoist paradox, Huichol reversal rites, and Hindu *coincidentia oppositorum*. Here gestures of denial and understatement, protesting far too much, succeed in hinting at the transcendent and ineffable, much like the mysteries concealed behind an iconostasis screen. Similarly, the plain walls and windows of a Puritan church confer an enormous emphasis upon pulpit and preacher, or the unseen therapist behind an analytical couch can elicit transference reactions perilously close to worship.

Two aniconic symbols with pronounced numinous implications are the Dhamma Wheel and stupa, which I shall now analyze in detail. In the texts cited above, Gautama explains that your sole refuge after the *guru*'s death must be yourself (*attasarana*) and the teaching (*dhammasarana*). "It may be, Ānanda, that in some of you the thought may arise, 'The word of the master is ended, we have no teacher anymore!' But it is not thus, Ānanda, that you should regard it. After I am gone, let the Dhamma-Vinaya which I have laid down for you all be your Teacher" (6:1). With the ascension of Jesus' physical body, early Christians gradually accustomed themselves to discover his more elusive sacramental body in the Church, in the preached apostolic Word, and in the Lord's Supper ritual. With Buddha's death, his first disciples in a similar manner began to view the Dhamma and *saṃgha* as a continuation of his numinous presence. In a key *Saṃyutta-nikāya* passage, Buddha asks, "What is there, Vakkali, in seeing this vile body? Whoever sees Dhamma sees me, whoever sees me sees Dhamma" (3:120).

What is Dhamma? Sanskrit *Dharma* becomes *Dhamma* in Pali, a Sanskrit derivative carried eastward by Indian Buddhists in their cultural and economic expansion, the official language of Theravāda scriptures. I have pointed out already the debt owed by a developed Hindu Dharma concept to Buddhist reform, so I now use the Pali term *Dhamma* in this chapter to suggest slightly divergent nuances between the two religious contexts. Two meanings of Buddhist Dhamma are especially important. First is the Hindu notion of *sanātana dharma,* eternal cosmic law, which the *Mahāpadāna-sutta* calls *dhammata.* Next is Dhamma-Vinaya, Gautama's teachings as a limited historical embodiment of the *dhammata,* replacing Hindu *varṇāśrama-dharma* common law.

Like the Judaic Torah, Dhamma-Vinaya has been formulated in a few deft inspiring phrases, or in turgid legal disquisitions marked by incantatory repetition, long checklists of virtues, and many other tricks of oral transmission, many of which petrify on the written page. A few remarks about Dhamma-Vinaya might clarify the basis for our later discussion. First, it welcomes all to the *saṃgha,* regardless of caste. Viewing Brāhmin ritual obligations as overrated or otiose, it mounts a prophetic critique, in the spirit of an ethical Axial Age, against all empty ritualism. Second, Gautama's Dhamma as expounded in the Theravāda Canon is called Vinaya or monastic discipline, and thus addressed principally to his wandering or settled *saṃnyāsin* disciples, but only on occasion also to the laity. It is possible to contest such an emphasis, and conjecture about a much wider original scope to the Dhamma, including a *bhakti* cultus, which was later trimmed and reinterpreted by partisan monastic redactors of the tradition. Or we might decide to view Gautama more restrictively as just a monastic founder, whose disciples after centuries of experience expanded his Dhamma into a universal gospel.

Third, Buddha seems to have endorsed the essential Hindu assumptions about karmic justice and the *saṃsāra* rebirth cycle. Convinced that human alienation, which Thoreau calls quiet desperation, is caused by our *taṇhā* craving to bend the world to self-centered needs, he lay down an eightfold discipline of moral action and *samādhi.* We charted this path of *niṣkāma-karma* in the preceding chapter—a life purified of selfish desire, culminating in *nirvāṇa* or an extinction of *taṇhā.* Buddha's direct handling of alienation, codified in his Four

Noble Truths, influenced the shape of Śaṅkara's Advaita *jñāna* rebuttal many centuries later, and also the *niṣkāma* activist ideal favored by the *Bhagavad Gītā* and Gandhi.

Fourth, pursuing this *taṇhā* theme so single-mindedly, the moral pragmatism in Gautama pushes aside unresolvable theological arguments about an immortal soul, cosmic origins, existence of the gods. The *Majjhima-nikāya* introduces a charming dialogue in which an elderly *saṁnyāsin,* directing these questions to Buddha one by one, threatens to defer entering the *saṃgha* until he gets every doubt resolved. Gautama compares this questioner to some patient dying of a poisoned arrow wound, stubbornly refusing surgical aid until he can track down the racial and caste pedigree of the assailant, the exact design of arrow feathers and bow. Why waste time on a question that makes no appreciable spiritual difference? It is "not useful, it is not concerned with the principle of religious life, does not conduce to aversion, absence of passion, cessation, tranquility, supernatural endowment, perfect knowledge, *nirvāṇa,* and therefore I have not explained it." Often naively misconstrued as atheistic or antitheistic, the Theravāda Dhamma is clearly *parahenotheistic,* in my opinion. Without denying them, it intends mostly to deemphasize and sidestep the popular Hindu *iṣṭas* and sectarian theological debates of its day.

My fifth and last comment on Dhamma centers on a distinctive insight Gautama always thought essential to his teaching. *Anatta* means no-*ātman,* no individual perduring self; *anicca,* the impermanence of all material and mental events. Sometimes these concepts seem to function in the manner just described—more to counterbalance and chasten attachment to the self and world than to deny their existence. Or they reaffirm a *niṣkāma* ethics, playing upon the familiar paradoxes of negation: *śūnyatā,* the void, is a condition of emptiness and perfection; self-denial leads to self-completion; or *nirvāṇa,* according to Gautama, suggests "the Isle of No-beyond, where there is No-thing to be grasped." In a more systematic mode, *anatta* and *anicca* can be woven into the intricate Buddhist cosmology of *pratītya-samutpāda*—the theory of interrelational genesis, or the social nature of reality. The evolving organismic universe discussed in the chapter on Sino-Japanese Tao implies that you become self-aware only by deepening at the same time your awareness of the world and others. "The reality underlying all phenomena is beyond all forms and is therefore often said to be formless, empty, or void . . . ," says Fritjof Capra, reflecting on quantum field theory in *The Tao of Physics.* "All things and events perceived by the senses are interrelated . . . manifestations of the same ultimate reality. Our tendency to divide the perceived world into individual and separate things and to experience ourselves as isolated egos in this world . . . is called Avidya or ignorance in Buddhist philosophy, and is seen as the state of a disturbed mind which has to be overcome."

A legend occurs in the *Anguttara-nikāya* about a Brāhmin disciple trailing Gautama on the road and discovering on each of his footprints the image of a thousand-spoked wheel. "These cannot be the footprints of a human being!" he concludes. In Hindu iconography, giant blank footprints are a widespread aniconic reference to Viṣṇu. The wheel mark signifies both divine kingship and the *dhammacakka,* singling out Gautama from Viṣṇu's many *avatāra* redemptive forms. In the early Buddhist tradition, meditation on Gautama's profound dictum "Who sees me sees the Dhamma" led eventually to theories about Buddha's double body *(dvikāya)* and triple body *(trikāya).* Eternal *Dhammata* is called *dharmakāya*—buddhahood or the transcendental Buddha-reality. Gautama himself becomes *rupakāya* or *nirmānakāya,* one but not the only historical physical embodiment of *dharmakāya.* Or Gautama is a transhistorical *avatāra* manifestation of *dharmakāya,* just a Docetic canvas portraying the ideal human life. In the later Mahayanist *trikāya* formula, a third glory-body *(saṃbhogakāya)* rank of heavenly Buddhas is added, symbolizing various personified aspects of *dhammata,* according to the modes of its alleged perception by non-mortal beings.

The *dhammata* reified and virtually deified, represents a prominent intellectual current in early Buddhist spirituality. An alternate stream, more devotional, seldom wavers in its attention to the finite body and biography of Gautama. The resurrection of Jesus prompted early Christian speculation about his heavenly preexistence and the attributes of his glorified body after death. Similarly, Buddhists argued that Gautama's achievement of *nirvāṇa* within a single lifetime must have been preceded by a lineage of heroic mortal Bodhisattvas (Buddhas-to-be) in previous samsaric births, accumulating karmic merit to make *nirvāṇa* a viable possibility for the future Gautama. Thus, the Pali Canon presents more than five hundred Jātaka myths about the Buddha in earlier animal, demigod, or human births, many of them centering on some crucial moment of renunciation. At first glance, an even stronger testimonial to belief in Gautama's mortal facticity is the veneration shown his relics, which by their visible enshrinement in stupas dotting the landscape steer the mind from Buddha's conjectured preexistence to his spiritual presence after *parinirvāṇa.* We should recall, too, the Pali Canon's depiction of other full-fledged historical Buddhas antedating Gautama, and the expectations of a future redemptive messiah, the Bodhisattva Maitreya. "Maitreya,

Come!" remains a perennial revolutionary slogan throughout Southeast Asia.

We have quoted the *Mahaparanibbana*'s guidelines for Gautama's funerary rites, for impartial distribution of his relics throughout India, and for meritorious devotions at stupa reliquary sites. Relics of the Buddha can be hair, a tooth, or some other piece of his body, or any object touched by or reminiscent of him. The architectural imagination of many nations and eras has transformed the stupa from a simple squat hemispheric burial mound into gargantuan urn and lampstand shapes, towers with multitiered roofs, and fragile umbrella pagodas. Memorializing Buddha's *parinirvāṇa* and thus his absence, the stupa, animated by his relics, paradoxically evokes Buddha's continuing presence. It symbolizes the *nirvāṇa* achievement, and therefore *nirvāṇa-dhammata* itself as an absolute. The word in Sri Lanka for a reliquary mound is *dāgoba,* derived from *garbha,* a chamber or womb, and *dhātu,* which means not only a relic but a person's very essence. The stupa contains Buddha's life force, then, a seed of great spiritual power. By proceeding reverently around the shrine, according to the prescribed circumambulation ritual, perhaps with garlands and chanting and music, one worships the person of Buddha and at the same time converges toward the numinous Center of cosmos and self. If aniconic footprints stamped with the *dhammacakka* associate Buddha with Viṣṇu, the stupa reliquary links him to the sacred phallus of Śiva.

A fascinating illustration of relics as a prominent feature in Buddha-*pūjā* is the *nētra pinkama* rite or Eye Festival, an imaginative Sinhalese Buddhist variation on the Hindu *pratīka* consecration ritual sketched in the last chapter. In many temples, the Buddha image becomes a formal object of worship only after its artist paints or carves the eyes, a gesture of delayed finality. He performs this act prayerfully, working sideways with the aid of a mirror, at a moment judged astrologically appropriate, while the large festival audience stand distant even from the outer doors. Just before the eye painting, after a *saṃgha* procession transporting the relic encased in a tiny silver stupa, one monk climbs the scaffold to insert this reliquary into the Buddha's head. While the artist chants in a high monotone and paints, *saṃgha* participants offer a background of uninterrupted *pirit,* the chanting of auspicious scriptural texts, which will continue throughout the night. The artist is led blindfolded from the temple, once his work is completed. The feet and hands of the consecrated statue are now covered with an ornamental cloth, and then public worship and festivities begin. A survey of those attending one Nētra Festival held near Kandy in 1965 prompted a surprising range of explanations for the efficacy of this consecration ceremony.

Most of the monks, dismissing the eye painting as a harmless, irrelevant folk tradition, view *pirit* as the single meaningful event. Listening devoutly to the texts and meditating on them can prove meritorious, and strengthen awareness of each person's inner Buddha-nature. A few monks and most laypeople treated *pirit* also as a sacramental charm exorcising the potential influence of evil spirits. The eye painting and insertion of relics were interpreted by most laypeople as the awesome culmination of all the rituals. Many believed the Buddha image had now been invested with the relic's life force—*budubalāya,* or the sacred power of Buddha-Śakti.

Probably the most articulate stupa theological statement is the Borobudur in Java, a mound 150 feet high, with a square ground plan 400 feet long. As you mount the five terraces gradually converging toward the massive stupa at its apex, you pass 72 smaller bell-shaped stupas, 505 Buddha statues, and innumerable carvings on the walls. This stunning monument combines a stupa, a cosmic mountain, a body and head of Buddha, and a map of the Buddhist universe. Guided by carefully planned iconography on the friezes, a pilgrim ascending the stairs is initiated into scenes of suffering in Dantean *purgatorios,* Jātaka preexistence legends, Gautama's biography, then celestial Bodhisattvas and a Buddhist *paradiso,* but at last the aniconic crest of *dhammata.* In a maturing Buddhist faith, you rise from the everyday phenomenal world to enter *nirvāṇa* and the void. Or according to the *trikāya* formula, you contemplate in progressive stages of *bodhi* the Buddha's earthly *rupa* body, his heavenly *saṃbhoga* body, and finally his Dhamma truth-body.

A Lay Buddhist Spirituality

American versions of the Buddhist legacy have consisted mostly of the congregational-style parish life adopted by Asian immigrants, retreat and meditation centers managed by Japanese and Tibetan monks, and the drop-out Zen popularized by Beat poets and the psychedelic counterculture. With the fall of Saigon, I worked the summer of 1975 as Catholic chaplain in a Guam relocation camp, a barbed enclosure designated specifically for refugees returning to their families in Vietnam. There for the first time I met some articulate young Buddhist militants who undercut my stereotypes. Offering Mass and Bible readings for Christians, I tried, with the aid of translators, to ditto classic passages from the Pali Canon, such as Gautama's Fire Sermon, to help a few dispirited Buddhist friends form their own meditation and support groups. To my surprise, they examined the texts but rejected them decisively. Though their hearts might have resented a patronizing meddler or a potential CIA spy, their embarrassed words had a plausible ring to them: this passive, otherworldly Buddha was irrelevant, even detrimental to their own contemporary Buddhist faith. They revered various heroic religious kings in Asian Buddhist history. They wanted to build a new postcolonial society where all could develop their own intrinsic Buddha-nature, without excessive dependence on religious institutions, customs, scriptures. They felt the colonial giant had taken cynical advantage of their gentle Buddhist faith and snatched from them the very wealth and functions of government their docile religious tradition had taught them to renounce. Admiring Gautama's insistence on democratic process and caste equality in the *saṃgha,* they preferred an engaged but cautiously restricted role for the contemporary *saṃgha* in education and politics.

Most of these Buddhists could be described as Mahayanist, endorsing a broader, more Platonic concept of the *saṃgha* community and Buddha-reality than the strictest Theravadist. Yet they represent an emphasis cutting across all Buddhist cultures with increasing emphasis, which I shall call lay, sometimes anticlerical; ethical, sometimes antiritualistic; and Aśokan, a term evoking the great Buddhist missionary-emperor, the Constantine of India. This spirituality now flourishes even in Theravāda countries alongside the canonical monastic ideal of *theras,* or the Elders. Here is a Buddhist version of the Hindu activist-contemplative, *karma-jñāna mārga* dialectic, more or less open to the élan and ritual of *bhakti* folk traditions. It has been suggested that some Buddhists have replaced the traditional Hindu *āśramas* with a developmental sequence of their own, based on widening exclusions from society: householder, lay devotee, cenobite, hermit. If much of the frustration and creative drive in Gandhi's career derives from his prolonged suspension between *gṛhasthya* and *saṁnyāsin* stages, so the average committed Buddhist wavers at the ambivalent boundary between lay devotee and monk.

The lay component in Buddhist spirituality is as multiform as its monastic correlative, varying in composition and authority from one monastery, nation, or historical epoch to another. For instance, though most Southeast Asian regimes expect their monks to transcend the bearpit of politics, Burma twenty years ago tolerated monk gangs trashing shops, overturning automobiles, and bludgeoning political enemies. Or again, Gautama's early *saṃgha* fitted readily into an established Indian tradition of reclusive yogins and *saṁnyasins,* supported dutifully by the *gṛhasthya* laity. Yet the *saṃgha* later shed much of this mendicant and celibate identity in China, which usually disdained beggars and yearned for male posterity to continue the chain of family memorial sacrifices.

It is instructive to hear the reasons why Dhiravamsa, Thai Theravāda leader of the Buddhapadipa Temple in London, gave up his robe in 1971 and ceased to be a *bhikkhu,* or monk. Monastic garb had become a symbol that "fragments life, creating a division between the holy and the ordinary, and tends to prevent the individual from experiencing the whole of life. . . . When we overlook simplicity, we shall not find the holy, but instead just find the idea of holiness and worship this in a religious way." Dhiravamsa decided to remain at the temple as a lay meditation master, a role that sounds similar to the *anagārika* function adopted by Dharmapala, the fiery nationalist of early-twentieth-century Sri Lanka. Dharmapala's vocation was to harass the colonial administrations and Christian missions, and also to synthesize Puritan bourgeois verities of thrift and hard work with the Buddhist traditional practice of meditation. The term *anagārika* in the Pali Canon means a homeless life, applied exclusively to the *bhikkhu.* Dharmapala redesigned it to describe an intermediate role between monk and layperson, the worldly celibate wanderer, actively involved in politics and society. "Lay *brahmacārin* for life" is his self-definition. "A life of a monk is suitable for a person who is concerned with his own self-welfare. But for those concerned with the welfare of others the *brahmacārin* life is suitable, useful for meaningful worldly work."

The Trungpa Chögyam, eleventh reincarnate Lama and head of the Surmang group of monasteries, tells in *Born in Tibet* that it took the threat of a Chinese invasion to make the clerical leadership worry how their overly dependent laity could survive the monasteries' immanent destruction. The Tantrayāna faith could perish unless each person became a separate repository of the tradition. Monks must leave their sanctuary and go out to teach Buddhist fundamentals to the laity. Their *guru* now began to reinterpret the standard monastic motifs. They must experience "the shock of re-entering the world and learn how to retreat within themselves," rather than within monastic hermitages. "They must give more help to the lay people who had no opportunity to study." In other words, people must try to build imperishable temples within themselves.

We might have expected a six-hundred-year-old Japanese Mahayanist lay tradition like Jōdo Shinshū to escape a Tibetan-style clericalism. In the Pure Land sect, Honen's disciple Shinran left the monastry, married, and accomplished a Lutheran sort of reform against celibacy and the legalistic dependence on scripture, ritual, and monastic directives. Yet the character Soshu, a Jōdo-Shinshū priest in Fumio Niwa's novel *The Buddha Tree,* contrasts his own neurotic undisciplined sexuality with Shinran's integrated humanity, and grieves over the decline of his Shin tradition into a decadent "temple Buddhism." Although the temple's business ought to be life and not just death, Soshu's priesthood consists mostly of funerary rites and *sūtra* chanting in a deserted temple. Ordinary geishas surely must view such temples as irrelevant to their own lives. "The absence of an imposing, traditional building compelled Buddhism to go out among the people," he concludes, "to become a lay religion—a religion which would make it natural for men and women to meet in fellowship and talk over their spiritual problems in a house no different from any other. Was not this the religion that Shinran had lived?"

These four voices, selected from the major Buddhist divisions of Theravāda, Tantrayāna, and Mahayāna, confirm the Buddhist lay manifesto I first heard from Vietnamese Buddhists. I shall now try to sift out the two most distinctive ingredients in this spirituality, its Aśokan legacy, and its subtle eschatology.

Filling the power vacuum left in the third century B.C.E., after Alexander's invasion of the Persian Empire, Aśoka will be immortalized as one of the few kings to repent publicly of his bloody climb to the throne. A fresh Buddhist convert, he renounced further war and violence, set up welfare funds for the poor and aged, built schools, monasteries, hundreds of stupas, and some of the world's first hospitals, sent Buddhist teachers throughout Southeast Asia, and left behind him rock inscriptions describing the vision and achievement of an ideal ruler. "The king, the friend of the gods, . . . honors all sects," he reassures his citizenry drawn from so many divergent religious backgrounds. "What little effort I make is from a debt I owe to all beings. I work for their happiness in this life, that in the next world they may gain heaven." A Buddhist king's duty, he believes, is to fashion a society where mature conscience and *samādhi* can flourish: "Mankind has been given as many blessings by previous kings as by me; but I have done this with the intent that people may practice the Dhamma."

Combine Aśoka's edicts with the image of the expected Maitreya messiah, and the model Buddhist royal *cakkavatti* or Dhamma-wheel-master, and you can glimpse outlines of a utopian Buddhist social order. The kingship and wealth that Gautama abandoned are now embraced by his lay disciple Aśoka, Gautama's own Lenin or Saint Paul, translating an essentially monastic charism into practical polity to nourish the Dhamma good life and protect the *saṃgha*'s existence. A few decades ago, most of these millennial hopes seemed close to fulfillment with the new postcolonial independent States of Burma, Sri Lanka, Laos, and Cambodia, and the approach of 1956, the 2,500th anniversary of Buddha's *parinirvāṇa*. The long apocalyptic era of Buddhist decline, foretold in the *Cakkavatti-sutta* of the *Digha-nikāya*, had ended, and now press editorials and campaign oratory in all these nations renewed the dream of *Dhamma-samaja*, a reign based on Dhamma.

The most articulate exponent of *Dhamma-samaja* has been U Nu of Burma, before his controversial regime was terminated by the army coup of 1962. His political addresses contain shrewd touches of folk wisdom, an evangelical eagerness to expound his Buddhist beliefs, and a sophisticated critique of both Marxist and capitalist fallacies. Establishing an early reputation as translator of *Das Kapital* and *How to Win Friends and Influence People*, he hoped to reconcile and transcend these two rival ideologies by his own Middle Path strategy of Buddhist socialism. The Utilitarian greed of nineteenth-century England, overflowing into its colonial subjugation of Burma, at the same time spawned Marx's revolutionary materialism, which in Asia later ironically aided Burma win its independence from England. Marx's polemic against bourgeois profit and acquisitiveness must be extended to uproot the grasping ego behind economic misery and all deeper spiritual *taṇhā*. Bourgeois attachment to property already owned and the proletarian lust for property not yet owned are based on a delusion that separate egos exist. The acquisitive principle that rules both the communist and the capitalist distracts them from their main spiritual task, to free themselves from *saṃsāra*.

The Wishing Tree myth is a perennial theme in Buddhist apocalyptic literature, and U Nu often recounts it in his speeches. This tree flourished during the Golden Age, before the origins of private property. "The inhabitants of the world found on it enough perfect, healthy, and comfortable things that were sufficient . . . and used them without clinging to them." When people first began to build fortunes in excess of minimal needs, they descended to greedy aggression, then extortion, hatred, murder, and the wishing tree vanished. "We wish to establish a Socialist state . . . to bring back successfully the era of the vanished Padeytha Tree." U Nu's reform, however, was blocked because of two distortions by Buddhists of their own ethical tradition, which he took every opportunity to correct. Too many rich rationalize their status quo separation from the poor as a consequence fixed by karmic merit and demerit from past lives. But the genuine redemptive Bodhisattva will labor to heal sources of social misery in this life. Second, *nirvāṇa* is not just a remote, individual goal of the spirit. It also means a material *lokanibbāna,* Judeo-Christian Paradise, Marx's Classless Society, a fellowship based on *bodhi, karuṇā,* and freedom that must begin in the present. This means a corporate *nirvāṇa* for future generations, among whom you can expect your own probable rebirth.

A crucial truism in comparative ethics is that divergent actions can stem from a single ideology, or a single action can be legitimated by divergent ideologies. The experimental socialist regimes and programs of land reform in Burma, Sri Lanka, and elsewhere are still too recent for adequate assessment. It is impossible to determine, too, the spiritual authenticity of this rhetoric, for it emerges during a postcolonial milieu of nascent nationalism, when leaders must grope for any ploys available to unite a people. Yet I think U Nu has proved himself a sincere, informed representative of the recent Buddhist Aśokan activist. The second principal feature of Buddhist lay spirituality has already been suggested by the *lokanibbāna* theme. In Buddhist eschatology, we can distinguish three different styles—*future,* associated conventionally with the *bhikkhu;* and *consequent* and *present,* applicable universally.

Nirvāṇa can be projected into the ultimate future, demanding a purgatorial climb through countless samsaric rebirths in this and other worlds, finally to broach the virtually unattainable condition where every selfish desire is extinguished. This future eschatology seems designed to motivate only the most rigorous *bhikkhu,* a status to which only those can aspire who have accumulated merit from many previous lay incarnations. Especially in some Theravāda cultures, *bhikkhus* are venerated by honorifics and bows normally reserved only for the stupa or the Buddha, are seated at public gatherings on a dais above the laity, are invited to chant *pirit* and receive alms at major family rituals, and are often consulted for spiritual direction. Every material privilege is offered them to facilitate renunciation and *samādhi,* for at least through them a spiritual remnant survives which most laity respect but feel too distracted or mortal to emulate. A classical Buddhist debate about the relative lay and clerical advantages in pursuit of *nirvāṇa* occurs in the influential postcanonic *Questions of King Milinda.* "What is the difference between the householder and the homeless wanderer?" Milinda asks Guru Nāgasena. "What is the use of inflicting pain upon yourself, if while remaining at ease you can win the ease of Nirvana?" Condemning the fraudulent *bhikkhu* who joins the *saṃgha* out of greed, political ambition, laziness, Nāgasena rates a worthy lay person higher than an unworthy monk. Yet none can surpass the committed *bhikkhu,* "unaddicted to society, energetic, independent, . . . skilled in all that concerns purification and spiritual progress. He is like Your Majesty's javelin. . . . He succeeds in doing it all rapidly" (IV,6:16–19).

By the term *consequent,* I refer to various practical accommodations devised by the popular religious imagination to find a place for the laity, banished to the footnotes of a future eschatology. For example, Vivekananda and other Advaitins, mentioned in the previous chapter, expect ordinary *Kali-yuga* people to follow an allegedly less perfect *karma-mārga,* a sort of *jñāna* for the nonelite. Similarly, the average Buddhist, for whom so wispy and remote a nirvanic goal drops simply out of sight, focuses on some more recognizable topography earlier on the long samsaric path. Not the cessation of rebirth but a better rebirth, not the extinction of *taṇhā* but its satisfaction in an improved earthly or celestial existence, not the *parinirvāṇa* of glorified *bhikkhus* but a participation in their generous accumulation of merit. Although all these can be defended as productive spiritual compromises, we can identify widespread abuses reminiscent of the clericalism and merit-grubbing in late medieval Europe. Contrast the eschatological attitudes of two Paganese queens in rock inscription prayers of the eleventh century. "Before I reach Nirvana," says Queen Caw, "by virtue of the work of merit I have done on such a big scale, I wish virtue and prosperity if born again as a human being. If I am born a spirit, I wish to be . . . beautiful, sweet-voiced, well-proportioned in limbs, the beloved and honored darling of every human being and spirit. . . . May I have lots of gold, silver, rubies, coral, pearls. . . . Wherever I am born, may I . . . not know one speck of misery. And after I have tasted and enjoyed the happiness of human beings and spirits, . . . may I at last attain the peaceful bliss of Nirvana." Another queen, Amana, asks that her own merit be showered upon the king and all his subjects, and even "Yama, king of death, and all creatures also share it. . . . I pray to cross samsara full of the good graces—modest in my wants, even-tempered, compassionate, wise, conscious of causes, large-handed, unforgetful, and affectionate." As a replay of the Christian parable about the Pharisee and the Publican, Amana's *nirvāṇa* is a generous Bodhisattva giveaway; Caw's is a narcissistic dream.

Merit accumulation and transference seem a subversive translation of the morality-meditation-wisdom injunctives listed in Gautama's eightfold Dhamma. For most imaginations, the *karma* ladder to *nirvāṇa* needs to be scaled in a quantified, reassuring manner—charter merit-increments, specific contractual fine print. A current Jōdo folk belief is that one seventh of the merit acquired by a memorial service of *sūtra* readings accrues to the dead soul, the other six-sevenths to mourning relatives. Someone has suggested that this spiritual arithmetic derives from the old custom of augmenting sums of money sent to exiles, in expectation that most of it could be written off en route for bribes and pilfering. Yet the careful wording of the memorial notice published in a Rangoon newspaper by U Thant suggests a more convincing explanation of merit transfer. *Pirit* and various other deeds of merit were to be offered on the anniversary of his son's death. "May the late Mg Tin Maung Thant rejoice 'Sadu, Sadu, Sadu,' and reap the full benefit of these merits in whatever plane of existence he now is." I think U Thant means that my own good deed can purify me of *taṇhā* and change my own *karma*, yet the dead, contemplating my deed, might be purified by empathy and thus reach deeper Buddha-realization.

For Theravadists especially, merit *(puñña)* is gained principally from ritual giving (*dāna*), and the donations most esteemed are usually those that reconfirm an extraordinary symbiosis between laity and *bhikkhus*. Lay donors venerate the monk as an invaluable merit field, and could imagine few worse deprivations than to be confronted by an upturned begging bowl, frustrating both *dāna* and the privileged karmic opportunity. This viewpoint precipitates a series of anomalies, similar to the potlatch gift excesses noted in an earlier chapter. Poor villages construct new monasteries that no monk will inhabit; they lavish costly, superfluous food on monks unable to consume it. The monk, meriting by a life of meditation and world withdrawal, is hounded away to retreats successively more remote, in order to escape being tempted by lay donors. The more austere and otherworldly a monk, the more sacred a merit field. And thus, the more cherished a recipient of the very *dāna* that this monk must continuously renounce. Lay generosity can twist itself into the very self-interest it was intended to dispel.

The perils of consequent eschatology include an impractical depreciation of the secular, yet at the same time a clinging to meretricious substitutes for a *nirvāṇa* that seems unreachable. This tragic confusion can be exemplified in the final months of U Nu's premiership, viewed with the unsympathetic eyes of his political adversaries. He had forced the passage of an amendment decreeing Buddhism the established religion of Burma, released for annual retreats and a daily prayer period those civil servants promising to meditate, paroled criminals who passed exams on the Buddhist basic catechism. He was disappearing more frequently from the administrative malaise mounting around him to meditate in a hut built on his estate or in a hermitage on Mount Popa. Finally, he announced his solution to the national economic and political crisis. Throughout Burma, sixty thousand sand pagodas would be constructed simultaneously at an astrologically determined hour, nine *bhikkhus* would be offered *dāna,* and *pirit* would be recited for three days. At this point, even many of his most devout *saṃgha* apologists began to doubt his lay vocation to politics and his sanity.

Future and consequent eschatology stem from the same traditional matrix, but *present* eschatology, perhaps the most suitable basis for a lay spirituality, demands a radical gestalt shift. "Before I was enlightened," says a familiar Zen *kōan,* "the mountains were mountains. When I began to be enlightened the mountains were not mountains anymore. Now, since I am enlightened, the mountains are indeed mountains." The impact of this eschatology can be caught through a careful reading of Herman Hesse's *Siddhartha,* especially the final paragraphs. The protagonist explains to his friend Govinda that we often speak about the sinner reaching *nirvāṇa* someday or becoming a Buddha someday. This *someday* is an illusion. The world is not slowly evolving toward perfection, but is perfect at every moment. The potential Buddha already exists in the sinner, every sin already bears grace within it. The river on which Siddhartha is ferryman, the Hindu sacred *Oṃ mantra,* or the serene smile of Siddhartha and Gautama—each contains within its microcosm every possible form of the cosmos. Siddhartha gives his own interpretation of the Zen *kōan* mentioned above. Once he thought each stone just a stone—*māyā,* without value; then he saw it also as animal, god, Buddha, everything. Now he has come to love it in its individuality, too. "I love it just because it is a stone. . . . I think it is only important to love the world, not to despise it." Siddhartha had come to this realization only after an experience of genuine human love for his spoiled, rebellious son. Once scornfully superior to the games and cares of ordinary people, "he now felt as if these ordinary people were his brothers. Their vanities, desires, and trivialities no longer seemed absurd to him."

Surely this eschatology in Hesse's novel, like the other two eschatologies examined, has its own misuses. One reason Hesse's book has never lost its loyal cult readership is that it can be oversimplified to justify the relaxed self-complacency and capriciousness of pseudo-Zen, or any political stasis without the spur of revolutionary messianism. Perhaps we can suggest its mature realization in another Burmese lay activist, U Thant, U Nu's close adviser and friend, third secretary general of the United Nations. Presiding with serenity and diplomatic finesse during the Cuban and Nigerian crises, convinced that Russia and the United States were still cold-war prisoners of their respective pasts, he drew upon long experience as spokesman for the nonaligned Third World. Less partisan a Buddhist than U Nu, and a self-described ethical Buddhist or even a Buddhist Unitarian, U Thant recommends Schweitzer, Teilhard de Chardin, and Gautama as a sound ethical basis for international dialogue. "As a Buddhist, I was trained to be tolerant of everything except intolerance," he says in *View from the U.N.* "Human life is one of suffering; hence, it is the duty of a good Buddhist to mitigate the suffering of others. . . . I was taught to control my emotions through a process of concentration and meditation, . . . cleansing the mind of impurities such as ill will, hatred, and restlessness." Acknowledging profound grief at the death of his only son, and exultation three years later at receiving the Nobel Prize, he detaches himself from these reactions and meditates daily to gain *upekka,* or equanimity. "To contemplate life, but not to be enmeshed in it, is the law of the Buddha."

A present eschatology contributes two crucial insights to any developing lay spirituality. Through intensive purification of awareness, we are asked to venture away from the *avidyā* and shadows of Plato's cave, and realize that *saṃsāra is nirvāṇa. Nirvāṇa* can be touched in the numinous present instant: a vase of flowers, a merchant's handshake, a plan for agrarian reform. An Upaniṣadic parallel is the *mantra "Tat tvam asi"*—"You *are* that!"—in its pantheistic or panentheistic interpretation. Nāgārjuna, the Yogācāra theologians, and other Mahayanists have expanded this notion into an intricate speculative system: all reality is *śūnyatā* or Dhamma or *nirvāṇa.* The second insight gained from present eschatology is trust in the continuous active presence of Bodhisattvas in the world, a theme which we shall now examine.

Vow of the Bodhisattva

"Let them hate or love me, accuse or wrong me, but let them share in enlightenment," is the prayer of the eighth-century poet Sāntideva. "May I be a protector for the unprotected, a guide for wanderers, a boat or bridge for those desiring the other shore, a lamp or bed to those in need, a slave for those who need a slave." In traditional Buddhist asceticism, one may reach a stage of contemplation and spiritual discipline where Sāntideva's vision and the Bodhisattva vow will no longer seem outrageous. Bowing before the *guru,* perhaps in the presence of images and scriptures representative of the Buddhist lineage, one then repeats a formula similar to that mentioned by Trungpa Chögyam in his autobiography: "I vow to proceed towards enlightenment. I accept all creatures as my father and mother with infinite compassion. . . . Let my master accept me as a future Buddha, but [let me remain] a Bodhisattva without entering Nirvana so long as a single blade of grass remains unenlightened."

The implications of such a vow are momentous. Like the Flying Dutchman, you chain yourself to perpetual *saṃsāra* on earth and even in future cosmic *purgatorios*. You forfeit for the sake of others whatever merit and wisdom you will ever acquire. Clearly this attitude constitutes a direct onslaught against the selfish brokerage abuses of a consequent eschatology. "As long as the enlightenment drama has a central character, 'me,' who has certain attributes, there is no hope of enlightenment," Chögyam explains in *Myth of Freedom*. The Bodhisattva vow means we are willing to share our own chaos and confusion with that of other sentient beings. "In the Mahayana we acknowledge that we are a Buddha, an awakened one, and act accordingly, even though all kinds of doubts and problems might arise. . . . The Bodhisattva is a very humble pilgrim who works in the soil of samsara to dig out the jewel embedded in it."

Now, this embedded jewel is surely our own acknowledged Buddha-nature, or the *nirvāṇa-saṃsāra* identity. It depends again on one's eschatological perspective. Notice Tantrayanist Chögyam's tendency in the combined citations above to use the terms *Buddha* and *Bodhisattva* almost interchangeably, so that it is hazardous to aim for a simple definition of *Bodhisattva,* or to distinguish it sharply from the flood of Buddha images in popular iconography. A Bodhisattva is literally a *bodhi*-being, someone enlightened already or in the process of aspiring toward enlightenment. Its more common usage means someone who has attained Buddhahood but postpones *nirvāṇa* to help others reach Buddhahood. According to a strict future eschatology, a Buddha has achieved literal *parinirvāṇa,* egoless and unreachable; but Bodhisattva saints, hovering at the brink of *parinirvāṇa,* share our same samsaric destiny and respond with empathic assistance. According to a strict present eschatology, on the other hand, represented by Chögyam's position, everyone begins as a partially aware Buddha-Bodhisattva. The Buddha-*dharmakāya* is already identified with all, or at least present and active within all. Once meditation has become an intuitive way of experiencing reality, the Bodhisattva dynamic comes alive. We feel paradoxical tension between the *prajñā* (spiritual wisdom), the awareness of our shared ontological Buddha-nature; and the *karuṇā* (compassion), that guides our hearts toward the more tangible misery and ignorance impeding an average person's Buddha-realization.

Partisan Mahayanists never tire misrepresenting the Theravāda privileged *arhat* monk, an isolated religious virtuoso confined to the pursuit of a selfish *nirvāṇa,* and at best, concerned only incidentally about others' cries for help. Carrying this naive dialectic one step further, we can juxtapose the Theravāda *arhat's prajñā* against the Mahāyāna Bodhisattva's *karuṇā*, both of which are transcended in the *prajñā-karuṇā* synthesis of Tantrayāna. Exotic Tibetan Buddhist liturgies exploit every imaginative *mantra, mudrā* (gesture), and visual design to celebrate this union of masculine *karuṇā* and feminine *prajñā*: the interpenetrating triangles of a *yantra,* spidery-armed divine couples in sexual *yabyum* embrace, a *dorje* scepter in the right hand plunged into a bell in the left hand, the chant of *Oṃ mani padme hum* (Amen to the jewel in the lotus). Committed lives of most Theravadists and Mahayanists, I suspect, give evidence that their accustomed theoretical polarities overlap, or actually include each other. World-denying phrases somehow reappear on the lips of many world-affirming activists. *Karuṇā* has been prized as the best way to extinguish the ego and reach *prajñā*. Through *prajñā* meditation one makes friends with oneself, and since this friendship is too joyful to be contained, it spills out into relationships with the world. Hard-won compassion for oneself, uncertain of its direction, can eventually sweep away boundaries between self and others.

The Bodhisattva's self-annihilating compassion is an ideal too ancient, widespread, and multidimensional to be appropriated exclusively by a single Buddhist school. The concept's most obvious roots can be found in Gautama's own life as a prolonged, resolute deferment of *parinirvāṇa*. The *Mahāvagga* of the Vinaya contains perhaps the earliest legend preserved by *saṃgha* disciples about Gautama's crucial decision to delay *nirvāṇa* and share the Dhamma. His instinctive inclination had been to give up preaching. "With great pains have I acquired it. Enough! Why should I now proclaim it? This doctrine will not be easy to understand for beings lost in lust and hatred." But he is soon persuaded otherwise by an inner theophany, or perhaps the personified *karuṇā* dimension of Gautama's spiritual consciousness. "Alas, the world will perish," the Hindu god Brahmā argues, "if the Tathāgata's mind decides to remain in quiet, and not to preach the doctrine. . . . As a man standing on a rock, . . . look down upon the people lost in suffering, overcome by birth and decay—you, who have freed yourself from suffering!" (I,5:2–7). Gautama's compassion later becomes characteristic of his gracious dialogic method of teaching, and recurs as a major Dhamma theme in such Vinaya sayings as the following: "If you are not concerned for one another, monks, who is there to be concerned for you? Whoever wants to tend me should tend the sick."

Many Jātaka tales, the Pali Canon pages most familiar in Theravāda cultures even today, present earlier incarnations of Gautama as an animal or human martyr Buddha-to-be. Each story opens with a dialogue between Gautama and his disciples, setting the didactic context. Then the tale is introduced as an exemplum, and concluded invariably by the formula "After this lesson, the Master summarized his theme and specified his incarnation: 'At that time the human king was Ānanda, the monkey's retinue the *saṃgha,* and the monkey king myself.'" What seems most arresting about these charming stories is not just the set of imaginative variations on a limited range of themes, but the incredible eagerness of so many Bodhisattva characters to sacrifice their lives. In a few representative animal tales, the monkey king stretches his body between two trees on either side of a river so that his troop can tread across his back to safety from pursuing hunters, whom his own body is too exhausted to escape. A deer king persuades a pregnant doe to let him replace her at the slaughtering block. An elephant permits an indigent forester to dig out and sell his prized ivory tusks. A rabbit shakes himself free of fleas to spare their lives, and surrenders his own life to the flames so that a fasting Brāhmin can enjoy his meal without having to slay animals: "Offering his whole body as a free gift, he sprang up, and like a royal swan, alighting on a cluster of lotuses, in an ecstasy of joy he fell on the heap of live coals."

A hermit in another Jātaka story is so intent on caring for animals ravaged by a drought that he almost starves. A person of low caste persists generously to share his food with a meticulous starving Brāhmin, who would rather die than eat something contaminated by the other's touch. In the final ten Lives, called *dāsajati,* Gautama's second-to-last incarnation is Prince Vessantara, whose alleged first words as a child were, "Mother, what gift can I make?" His life becomes almost a parody of Bodhisattva self-abandonment—he gives away a kingdom, then his two children, and even his wife. Like the Book of Job, this tale ends with the gods restoring all his gifts a hundredfold.

Besides Gautama's renunciation of *nirvāṇa* and the accounts of his legendary Jātaka births, we have already explored a third Bodhisattva context in earlier sections of this chapter. Many Buddhist kings throughout the history of Southeast Asia perceived themselves as Aśokan Bodhisattvas, *dhammacakkavatti* incarnations of the Maitreya messiah, restoring the Golden Age of Dhamma. For example, the epithet Bodhisattva-*avatāra* was added to later medieval Sinhalese kings, and one ruler a few centuries earlier described the ideal of his reign, "to be able in every successive rebirth, . . . with my hand of great compassion, to deliver suffering humanity from the extensive quagmire of samsara." In common dreams of a Buddhist utopia, the State would dissolve into the monastic *saṃgha,* with its standard of shared community property. It is significant that U Nu, to celebrate in 1956 the 2,500th anniversary of Buddha's *parinirvāṇa,* staged a celebration in Rangoon, at which 2,500 men in uniform simultaneously donned the garb of *bhikkhus,* a sign for many that the *cakkavatti* millennium had indeed arrived. Unmasking these Bodhisattva pretensions, his wily opponents would later urge people not to vote U Nu back into the premiership, for worldly power might impede his achievement of complete Buddhahood.

The fourth and most essential contribution to the developing Theravāda Bodhisattva concept is its Mahayanist interiorization. A Bodhisattva is not just Gautama or an external royal exemplar to be emulated, but an enabling spiritual dynamic within everyone. The cosmos is throbbing with millions of helping hands, various heavenly Bodhisattva *saṃboghakāya* manifestations, omniscient and compassionate. Among Mahayanists, the Nichīren and Jōdo traditions claim more than sixty percent of Japanese Buddhists, according to 1976 statistics in the *Japanese Yearbook of Religions.* Since Nichīren is based on the Lotus Sutra and Jōdo on the three Amidist Sutras, perhaps the best way to grasp the Mahayanist Bodhisattva motif is to trace its embodiment in these authoritative scriptures.

The most influential of all Mahayanist scriptures is the *Saddharmapuṇḍarika-sūtra* (Lotus Sutra of the True Dharma). Written in plethoric second-century Sanskrit prose and verse, it introduced the glorified Gautama, virtually deified, presiding over a heavenly court of Buddhas and Bodhisattvas. Like Viṣṇu-Kṛṣṇa in the *Bhagavad Gītā,* the transcendent Buddha will save any *bhakta* invoking his name or paying special respect to this *sūtra*: "I am all-knowing, all-seeing. Come to me, gods and mankind. Hear the law! . . . Having reached the shore myself, I carry others to the shore; being free I make free, being comforted I comfort" (5c). Again like Viṣṇu, quick to reappear as redeemer whenever the world needs him, the Buddha admits he adopted the *avatāra* form of Gautama, simply to make himself tangible and accessible to our weakness.

The twenty-fourth chapter of this *sūtra* is a lyrical ode to Avalokiteśvara and his loving transformations, one of the two Bodhisattva attendants to Buddha Amida. Two meanings of Avalokiteśvara's very name sum up the Bodhisattva essence—the lord looking down with compassion, or being looked up to for help. His standard epithet is Mahākaruṇā, which gives him a widespread reputation for numinous power to save people from natural disasters, infertility, and especially deathbed terrors. He becomes Kuan-yin in China, Kannon in Japan, and often assumes an androgynous or feminine identity there, notably the archetypal madonna with child. In iconography Avalokiteśvara is given many arms and faces to show his vigilant compassion, directed to all points of the compass. The endless lines of many-armed Kannon statues in the Kyoto Sangyusangendo Temple evoke an awesome impression of his thousand helping arms. Tantrayāna Buddhists view the Dalai Lama as the continuous reincarnation of their national patron Avalokiteśvara to protect and lead his people.

Three themes dominate the Lotus Sutra. "Like a cloud shedding its water without distinction," the Buddha's salvation is universal. And powerful Bodhisattva multitudes are poised with their aid, eager simply to be asked. Second, the Dhamma of this *sūtra* replaces all preceding versions of the Dhamma—others were simply temporary mirages, toys, endearing compromises to lure us beyond our hesitant anticipations. In other words, the Theravāda Canon is discounted, or patronized for its restricted relevance. *Arhats* are expressly disparaged who feel themselves "too high for this Buddha-vehicle." Third, this Dhamma of mercy has been revealed to guide us through an urgent apocalyptic period that now approaches, "the last period, the last five hundred years, when the true law is in a state of decay" (13:25).

Chinese T'ien-t'ai Buddhists of the sixth century and their later Japanese Tendai disciples were attracted to the inclusive vision of this *sūtra,* and used it as the cornerstone for a Buddhist synthesis that left space for an exciting diversity of Dhamma emphases. Breaking with this established school, the stormy medieval patriot Nichīren turned back to the second and third themes noted above, the *sūtra*'s apocalyptic condemnation of any Dhamma other than its own. His famous Daimoku *mantra—Namu myoho renge kyo* (Amen to the Lotus Sutra of the Mystical Law)—is still the battle cry of Sōka Gakkai and other controversial militant Nichīren groups today. The centrality of Gautama and of a single transcendent *dharmakāya* must not be jeopardized by the excessive clutter of devotions to negligible Buddhas like Amida or other celestial intermediaries. Nichīren added a touch of strident Puritan aggressiveness to the Bodhisattva image. Believing himself a reincarnation of Jogyo, one of the chief Bodhisattvas introduced in this *sūtra*, he tried to embody the more selective judicious compassion of a father, rather than the forgiving unconditional compassion of a mother. A hard but authentic mercy must be intolerant of vice and error, he told his followers. An uncompromising moral prophet will use *shakubuku*, or forceful persuasion, if necessary, in the service of Daimoku and the True Lotus.

The epitome of Buddhist *bhakti,* Jōdo Shinshū, the second major Buddhist movement in contemporary Japan, traces its antecedents to the fifth-century Ching-t'u or Pure Land School of China, and reached its present doctrinal identity under Honen and Shinran in the thirteenth century. The presumption of both Nichīren Shōshū and Jōdo Shinshū is that faith has crucially eroded in this final age. So much deadening *karma* has accumulated through past births that the average person needs a concise practical spiritual strategy, not the athletic concentration of Ch'an or Zen professionals. The Jōdo tradition believes that a simple *bhakti* gesture of faith in Amida Buddha will carry you at death to a Buddha-field, the Pure Land or Western Paradise. In some scenarios, this condition is *nirvāṇa* itself; whereas in others it is a mild *purgatorio* interlude, the length of which depends first on your stage of spiritual growth and second on your decision to enter *nirvāṇa* or return to earth as a Bodhisattva. For Shinshū, the True Pure Land Sect founded by Shinran, faith alone is sufficient for *nirvāṇa,* faith without works—just a single invocation of the Nembutsu *mantra, Namu Amida Butsu* (Amen to the Buddha of Infinite Light).

The basic Jōdo scriptures are the Major and Minor *Sukhāvatī-vyūha-sūtras* and the *Amitāyurdhyāna-sūtra* (Amida Meditation Sutra), ascribed to the same second-century Sanskrit context of the Lotus Sutra. The dramatic setting of all three texts is a dialogue from Guatama's earthly teaching career, in which he commends both the nirvanic path of *sukhāvatī* or Pure Land, and the Buddha Amitābha, who established it earlier in "an enormous, immeasurable, incomprehensible *kalpa* before now." The Major *Sukhāvatī* lists all exhaustive forty-six provisions of Amida's original vow, which can be summarized briefly. Long ago, Bhikkhu Dharmakara vowed to achieve *nirvāṇa,* but only on condition that his karmic merits could be transformed into a prenirvanic sanctuary for all who put their trust in his promise. His perfect Bodhisattva vow granted, he now reigns as the most available of all *saṃboghakāya* Buddhas, lord of eternal life *(amitāyus)* and eternal light *(amitābha)*, often portrayed with a nimbus of great light or fire. It is significant that the Minor *Sukhāvatī* does not require the strict moral life and "stock of merits" specified by our larger text. But in a passage that would later provoke endless Buddhist controversy, it insists that "beings are not in that Buddha country of the Tathāgata Amitāyus as a reward and result of good works performed in this present life" (10). The Meditation Sutra views Amitābha's very nature as absolute compassion, welcoming at the instant of death even the greatest sinners, who have only to utter the Nembutsu, the *triratna* formula, or simply the Buddha's name.

A few remarkable lines in the *Amitāyurdhyāna* may bring some clarity to the parallels often cited between Shinran's Nembutsu, Luther's justification by faith, and Zen *satori*. Who is the Buddha Amida? "Every Buddha Tathāgata is one whose spiritual body is *dharma-dhatu-kāya*. . . . Consequently, when you have perceived Buddha, it is indeed your own mind that possesses those . . . marks of excellence which you see in Buddha. In other words, it is your mind that becomes Buddha, it is your mind that is indeed Buddha" (17). Therefore, the argument concludes, the most appropriate way to achieve *sukhāvatī* and *nirvāṇa* is *samādhi* meditation, facilitated by an active creative imagination.

Obvious theological differences separate Shinran's inner Buddha-dynamic from Luther's transcendent-historical Christ, but the religious anxiety and trust, the prayers and images from both traditions look scarcely distinguishable. An accurate contemporary sample of Jōdo confessional literature, Niwa's *Buddha Tree* novel, despite its misogyny and clumsy homiletic style, presents the credible character of a Jōdo priest, trying to extricate himself from a sinful love affair. He wanders through all the classical psychological labyrinths of Paul, Augustine, and Luther. To save his soul, he forces himself to kneel in the temple all night, intoning the Three Sutras; he mutters the Nembutsu but fears it has become a shallow habit; he distrusts any repentence that comes too cheaply. Like Shinran himself, he at last "felt himself to be so hardened and steeped in sin that he was beyond even the hope of being saved—but it was this very despair of self that proved to be the beginning of his salvation." There must be no mistake that Shin or Lutheran surrender means an easy salvation, as its critics caricature it. Faith still demands deeds, not as meritorious cause but as plausible consequence. Neither the simple Nembutsu prayer nor the technique of any other world religious tradition can guarantee peace for the obsessive self-punitive conscience. Authentic Zen, too, means not just instant enlightenment or *satori* ecstasy, but a sustained transformation of life based on such experiences.

In the controversial dichotomy between *jiriki* and *tariki*, self-power and other-power, the resolute self-reliance of Zen is usually pitted against the *bhakti* self-abandonment and absolute dependence of Jōdo Shinshū. Yet I think both traditions actually draw much closer. Clouded by *avidyā*, or ignorance, the ego in routine experience, crystallized by social conditioning and personal character armor, confronts a severe spiritual crisis or a series of *kōans* designed by a Zen master. Exhausting its usual resources in trying to reach a solution, the mind breaks down in desperation and at last, empty and objectless, breaks through to a wider consciousness. This is the dramatic *satori* awakening—the fiction of an isolated autonomous ego dies, replaced by an experience of cosmic unity, the paradoxically empty yet complete *śūnyatā,* a more inclusive relational *self.*

D. T. Suzuki, in his ingenious shorthand attempt to narrow the gap between Jōdo Shinshū and Zen, explains *satori* as a numinous experience of the *ho* or absolute self, reached by the breakthrough of the *ki* or relative, conceptual self. Similarly, in the Nembutsu formula, *Namu* is *ki,* Amida-Butsu is *ho,* and one suddenly realizes the absolute dependence of *ki* on *ho,* or more profoundly still, their transcendental unity. According to the *Amitāyurdhyāna* text quoted, I am already Buddha, and all the attributes perceived in Amida are projected and mythologized attributes of my own unconscious Buddha-nature. The distant Pure Land can be remythologized into an alternative spatial myth of depth, interiority, and ultimacy. Saved because of my trust in Amida's compassionate Bodhisattva vow long ago to save me, I am also saved because I now appropriate and reenact his vow. The Nembutsu *mantra* is just one way to give ritual utterance to my own redemptive Bodhisattva care for the world.

FURTHER READING

1. **Overview.** An enormously well-annotated bibliography is Frank Reynolds et al., eds., *Guide to Buddhist Religion* (Hall, 1981). In addition to the *Dictionary of Buddhism: Indian and South-East Asian* (Bagchi, 1981) by Trevor Ling, it is the best starting point for research. Ling's entries are succinct and accurate.

2. **Buddhist Religious Life in Its General Context.** The best way to get beyond the accepted charts and dichotomies of textbook Buddhism is to study the Buddhist phenomenon through various cultural adaptations. Follow the graphic plates and text of Dietrich Seckel, *The Art of Buddhism,* tr. Ann Keep (Crown, 1964), and Philip Rawson, *The Art of Southeast Asia* (Praeger, 1967); and observe the complex interrelationship of Hindu-Buddhist themes in Albert Moore, *Iconography of Religions: An Introduction* (Fortress, 1977). Moore gives helpful information on the stupa, *dhammacakka,* and the protean figure of Avalokiteśvara. A more specialized essay on early Buddhist aniconic symbols and their slow transformation into iconic is Sukumare Dutt's *The Buddha and Five After-Centuries* (Luzac, 1957). A summary of the intellectual and

religious environment during these first five Buddhist centuries, and some suggestions on reading texts critically, are found in Richard Drummond's *Gautama the Buddha: An Essay in Religious Understanding* (Eerdmans, 1974).

3. **Buddhist Adaptations within Specific Cultures.** John Koller's *The Indian Way* (Macmillan, 1982) shows the Hindu matrix of Buddhist thought; Ananda Coomaraswamy, *Hinduism and Buddhism* (Wisdom Library, n.d.), gives a Hindu view of the Buddhist reform as part of a more inclusive esoteric *philosophia perennis*. Roderick Hindery, *Comparative Ethics in Hindu and Buddhist Traditions* (Motilal Banarsidass, 1978), suggests links between the *Gītā* and early Mahayanist scriptures.

In the Theravāda schools, you can trace conflicts between kammic and nibbanic attitudes, and also the social psychology of merit-transfer in Melford Spiro's *Buddhism and Society: A Great Tradition and Its Burmese Vicissitudes* (Harper and Row, 1970). Sri Lankan practice is analyzed in Richard Gombrich's *Precept and Practice: Traditional Buddhism in the Rural Highlands of Ceylon* (Clarendon, 1971); Gombrich develops details of the *nētra pinkama* festivities and surveys lay and *bhikkhu* reactions in "The Consecration of a Buddhist Image." *Journal of Asian Studies* 26:1 (November 1966), pp. 23–36. In "Religion and Psychosocial Development in Sinhalese Buddhism," *Journal of Asian Studies* 37:2 (February 1978), pp. 221–32, John Halverson tries to sift out the Buddhist dimension of the eclectic religious context there. The synthesis of Christian and Buddhist ethical components can be observed in the writings of Dharmapala—see Gananath Obeyesekere's "Personal Identity and Cultural Crisis: The Case of Anagarika Dharmapala of Shri Lanka," in Frank Reynolds and Donald Capps, eds., *The Biographical Process* (Mouton, 1976), pp. 221–52.

Buddhist schools in China are surveyed in Howard Smith's *Chinese Religions* (Holt, Rinehart, 1968); but the most interesting study in this area is Leon Hurvitz's "The Mind of the Early Chinese Buddhist," in *Developments in Buddhist Thought,* ed. Roy Amore (Canadian Corporation for Studies in Religion, 1979), pp. 114–61.

Buddhist interactions with Shinto and Neo-Confucian traditions are analyzed in Joseph Kitagawa's *Religion in Japanese History* (Columbia University Press, 1966). In *Buddhist-Christian Empathy* (Oriens Institute for Religious Research, 1980). Joseph Spae, CICM, explores the Bodhisattva motif in Japanese religious attitudes, especially those of Jōdo and Zen. Two outstanding Zen studies by D. T. Suzuki are "What Is Shin Buddhism?" *Eastern Buddhist* 5 (October 1972), pp. 1–12; and "Lectures on Zen Buddhism" in *Zen Buddhism and Psychoanalysis* (Harper and Row, 1960), pp. 1–76, a symposium with Erich Fromm and Richard De Martino. In the latter, Suzuki develops his *ho-ki* dialectic, here as the *sho-hen satori* synthesis. Daiei Kaneko's "The Meaning of Salvation in the Doctrine of Pure Land Buddhism" *Eastern Buddhist* (September 1965), pp. 48–63, is a helpful brief introduction to the three Amida scriptures.

John Blofeld's *The Way of Power: A Practical Guide to the Tantric Mysticism of Tibet* (Allen and Unwin, 1970) gives a clear Mahāyāna setting for this relatively inaccessible Buddhist synthesis. In *My Land and My People* (McGraw-Hill, 1962), the Dalai Lama includes a fine brief compendium of Tantrayanist doctrine.

Emma Layman's *Buddhism in America* (Nelson-Hall, 1976) presents the detailed Oriental setting for each Buddhist sect and then its adaptations to the American scene. The Jōdo and Nichīren sections are most illuminating, especially the apparent efforts by Sōka Gakkai to modify its aggressive tactics. Nolan Jacobson's *Buddhism and the Contemporary World: Change and Self-Correction* (Southern Illinois University Press, 1983) exemplifies an attempt to correlate Buddhist and Whiteheadean process philosophy.

The new Buddhist activism is documented in *The New Face of Buddha: Buddhism and Political Power in Southeast Asia* (Coward-McCann, 1967) by Jerrold Schecter, who focuses especially on Vietnamese monks, Sōka Gakkai militants, and U Nu. Emanuel Sarkisyanz's *Buddhist Backgrounds of the Burmese Revolution* (Nijhoff, 1965) is an outstanding collation of Neo-Aśokan rock inscriptions, editorials, and political oratory, culminating in the U Nu phenomenon. See also *U Nu of Burma* (Stanford University Press, 1963) by Richard Butwell; and a sample of his speeches during a visit to the U.S. in *An Asian Speaks* (Burma Embassy, 1955). In "Toward a Buddhist Anthropology: The Problem of the Secular," *Journal American Academy of Religions* 36 (1968), pp. 203–16, Bardwell Smith sketches the rudiments of an activist lay theology.

4. **Buddhist Scriptures.** Two standard introductory anthologies are Edward Conze, ed., *Buddhist Scriptures* (Penguin, 1968); and the older *Buddhism in Translations* (Atheneum, 1896), ed. Henry Warren. See the Max Müller fifty-volume series, *The Sacred Books of the East,* originally published in the 1890s, reissued in the UNESCO Collection of Representative Works, Indian Series (Motilal Banarsidass, 1960–), for translations of selected Pali and Sanskrit classics. In the Theravāda tradition, there are the Vinaya texts (vols. 13, 17, 20), *The Dhammapada* (10), *Questions of King Milinda* (35–6), and assorted *suttas* (11), including the important *Mahāparinibbāna.* In the Mahāyāna tradition there are the Lotus Sutra (21), and the collected *Amida Suttanta* (49).

The Jātaka stories are most widely read in their Pali Text Society edition, ed. E. B. Cowell, 3 vols. (Luzac, 1957). Elizabeth Wray et al., *Ten Lives of the Buddha: Siamese Temple Paintings and Jataka Tales* (Weatherhill, 1972), gives a popular retelling of the last ten stories, with interesting Thai illustrations.

5

Humanist Rights

Bertrand Russell one day in 1901 had a sudden taste of the lonely futility in most people's lives, much like the shock of death and samsaric misery that first met Gautama outside his protected palace garden. With characteristic understatement, Russell would later refer back to this shattering awareness as "not unlike what religious people call 'conversion,'" an experience that drove him from contemplative mathematics into a career of militant public advocacy. He concluded that all of us, doomed to extinction in a dying solar system, must first accept this tragic verdict without flinching, and then at least help those suffering alongside us by our sympathy, encouragement, and untiring affection. "Three passions, simple but overwhelmingly strong, have governed my life: the longing for love, the search for knowledge, and unbearable pity for the suffering of mankind," he writes at the head of his three-volume autobiography. "Love and knowledge, so far as they are possible, led upward toward the heavens. But always pity brought me back to earth. Echoes of cries of pain reverberate in my heart. . . . " Here are the essentials of a traditional Bodhisattva, except for a single important detail, expressed with vigor and clarity in Russell's *Why I Am Not a Christian:* "I think all the great religions of the world—Buddhism, Hinduism, Christianity, Islam, and Communism—both untrue and harmful. . . . What the world needs is not dogma but an attitude of scientific inquiry combined with a belief that the torture of millions is not desirable, whether inflicted by Stalin or by a Deity imagined in the likeness of the believer."

With Russell's apologia as a point of departure, we can conjure a loose fellowship, selective and mostly implied, of various people trying to be authentic human beings. Their origin lies in the fringe of outsiders, drop-outs, and partly-ins surrounding all the charted world religious systems. We shall name this inchoate but perennial tradition *Humanist*—the concern to humanize the world, to celebrate, secure, and extend human values. These liberties we call the basic *human rights,* conceived by most Humanists as inherent not in each isolated ego, but in communal humanity itself, at the service of which governments can be conditionally summoned or dismissed. One of the most touching exchanges in Camus's *The Plague* occurs during a brief swim taken by Tarrou and Dr. Rieux as respite from their work with plague victims. "What interests me," Tarrou confides, "is learning how to become a saint. . . . Can one be a saint without God?" Rieux replies, "Heroism and sanctity don't really appeal to me, I imagine. What interests me is being a man." The two men's shared code constitutes a Humanist compendium. They treat the plague, whether it be physical microbes, the taint of Nazi collaboration, or some other moral flaw, as something within us all. They are vigilant not to contaminate others less infected, and "while unable to be saints, but refusing to bow down to pestilences, strive their utmost to be healers."

Our Humanist model must be wide enough to include both civil libertarian activists and more contemplative figures like Rilke and Faulkner. It implies complete human nature, not just the desiccated intellect caricatured in rationalist, free thinker, and village atheist stereotypes. Notice Russell's use of the word *passion,* the intensity of feeling pervading his statement, and his struggle to combine knowledge, love, and pity. Moreover, human nature must not be viewed as separable from the unfathomable, numinous matrix of cosmic Nature within which it is only one evolving component. Responding to a questionnaire once sent him by *Humanist* magazine, Russell hesitated to identify himself with the Humanist tag used by this organization because he had been finding "the nonhuman part of the cosmos is much more interesting and satisfactory than the human part." We shall expect outstanding representative Humanists, by the way, to distrust labels of Humanist orthodoxy, constitutions and manifestos, hierarchies, journals, Humanist rallies and political lobbies, as demonic substitutes for the religious baggage from which most have long strained to free themselves.

If we are searching for a Humanist tradition that is patently *alternative,* it is convenient that Russell should comply by attacking all our classical world religious traditions. Two phases can be distinguished in the average Humanist credo—positive disclosure and then, as a corollary, prophetic iconoclasm. First, the human rights and responsibilities endorsed by a Humanist consensus; then, an aggressive campaign against specific counterfeit humanisms allegedly hostile to these verities. Adding Marxist Humanists to Buddhists and Christians, Russell would be more consistent to include any "ism," even his own Humanist philosophy, insofar as it has the power to become an end in itself, to shut off inquiry, to be twisted into a sanction for antihuman ignorance and injustice. In this chapter, we are interested in both phases of any Humanist self-definition: its affirmative identity, and also the major perceived adversaries with which it disidentifies. We presume the ideal of an open Humanist, resolutely tolerant by definition though often anticlerical and antiscriptural by temperament, alert to discover anonymous Humanists anywhere, even among those with a traditional religious affiliation. After sketches of the Marx and Freud Humanist legacy, I shall attempt to reconstruct a Humanist spirituality.

The Marxist Humanist

U Ba Yin, former Burmese minister of education, once remarked that Buddhists and Marxists have much in common. Both had long dismissed the Great Dictator God, omnipotent and imperialistic, fashioned by religious believers in the West. Whereas Soviet Marxists admittedly show a pattern of totalistic command in Russia, mostly to fill the power gap left by an autocratic God and Church, the more immanentist Buddhist traditions of Asia seem to offer better prospects for a truly Communist egalitarian society. Despite Yin's prognosis, however, we can take the less sanguine situation in contemporary China as a paradigm. In the Mao era, only a private esoteric Buddhist spirituality had been allowed to flourish. The long-suppressed exoteric forms of Buddhist ritual, preaching, proselytizing, and social activism, nevertheless, give recent indications of a nascent, scrupulously monitored revival. The theocratic structures of Tibet and Mongolia now lie dismantled, much like the once-powerful Catholic Church in parts of eastern Europe and the Orthodox Church in Russia, both of which seemed to impede the Soviet Marxist advance.

Chinese Marxists took over Tibet purportedly to vindicate longstanding territorial claims and to liberate peasants from feudal exploitation by the lamas. Shortly before his invasion, Mao Tse-tung attended a New Year's celebration honoring the Dalai Lama during his visit to Peking. Tibetan Buddhists customarily break off a piece of special New Year's cake and toss it to the ceiling as an offering to Buddha. When the meaning of this ritual had been explained to Mao, he threw one piece above, and then with a grin of mischief, dropped another piece onto the floor. In his autobiography, the Dalai Lama mentions that Mao on another occasion expressed admiration for Gautama, who, though a prince, had at least concerned himself with problems of common people. "But of course," Mao concluded, "religion is poison. It has two great defects: it undermines the race, and secondly it retards the progress of the country. Tibet and Mongolia have both been poisoned by it."

A century before this crucial conversation, Karl Marx wrote an article on British Indian imperialism in which he analyzed two Hindu social abuses—caste inequities and the alleged human diminishment caused by exaggerated reverence for the cow and other animals. Although he generally showed little knowledge or curiosity about the religious phenomenon beyond his own European Judeo-Christian milieu, he was convinced that exposure to other religious traditions could at least sabotage uncritical loyalty to one's own faith. "Bring your gods to a land where other gods prevail . . . and everybody will laugh at your subjective imagination." Repeated experiences like this could prepare people for the country of Reason, where no gods exist at all. In all these situations, we view Marx and his disciples handling religion first as a perilous socioeconomic epiphenomenon, and then less directly, as a cognitive position to be discredited. Lenin once cautioned that direct battles against religion might succeed perversely in preventing its death by reviving an interest in it. For Marx had predicted that once the sources of social alienation were healed, the religious illusion would die without its essential fuel in human misery.

Marx's perception of religious distortion cannot be separated from his outrage over the global bourgeois malaise of his era. His essay "On the Jewish Question," groping for an image of vile haggling and greed, settles on the nineteenth-century Yankee stereotype, supposed to be pious and politically free. Commercial exchange and bargaining dominate his mind. When he travels, he carries his shop or office on his back and talks of nothing but interest and profit. If he grows silent about his own business for an instant, you can presume he wants only to sniff out the business of someone else. "Mammon is his idol to whom he prays not only with his lips but with all the power of his body and soul. In his eyes, the world is nothing but a stock exchange, and he is convinced that here below he has no other destiny than to become richer than his neighbors."

The *Communist Manifesto* a few years later traces in sharp apocalyptic terms the impact of this naked self-interest on the rest of society. Personal links between people are debased into mere exchange value, exploitation, egotistic calculation. The countless chartered human freedoms are reduced to a single inhuman freedom, the right to property and free trade. Male laborers have become mere appendages to the machine, worth no more than the cost to feed them; their wives commodities, public and private prostitutes; their children a burdensome debt or investment for later security. The *Manifesto*'s most penetrating insight, in my opinion, is the following distillation of Marx's historical dialectic, addressed to the ruling classes: "Your very ideas are but the outgrowth of your bourgeois production and property conditions, just as your jurisprudence is but the will of your class made into a law for all. . . ." From a distance someone might recognize the rationalizations used by ancient and feudal property owners to justify their status. These are selfish misconceptions that "you are of course forbidden to admit in the case of your own bourgeois forms of property." The most glaring deceptions Marx and Engels have in mind here are the property owners' smug religious alibis.

Victorian England, of course, provided Marx with a showcase of religious rationalizations, richly illustrated in the fiction of Dickens, Trollope, and George Eliot. Marx once witnessed a Hyde Park demonstration in 1855 by lower classes against the passage of the Beer Bill and Sunday Trading Bill. Both laws were enacted by business lobbies, ostensibly to preserve Sabbath rectitude by closing pubs and stores, but actually to instill habits of temperance and thrift among workers, and discriminate against small shops and against those laborers too harried to shop except on Sundays. This ingenuous interweaving of capitalist and Christian motifs can be sampled in the popular Protestant hymn "Rock of Ages," which its composer, Toplady, once explicated with an analogy from economics. The debt incurred by each sinner before God, computed at the rate of one sin per second, results in a national debt so enormous that all Europe could not pay it off. We can only abase ourselves before the Great Creditor's mercy: "Not the labors of my hands / Can fulfill Thy law's demands." This is the bourgeois God-image that Marx calls "my Lord Capital." "Money degrades all the gods of mankind and converts them into commodities," he argues, developing Feuerbach's perception of religion as a form of self-alienation. "It has robbed the whole world, the human world as well as nature, of its proper worth. Money is the alienated essence of human labor and life, and this alien essence dominates human beings as they worship it."

Born into this grossly materialistic period of history, the Marxist and Christian both begin with an honest acknowledgement of the circumstances in which they find themselves: "corrupted by the entire organization of our society, lost to themselves, alienated, oppressed and dominated by inhuman relations and elements." They both yearn passionately for an ideal human future of liberation. But here their positions sharply diverge. The traditional Christian presumes this alienation inherent and necessary, calls it a condition of original sinfulness, and searches beyond every possible human remedy for divine redemption. The Marxist, striving directly to uproot the social sources of this alienation, treats the Christian's recourse to God as a harmful delusion, which defers immediate efforts to an indefinite future, and narcotizes anxiety that might otherwise prove an inducement to action. "People make religion," says Marx in a few of his most famous lines, "religion does not make people. . . . Religion is the sigh of the oppressed creature, the heart of a heartless world. . . . The abolition of religion as people's illusory happiness is the demand for their real happiness. The demand to abandon illusions about their condition is a demand to abandon the condition which requires illusions." In other words, the religious dynamic, outcome of a flawed societal structure, will be retrojected back and dissolved into its original human components after the social revolution.

Marx throughout his life composed various platforms and broadsides on civil liberties, including the right to humane working conditions, a living family wage, universal suffrage, and a free education; heavy progressive taxes, restricted inheritance rights, state-controlled utilities; and a secular state government permitting the unhampered existence of privately supported voluntary religious groups. A convinced heir to the Age of Reason, he disdains the scriptural revelations proclaimed by contentious religious groups and, especially in the first four decades of his life, trusts philosophy and political recruitment as the two principal allies to implement his radical vision. "Who should decide the limits of scientific inquiry if not scientific inquiry itself?" he argues against an editor advocating ecclesiastical censorship. "Philosophy asks what is true, not what is accepted as such; what is true for all people, not just individuals. Its metaphysical truths do not recognize the boundaries of political geography. . . . You demand faith in your faith, whereas philosophy demands not faith in its own results but the test of doubt."

Stripped of their traditional religious dreams, how shall people find strength to bring about a future classless society? This is the exact question pondered by Nietzsche in *Joyous Cosmology:* "You will never pray nor adore again, nor rest in endless trust. . . . There is no avenger for you, no eventual solution. . . . People of renunciation, do you want to renounce all this? . . . Perhaps this very renunciation will also lend us the strength to bear the renunciation itself. Perhaps the human race will rise ever higher once they cease to flow out into a god." Marx reaches the same conclusion. With property and political clout so negligible, the proletarian class has nothing left to renounce except its seductive religious evasions. "By heralding the dissolution of a hitherto existing world order," says Marx, "the proletariat merely proclaims the secret of its own existence. For the proletariat is a factual dissolution of that world order." Reinhold Niebuhr thinks Marx's lasting significance is this imaginative religious interpretation of proletarian destiny. Society's brutalized victims are transformed into its moral saviors. To make deprivation and social defeat of the proletariat the very presage of its final victory, to foresee in its loss of all property the fate of a civilization in which no one will have privileges of property—this is to snatch victory out of defeat in the style of classical drama and of all major religious traditions.

The century after his death has witnessed extraordinarily varied uses of Marx. The Soviet Union and China claim to be rival laboratories testing his social theory, and today there exist Buddhist, Muslim, even Christian Marxist theologians. Yet a persistent critique against many of those regimes invoking the name of Marx decries their apparent betrayal of the revolution. Autocratic provisional five-year plans become permanent policy. The millennium, if portrayed as too near, proves disillusioning; if too remote, then beyond imagination. And Marx's vision, of course, hardens into orthodoxy.

The character of Spina, disguised as a priest in Ignazio Silone's *Bread and Wine,* a novel originally written at the time of Mussolini's Ethiopian War but revised in 1962, once abandoned the Catholic Church because of its identification with the Italian Fascist establishment, and became a Marxist revolutionary. "Why have all revolutions, every single one of them, begun as movements of liberation and ended as tyrannies?" a disillusioned ex-Marxist now taunts him. "The present black inquisition will be followed by a red inquisition. . . . Your future bureaucracy will identify itself with labor and socialism and will persecute all those who continue to think with their own head. . . ." Also Nunzio, Spina's old friend, suggests an intriguing analogy: "You're the best part of all of us. . . . You don't believe in God anymore, but in the proletariat, with the same absolutism as before." Spina never fully internalizes these insights until actually threatened with dismissal from the Communist party for his dissent over some inhuman tactics. "Leaving the party means abandoning the idea," he is warned. Spina responds, "I can't sacrifice to the party the reasons that led me to join it. . . . It would be like putting the church before Christ." Spina, like Silone in his own life, must finally break with every orthodoxy in order to retain his Humanist integrity. Confirming this same theme, Camus's *The Rebel* recounts the myth of Prometheus rebelling against human misery, leading people enthusiastically away to the desert. But this messiah gradually develops into an authoritarian caesar, requiring the challenge now of yet another Prometheus, in a continuous succession of rebellions by rebels against their own unconscious totalitarian impulses. For the same reason, Mao instigated his Red Guard revolution to slap down the complacent illusion that social injustice had been eradicated and the revolutionary process completed.

Marxist Realpolitik, Nazism, and the authoritarian churches are perceived as differing pseudonyms of a single totalitarian specter by Silone, Camus, and especially George Orwell in *Animal Farm* and *1984*. In an essay, "Notes on the Way," written at the outset of the Second World War, Orwell sustains Marx's attack against bourgeois religion. By the nineteenth century it had become a lie, a semiconscious device to keep the poor contented with their poverty, which would be redressed only beyond the grave. However, the soul that Marx tried to cut away required not just a simple appendectomy, but a major amputation that grows daily more septic. This is a generation of wasps cut in half, still wriggling, unaware of dismemberment until their attempt to fly. Or, in another vivid metaphor, after sawing for many years at the branch they were sitting on, finally down they came, not onto a rose garden but into a cesspool of robbers, torturers, Grand Inquisitors. "There is very little chance of escaping it unless we can reinstate the belief in human brotherhood without the need for a 'next world' to give it meaning. . . . The Kingdom of Heaven has somehow got to be brought onto the surface of the earth." Religious believers maintain that without belief in God's common fatherhood, it is impossible to develop a sense of community. Yet people often sacrifice themselves for the sake of such fragmentary communities as nation, race, class, family, "and only become aware that they are not individuals in the very moment when they are facing bullets. A very slight increase of consciousness, and this sense of loyalty could be transferred to humanity itself, which is not an abstraction. . . . Man is not an individual, he is only a cell in an everlasting body. . . ."

The Freudian Humanist

Fifteen years after the Bolshevist Revolution, Freud in his *New Introductory Lectures on Psychoanalysis* offers a cogent rebuttal to what he calls the European Marxist experiment. Though commending its nobility of purpose, he first of all denounces its bloody implementation by commissars, "unshakable in their convictions, inaccessible to doubt, without feeling for the sufferings of anyone standing in the way of their intentions." Second, Marxist ideology strains to compensate Communist believers for their present deprivations. It promises a utopian human community that seems even less plausible than the Judeo-Christian heavenly illusions that Marxists disclaim. Hoping to alter human nature within a few generations so that people will work freely and live without aggression and hatred, nevertheless it ironically harasses and slays them today for their selfish disobedience and reluctance to change.

Third, Marx exaggerates the role of economic motives as determinants of social behavior. Though economic factors are important, we must never underestimate the "self-preservative instinct, aggressiveness, the need to be loved, the drive toward obtaining pleasure and avoiding pain," and most of all, the demands made by each individual "superego, which represents tradition and past ideals, and would for a time resist the incentives of a new economic situation." Finally, Marxist orthodoxy has developed an uncanny likeness to the authoritarian religious systems from which it claims to liberate a new humanity. "Any critical examination of Marxist theory is forbidden, doubts of its correctness are punished in the same way as heresy was once punished by the Catholic Church. The writings of Marx have taken the place of the Bible and the Koran as a source of revelation. . . ."

Marxist idealization of the proletariat, under Freud's hard scrutiny, is deflated to a dangerous sentimental daydream. And Marx's outraged impatience at human depravities finds little resonance in Freud's controlled temperament. He is both more pessimistic and paradoxically more optimistic than Marx about the decay and cure of middle-class civilization. He believes nature inherently Hobbesian and violent. The First World War simply peeled away a hard-earned civilized veneer to expose our innate viciousness, just as the subsequent League of Nations could not be expected to sustain peace without support of a massive armed police force. Despite its cruel child-labor customs, the bourgeois religious imagination had long idealized the cult of childhood innocence. But "children are completely egotistic," *The Interpretation of Dreams* asserts. "They feel their needs intensely and strive ruthlessly to satisfy them—especially against other rival children, and foremost against their brothers and sisters." With modest optimism, Freud trusts that by sound ethical training, "altruistic impulses and morality will awaken in the little egotist, and a secondary ego will overlay and inhibit the primary one." Achieved only much later in life, if ever, love for the stranger, or especially the enemy, can by no means be called spontaneously human. For as Heine confesses, we might instinctively imagine forgiving our enemies, but only after they have been hanged. "Aggressiveness," Freud states repeatedly, "was not created by property."

His vision of human destiny as an indeterminate conflict between Eros and Thanatos, with no afterlife, represents an unpalatable conviction forced upon Freud by experience. "The question is not what belief is more pleasing, comfortable, or advantageous to life," he writes Pastor Pfister, "but what may approximate more closely to the puzzling reality ouside us. . . . Thus, to me my pessimism seems a conclusion, while the optimism of my opponents seems an apriori assumption." Yet human life scraped clean of utopian and religious illusions has its own unique savor. In his essay "On Transience," Freud tells of a summer walk with two friends through a radiant countryside, months before the eruption of war. All three felt sobered by the inescapable fact that this natural splendor, like human achievements, too, would someday perish. How can a person come to terms with this fact? One reaction is an inability to enjoy beauty shorn of its worth by the transience looming into perception. Another is a rebellious leap beyond the evidence, affirming that anything so beautiful shall never die, but must somehow persist forever. Freud's own response uncovers a singular charm in evanescence itself. The aesthetic emotion is intensified precisely because of its precariousness. For even the destruction caused by war can render ephemeral what once was taken for granted as immutable, and cause us to prize our friends and country more than before.

Freud's analysis of religious experience offers a creative amalgam of Feuerbach and Comte. The religious symbol for Feuerbach, like any other human construct, reveals first of all the needs and drives of whatever human imagination projected it. "The more empty life is," says his *Essence of Christianity,* "the fuller and more concrete is God. The impoverishing of the real world and the enriching of God are a single act. Only the poor have a rich God." Comte's threefold schema, tracing the historical evolution of consciousness toward his so-called Religion of Humanity, is replicated closely in the armchair anthropology of Freud's *Totem and Taboo:* "Spirits and demons are only projections of one's own emotional impulses. . . . At the animistic phase people ascribe omnipotence to themselves. At the religious phase they transfer it to the gods but . . . reserve the power of influencing gods according to human wishes." Thirdly, our present scientific phase no longer encourages a sense of human omnipotence, except for faith in the power of our mind, which must discover and reconcile itself with the laws of reality. With mounting wariness, we follow Freud's conjectures about the slim phylogenesis-ontogenesis parallels between evolving civilizations and an individual's maturation process. He eventually settles on three contentious myths: an infantile "primitive" society, an adolescent or even obsessive-compulsive era of collective religious belief, and an approaching millennium of adult Science.

This utopian trust in human rationality, shared by both Freud and Marx, receives far more self-conscious critical appraisal from Freud than it does from Marx. Freud carries on a witty caustic dialogue with the religious believer in *Future of an Illusion:* Freud's hopes are perhaps illusory, but so are the believer's. The admitted weakness of Freud's own position does not imply the strengthening of anyone else's. At least he does not impose his opinion on others, through the censorship and persecution used perennially by religious people. In years of casework, he has noticed simply that religion is comparable to a childhood neurosis, and he is optimistic enough "to suppose that mankind will surmount this neurotic phase, just as so many children grow out of their similar neurosis. . . . The voice of the intellect is a soft one, but it does not rest till it has gained a hearing."

The dialogue continues by playful disclosure of the Freudian god's identity—*Logos* or Reason. Scientific inquiry is a self-correcting process, capable of purifying all Freud's expectations. If they prove mistaken, he will drop them immediately. Prepared to renounce as many childish wishes as necessary, he can bear losing a few helpful but unfounded hopes. Yet you, on the contrary, are so impatient, exacting, and self-seeking for heavenly rewards after death that "you have to defend the religious illusion with all your might. If it becomes discredited—and indeed the threat to it is great enough—then . . . you despair of everything, of civilization and the future of mankind." He recognizes that most people will not be able to sacrifice their religious addictions and face the cruelties of reality, but perhaps an "education to reality" from childhood onward will help later generations renounce this infantilism. They shall have to realize, of course, "they can no longer be the center of the universe, no long the object of tender care by a loving Providence. They will be in the same position as children who have left their parents' house where they were so warm and comfortable."

Freud's strong suit is less a constructive ethics than a prophetic and often demolishing analytical scrutiny. The immature religious projection must be retrojected back to its origins in the authoritarian middle-class family structure. A Provident God symbol, for instance, invites adults regressively to recover children's relationship to their father as a shield against the horrors of the night. A devil represents the terrifying doppelgänger half of this same father, toward whom the child feels ambivalent love-hate, an emotion too threatening for anything other than dualistic expression. Guilt in a neurotic conscience is a superego-imprint of the father's value system, self-punitive because of the child's unresolved rebellion and hostility. The sense of ecstatic union experienced in the widespread religious "oceanic feeling" is actually a reversion to the earlier mother-child symbiosis, a time when the sharply demarcated adult ego was still permeable and more inclusive.

These theories are woven into plausible case studies that read like first-class detective fiction. Freud's analysis of the psychotic Dr. Schreber's autobiography brings some intelligibility to this patient's garish religious symbolism. Basically a "soul-murderer," Schreber's God professes to love him and thus to choose him as a special redeemer, a mission he cannot achieve except by changing sex to become God's wife. Freud interprets this myth ingeniously as a condensed projection of covert homosexual shame, narcissistic messianism, contempt for his unfeeling physician-father, and transference-fear of seduction by his therapist, Flechsig. The famous Wolf Man and Rat Man cases give details of a prolonged pseudoreligious phase in both boys' early adolescence. They showed obsequious exactitude in performing religious ritual. Yet alternating between masochistic guilt and Oedipal rebellion, they continued to toy with doubt and blasphemy.

Regressive and neurotic religious responses of this type, prevalent throughout the era, prove the worst imaginable ethical foundation for a new Age of Science. People have connected the moral consensus against murder, for instance, with commandments issued by God, and thus invest this human prohibition with a holy solemnity and immutability it would otherwise lack. Yet at the same time, they risk making its observance seem to depend exclusively on a belief in God. Freud suggests that this religious prop be left out entirely, and that the ethical prohibition depend on sheer consensus or on inherent human rights. This is an adamant theme in *The Future of an Illusion.* "If the sole reason why you must not kill your neighbor is because God has forbidden it, and will severely punish you for it in this or the next life—then, when you learn that there is no God and that you need not fear his punishment, you will certainly kill your neighbor without hesitation."

Therapists of the strict Freudian persuasion have preferred not to view themselves as spiritual guides, ethicians, or educators. Their hope is to release a person from internal bondage and establish only the preconditions for choice. A reluctant description Freud himself later adopted in *Question of Lay Analysis* is the term "secular pastoral worker," suggesting parallels with those who heal by integrating the client into a church community. "We seek rather to enrich them from their own internal sources, by putting at the disposal of their ego those energies which, because of repression, are inaccessibly confined in their unconscious, as well as those which their ego is obliged to squander in the fruitless task of maintaining these repressions. Such activity is pastoral work in the best sense of the words."

The Freudian therapeutic relationship aims to create a situation of strict confidentiality, trust, support, candor, and, especially, a progressively more uninhibited "free association" self-disclosure. Clients are invited to lift the filter of social and personal censorship and give relaxed expression to their most forbidden wishes and fantasies. What eventually emerge are the values unconsciously guiding one's past, with the added privilege now of reassessing this moral inheritance from family, church, society, and other sources. Making this value system conscious is a first step toward liberating oneself from it. With this precondition achieved, each person must finally piece together and put into practice a more mature ethics, deciding what to reaffirm, discard, and transform from before.

The vicissitudes of Freudianism illustrate again how a vital charism crystallizes into orthodoxy. At a meeting of the Vienna Psychoanalytic Society in the 1920s, Freud once showed remarkable prescience about the caliber of his disciples. "Here you are debating among yourselves about what I once said. I sit at the head of the table, and not one of you thinks of asking me, 'What do you think *now?*' If this is the way you treat me while I am still alive, I can well imagine what will happen when I am really dead." Sample psychology articles today often begin with ceremonial repudiation of some Freudian dogma, then perhaps gloat at the tragic history of apostasy and mutual excommunications within the tradition. Then they proceed, at times unaware, to turn Freud's own psychoanalytic tools back upon an analysis of the master himself. Many of his biographers offer proof that Freud unconsciously encouraged the formation of a religious cultus around himself. For instance, he selected, groomed, and banished one disciple after another; in subsequent editions of his books, he obliterated names of recent heretics from established footnotes; he even bestowed a symbolic ring on each of his closest lieutenants.

A biased but plausible study of Freud's suppressed religious dynamic occurs in Jung's *Memories, Dreams, Reflections*. The Eros theory of Freud, though couched in antiseptic sexual terminology, reminded Jung of the intensity usually associated with religious revelation. "When he spoke of it, his tone became urgent, almost anxious, and all signs of his normally critical and skeptical manner vanished." This spiritual élan seemed unable to express itself in his narrow biological vocabulary, and he gave the impression that at bottom his words were betraying the *daimon* within himself. "Freud, who had always made much of his irreligiosity, had now constructed a dogma, . . . scientifically irreproachable and free from all religious taint. . . . In the place of a jealous God whom he had lost, he had substituted another compelling image, that of sexuality . . . , no less insistent, exacting, domineering, threatening, and morally ambivalent than the original one."

In an earlier chapter, we examined the Japanese *amaeru* concept, a need to be cherished, protected, and indulged. It is evident that Freud viewed this tendency in himself and others as shamefully regressive, a neurotic dependence and transference—precisely the attitudes to be exploited by religious cults and totalitarian regimes. Yet many Humanist critics of Freud think the most proficient therapy can replace a malfunctional God-image only by one more maturely functional. They find it neither desirable nor possible to eradicate the *amaeru*-drive from a personality. Arthur Koestler's ideological novel *Arrival and Departure,* written in the early years of the Second World War, addresses this dilemma persuasively. The setting is Neutralia, a politically nonaligned halfway house where the ex-Communist Peter Slavek faces various characters, each representing a different ideology competing for his allegiance. His options are to rejoin the Party, which now does not want heroes but iron civil servants, or to sail for neutral America, Fascist Germany, or capitalist Britain. Caught in a paralysis of choice, he develops a paralyzed leg and thus consults the analyst Dr. Sonia Bolgar.

The few surviving shreds of Marxist faith are snatched away from Peter by his therapist. She helps him discover that his unconscious guilt over a rival brother's death in childhood had been the root of adult masochistic search for humiliation—his crusade for the workers, for example, or his heroic suffering in a Fascist prison. This harrowing insight leads Peter to recognize some characteristic pathological abuses of Marxist labels. So many of his colleagues had been "hair-splitting dialecticians advocating proletarian simplicity, the atoning Oedipuses, the jealous younger brothers in search of an abstract fraternity, the male spinsters to whom Power had never proposed." Never again would he make a fool of himself. He was cured of his illusions, those fictitious allegiances and debts he had hung on the childish "Christmas tree of his guilt. With a cool delight and only a shadow of sadness, he took them down one by one, the stuffed idols of his past dangling from the withered branches." To his despair, however, the scars remaining after therapy leave Peter in a moral burn-out, with every past ideal analyzed to death. In the remaining pages of the novel, he achieves only a partial dubious recovery from this inner cataclysm. "She had promised to restore his appetite for life, but instead he experienced only pangs of greed, alternating with weary satiety. . . . He roamed through the empty rooms, shivering in the cold draft of his newly attained freedom. He had abandoned the fraternity of the dead, and the fraternity of the living had not yet received him."

Demolition therapy is only the prelude to complete character transformation. "Criticism has plucked the imaginary flowers from the chain," says Marx, "not so that people will wear the chain without any fantasy or consolation, but so they will shake off the chain and cull the living flower." For a confirmed Marxist, the Freudian phenomenon is an inviting target for dialectical critique. The entire system seems designed to smoke out rebellion and smother it, then to reinstate authority of the bourgeois father in oneself and in society. Freud's ideology and therapeutic practice rationalize a role for the conservative intellectual elite: to heal the pathology spawned by an alienated society, without healing the social alienation itself. Two figures meet in a private contractual relationship, a purchased hour of friendship, and isolated from the public shamanic healing ceremonies we delineated before in primal societies, focus on the trivia of middle-class existence. Perhaps there is an impending career decision, work stress, a stale love affair, or failure in exams. At best, the client gains release from the bondage of personal self-deceptions, only now to be left more vulnerable to the larger social evils that once made these unconscious defenses necessary.

Marx believes "the past dominates the present in bourgeois society, whereas in Communist society the present dominates the past." Freud's therapeutic method is principally an act of excavation and restoration, searching for a truth lying in an individual's archaic past, which has been covered over fearfully with many disguises. If the Freudian bias can be termed a recoil backward and inward, the Marxist bias is a plunge ahead and outward. Freudian determinism is caused by a sense of repeated, powerless confrontations within a fixed bourgeois gravitational field. Yet according to Marx's most quoted aphorism, "philosophers have merely interpreted the world in various ways; the point, however, is to change it." The Marxist, therefore, must first transform the world through revolutionary action, liberate people from enslaving present structures, create free new institutions, and only then try to understand this new human transformation.

Transvaluation of the Secular

In the effort to reassess and appropriate their own heritage, contemporary Humanists usually recognize the need for a Marx that is more introspective, a Freud more communitarian, and for an increasingly broader openness to the religious and human dimensions in society. We distinguished earlier between two implicit phases in every Humanist position: the constructive, or what it affirms; and the iconoclastic, or what it denies. We shall now examine these two phases more carefully in the current aftermath of Marx and Freud.

The neo-Freudian Erich Fromm represents one attempt to combine Marx and Freud into a new secular iconoclasm, despite demurrals by orthodox proponents in each school against facile synthesis. First, he disparages a mere adjustment therapy, content only to help clients cope with societal pressures left mostly uncriticized. Genuinely curative therapy, on the other hand, taking a normative stand on social values, expects clients to challenge, change, and even to experience creative frustration over their total therapeutic milieu. The sanity of a society itself, not just the relative sanity of an individual within it, should be evaluated by a criterion of human rights transcending any particular culture. Normalcy "must be defined in terms of the adjustment of society to the needs of man," says *The Sane Society*. An unhealthy society is one that creates mutual hateful competitiveness and distrust, transforming a person into an instrument of exploitation for others, and depriving the person of self-worth. Second, Fromm redefines a number of stock psychoanalytic concepts. Therapy is needed not so much for individual neurotic symptoms as for the deeper existential malady of alienation from oneself and others and nature. Freud's classical anal-phallic developmental phases now become each individual's growth from the receptive infant, through the cruel stingy child with an exploitative marketing orientation, finally to the active productive adult. The reified Unconscious is translated into stages of relative unawareness or what Marxists call false consciousness.

A corollary to this relativity of consciousness offers Fromm a third theme. Projecting its own specific social values, each society, by a filter of language, logic, and taboos, shapes the unaware consciousness of every individual within it. For example, some subtle aesthetic experiences are almost impossible to imagine if a given community does not cultivate these experiences, or lacks the words to express them. People are not truly free unless helped first to reach awareness of their lifelong social indoctrination. Then they must still transcend nationalism, xenophobia, and the other moral limitations sanctioned by this specific value system.

Fromm's most detailed insight is a Humanist reinterpretation of conventional religious language. Describing himself as a nontheistic mystic, he prefers the inclusive definition of religion as *any* profound devotional commitment. His God-image is not the separate Supreme Being common to Western Theism but the Hindu *Brahman* or Tillich's Ground of Being. "God is a symbol of all that which is in man and yet which man is not," he says in *Psychoanalysis and Religion,* "a symbol of a spiritual reality which we can strive to realize in ourselves and yet can never describe or define. God is like the horizon which sets the limitations of our sight." Religions are humanistic or authoritarian, insofar as they nourish or thwart the model sane society and mature individual already defined. Cutting a swath through world religious traditions, Fromm collates a Humanist *philosophia perennis.* Zen and Taoist aphorisms, and carefully selected teachings of Isaiah, Jesus, Socrates, and Spinoza, constitute the canon; excluded are most other faiths, especially every totalist racial and political system. "Inasmuch as humanistic religions are theistic, God is a symbol of man's own powers which he tries to realize in his life. God is not a symbol of force and domination, having power over man. . . . What matters in all such systems is not the thought system as such, but the human attitude underlying their doctrines."

Whereas the great Judaic prophets condemned idols of stone and wood, Fromm carries this iconoclastic impulse to the modern idols of capitalist and Communist society. "God as the supreme value and goal, is *not* man, the state, an institution, . . . possession, sexual powers, or any artifact made by man . . . ," he explains in *You Shall Be As Gods.* "The idol is the alienated form of man's experience of himself." To worship an idol is to sacralize a diminished shadow-image of oneself—intelligence, physical strength, fame. By identifying themselves with a partial aspect of the self, people limit themselves to this aspect. They lose their totality as human beings and cease growth. Despite all the different religious affirmations that separate human beings, Fromm believes most of the world can unite on this single common religious *negation*—the unmasking of contemporary idolatry or alienation. No theistic or atheistic ideal exists that has not been twisted into an excuse to exploit and oppress people. Without denouncing the ideal itself, a really sophisticated iconoclast must show how it got transformed into an abused ideology, and then challenge this distortion in the name of the betrayed ideal.

The most productive task of Fromm's secular iconoclast or of any prophetic critic is to keep the religious believer honest and accountable. It seems fair to observe that most religious institutions need to be more deeply humanized, so they act on their own professed ideals. They have to respect the civil liberties of their disciples, especially the right to due process. They require constant prodding from the outsider to become more self-critical of their own belief, tolerant of other traditions, and more responsive to serious injustices in the societies with which they interact. At the same time, the ultimate responsibility of any iconoclast is consistent, exacting *self*-criticism. Richard Gill's superb short story "The Code" recounts the tragic experience of a boy who cannot accept the snuffling religious platitudes offered by his mother and aunts to help him bear his brother's death. Instead, he identifies with the honest distress and atheism of his father, which the boy for many years afterward idealizes as a Humanist code. His father and he share this unflinching disbelief as a macho secret binding them closely. "I considered it a disloyalty to him, to myself, to the code we had lived by, to alter my position in the least." The narrator is appalled one day, when called to his dying father's bedside, to observe him wavering from the code, pleading with his eyes for implicit permission to talk with the Methodist minister, who waits outside the sickroom for a signal from the patient. By his terse, detached response to his father's pain, he tacitly refuses to support this betrayal. The father dies, straining to remain loyal to a frozen ideal of disbelief that probably is no longer his own.

Once all idols have been shattered, the Humanist must decide whether nothing is sacred anymore, or everything is sacred. This is the recurrent dilemma posed by almost every responsible Humanist encountered, especially the disillusioned antihero of Koestler's novel. Thus we turn to what seem the most constructive attempts by modern Humanists to fashion a secular spirituality. In earlier chapters we observed the pervasive apophatic path to the numinous, notably in those Buddhist movements that emphasize present eschatology. This approach is also suggested by Fromm's description of the Humanist God-image as that which humanity is not, the horizon that cannot be defined. The Zen symbol of an empty circle captures the *śūnyatā* paradox of renunciatory fulfillment, unworldly worldliness, the interpenetration of sacred and profane—an immanentist Humanist spirituality common to the East, which many secular pilgrims in the West reach only after prolonged bouts of iconoclasm.

This experience of numinous emptiness might be called a secular Dark Night of the human spirit. Keats spoke of it as Negative Capability, a disposition to remain immersed in doubts and mysteries without any precipitous reaching after fact and reason. Rilke writes to a young poet, "Do not now seek the answers, which cannot be given you because you would not be able to live them. Live the questions now. Perhaps you will then gradually, without noticing it, live along someday into the answers." Similarly, there is Kafka's description of himself as an attendant upon grace—whether this waiting is a harbinger of grace or grace itself, he cannot decide. But most important, he has befriended his ignorance. Vladimir in Beckett's *Waiting for Godot* tries to uncover the minimal human significance in mankind's endless waiting: "We are not saints, but we have kept our appointment." Neo-Marxists Roger Garaudy and Ernst Bloch explain the God-image as a projected hope for our long-awaited future, an exigency within our depths crying out for perfect justice and the Absolute. This hope is an image worthy of contemplation and religious awe—a holy transcendental vacuum always deferred, evolving like humanity itself. What we sometimes picture as an absent God is in fact our humanity itself in the process of being born.

Each poet, novelist, and philosopher adds slightly different nuances here to what is actually a fragile, intensely paradoxical spirituality. To sustain itself, it needs a tough asceticism, able to face the tragic dark side of humanity. In E. M. Forster's *A Passage to India,* the "frank blank atheist" Fielding believes the world is a globe of people trying to reach one another, aided by culture and intelligence. The path is "kindness, more kindness, and even after that more kindness." A sudden realization of the resistant ignorance and cruelty of Indians and British, Muslims and Christians toward one another draws limits to his optimism. "He felt dubious and discontented suddenly, and wondered whether he was really and truly successful as a human being." He reflects on his effort for forty years to educate himself, develop his personality, explore his limitations, control his passions. "A creditable achievement, but as the moment passed, he felt he ought to have been working at something else the whole time—he didn't know at what, never would know, never could know, and that was why he felt sad."

"I travel light," Fielding once said confidently. "I'm a holy man, minus the holiness." An increasing number of Humanists, however, respecting the charisms but seldom the institutions of traditional world faiths, are reluctant to surrender the holiness. In *Religions, Values, and Peak-Experiences,* Maslow deplores the error of permitting sects and cranks to usurp for their exclusive use the rich language of patriotism and religion. "I had let them redefine these words and then accepted their definitions. And now I want to take them back. I want to demonstrate that spiritual values have naturalistic meaning, that they are not the exclusive possession of organized churches, that they do not need supernatural concepts to validate them...." He tests out a marked prevalence of peak and plateau experiences characterized by awe, wonder, and cosmic engulfment among many people dissociating themselves from any institutional religion. In a similar situation, Dewey once explained that his *Common Faith* was written to assist those who had abandoned supernaturalism, and were thus reproached by traditionalists for turning their backs against anything religious. "This book was an attempt to show such persons that they still have within their experience all the elements which give the religious attitude its value." Dewey reconstructs religion as an adjective or adverb modifying ordinary experience. To be irreligious is to treat people in isolation from physical nature and the human community or to lack what he calls *natural piety*.

Some aggressive forms of Humanist secularity originating in Europe and the United States have been exported to Eastern and primal civilizations with extremely disruptive results. Many of these victim cultures are permeated by the religious adverb and adjective to such an extent that the religious phenomenon has become an integrated quality and not just a distinct sector of life. To give up one's traditional religious faith is to destroy the Center from which everything else derives its meaning. Dewey and Nehru, the final two Humanists in our discussion, shared an unusual sensitivity to this transcultural problem. Somehow they sensed sympathetic parallels between their own Western empiricist secularity and the Humanist dynamic already emergent within the Chinese and Indian religious traditions.

At the apex of his career as a reformist and educator at Columbia University, John Dewey for two years after the First World War lectured throughout China at the invitation of his many former students, who had become influential college teachers and administrators. With the fall of the imperial system in 1911, China was experiencing an era of ideological turmoil, trying out various styles of philosophy, educational reform, and democratic process. During Dewey's 60th birthday celebration, the president of National Peking University contrasted him with Confucius, also enjoying his 2,470th birthday, though in current disfavor: "Confucius said respect the Emperor, yet this learned doctor advocates democracy; Confucius said women are a problem to raise, yet the learned doctor advocates equal rights for men and women; Confucius said transmit and not create, yet the learned doctor advocates creativity." Dewey's books were widely translated during the next decade, alongside works by Bertrand Russell, Darwin, and Spencer. The impact of his disciples can only be gauged by the rapidity with which his ideas were adopted and modified by later Chinese Kuomintang reform programs, and the vehemence with which Dewey's moderate bourgeois reforms were subsequently condemned by Mao and other Communists. Three volumes of his China Tour lectures, interpreted into Chinese as they were delivered, have only recently been translated back into English.

It is impossible to chart the staggering range of topics Dewey covers in these lectures, but their consistent emphasis is unmistakable. The way to create a new society is primarily to educate a new generation in the classroom. Both laissez-faire capitalist individualism and Marxist totalitarianism are polarized fallacies. Traditional Chinese values should not be rejected, but reevaluated by methods of public discussion, honest openness, and scientific inquiry. Paging through a number of student magazines, Dewey lists the topics that apparently concerned them most: "the need for educational change, attacks upon the family system, discussion of socialism, of democratic ideas, of all kinds of utopias." In place of a detailed blueprint for revolutionary action, which some impatient leftists demanded, Dewey offered only a Humanist *method*—three bland words, evoking three self-validating, idealized, almost sacred rites: *science* and *democracy* and *education*. Sometimes it is hard to connect these grand verities with the flawed empirical matrix from which they derive: actual chemistry labs, town meetings, and urban classrooms.

A few representative lines from Dewey's brief talk on "Science and Knowing" may explain why his Experimentalism is sometimes credited later with the preliminary softening blow before Marxist overthrow. "It is only after we have acted upon a theory that we really understand it. There can be no true knowledge without doing." The Golden Age of China is not in the past but in the future. "Everything is subject to change in time and circumstance." Scientific inquiry is "planned, confident adventure, . . . subjecting traditional theories and established truths to examination by experiment." In Dewey's entire system, there are frequent echoes, not only of Marx, but especially of classical Chinese holistic cosmology. Like the young Marx, Dewey began as a Hegelian, but he did so for significant personal reasons: "Hegel's thought . . . supplied a demand for unification that was doubtless an intense emotional craving. . . . The sense of divisions and separations that were, I suppose, borne in upon me as a consequence of a heritage of New England culture, divisions by way of isolation of self from the world, of soul from body, of nature from God, brought a painful oppression. . . ." Words like *organic interaction, transaction, situation, communication,* and *context* resound throughout his lecture notes. Dewey's Humanist platform demands revolutionary reconstruction, contemplation that is at the same time action, classrooms that are playgrounds and model societies, and the ideal of comprehensive human experience in which aesthetic, religious, and moral dimensions all interweave.

No less than Dewey, Nehru could describe himself as a votary at the shrine of science, ever since the years of his studies in England, where he haunted the laboratories of Harrow and Cambridge. There he first experienced the conflict between religion and science, "between the intellectual tyranny imposed by what was deemed to be religion and the free spirit of man nurtured by the scientific method. Between the two there can be no compromise." This is the text of his address before the Academy of Sciences at Allahabad in 1938. He is convinced no real conflict need exist between true religion and science if both agree not to place blind faith in someone else's faith. "Religion must put on the garb of science and approach all its problems in the spirit of science. A purely secular philosophy of life may be considered enough by most of us. Why should we trouble ourselves about matters beyond our ken when the problems of the world insistently demand solution?"

To the exiled Dalai Lama, Prime Minister Nehru seemed an urbane host and brilliant practical statesman, but "although the mantle of Mahatma Gandhi had fallen on him, I could not catch any glimpse of spiritual fervor in him." Yet we can discover a deeper Nehru behind the astute handsome facade, especially in his personal letters and prison journals. It is incredible that he and Gandhi managed to preserve their friendship and political alliance, despite major religious differences. Gandhi's tactics at times struck Nehru as "sheer revivalism. . . . Gandhiji did not encourage others to think; his insistence was only on purity and sacrifice. . . . He had the flair for action, but was the way of faith the right way to train a nation?" Gandhi wants a new India, uncontaminated by Western materialistic technology, whereas Nehru's autobiography states: "These defects are not due to industrialism as such, but to the Capitalist system which is based on exploitation of others." Gandhi wants to share in the poverty of India's poor, yet Nehru doubts very much "if the fundamental causes of poverty are touched by it.... Renunciation has always appealed to the Indian mind.... I prefer the active virtues to the passive ones, and renunciation and sacrifice for their own sakes have little appeal for me." Nehru was one of the principal architects of an Indian secular State, which seemed the only plausible foundation for so many differing religions. Such a State "honors all faiths equally and gives them equal opportunities.... No real nationalism can be built up except on the basis of secularity. Any narrower approach must necessarily exclude a section of the population."

What we observe in Nehru is a disciplined attempt to reconstruct a secular spirituality of his own. First, he abhorred the whole religious spectacle in India and wished it were possible to make a clean sweep of it—"blind belief and reaction, dogma and bigotry, superstition and exploitation, and the preservation of vested interests. And yet I knew well that there was something else in it...." Second, he therefore distinguishes between the rituals and dogmas that are assigned the name of religion, and a deeper essence in all religions, this "something else," which he calls *spirituality*. On another occasion he names it "this indefinable and indefinite urge, which may have a tinge of religion in it and yet is wholly different from it." The idea of God, as usually conceived in Western religious traditions, does not attract him. "But the old idea of Hindu philosophy in the Vedanta that everything has some part of the divine essence does appeal to me." Third, this Upaniṣadic insight confirms an experience that Dewey would call natural piety: "Often, as I look at this world, I have a sense of mysteries, of unknown depths." And again, "One main trouble is a lack of organic connection with nature or life. We have gone off at a tangent from the circle of life, uprooted ourselves and thus lost the sense of fullness and coordination with nature." In his prison journal, he writes during a bout of depression that he is ready to die, but only for some good cause. "I have loved life—the mountains and the sea, the sun and rain and storm and snow, and animals, and books and art, and even human beings—and life has been good to me."

Gandhi's famous karma-yogin ideal becomes in Nehru's reinterpretation "the true scientist, . . . the sage unattached to life and the fruits of action, ever seeking truth wheresoever this quest might lead him. To tie himself to a fixed anchorage, from which there is no moving, is to give up that search and to become static in a dynamic world." Gautama Buddha, too, is translated into a contemporary model of tolerance and compassion, but also something more revolutionary: "The Buddha asked no man to believe anything except what could be proved by experiment and trial. All he wanted men to do was to seek the truth and not accept anything on the word of another, even though it be of the Buddha himself."

Nehru admirably sums up in himself both the glory and the burden experienced by the Humanist, and anyone else, who tries to carve out and then remain faithful to a tradition that is fully one's own. "I have become a queer mixture of East and West, out of place everywhere, at home nowhere," he confides in his autobiography. Nehru's national and intellectual heritage have left him with "a feeling of spiritual loneliness not only in public activities but in life itself." In his Last Will and Testament, he asks that no traditional religious rituals be performed at his cremation because he does not believe in them. But he does want a handful of his ashes thrown into the Ganges, as a symbol of his desire to remain an indistinguishable part of India's past, flowing into the ocean of the future. "Though I have discarded much of past tradition and custom, and am anxious that India should rid herself of all shackles that . . . prevent the free development of the body and the spirit, . . . yet I do not wish to cut myself off from that past completely."

FURTHER READING

1. **Marxist Legacy.** The best single introductory anthology of his shorter pieces is Saul Padover, ed. *The Essential Marx: The Non-Economic Writings* (Mentor, 1978); and an anonymously edited edition of *Karl Marx and Friedrich Engels on Religion* (Schocken Books, 1964), which collects fragmentary comments on the topic. Two other standard collections are David Caute, ed., *Essential Writings of Karl Marx* (Collier, 1967); and David McLellen, ed., *Karl Marx: Selected Writings* (Oxford, 1977).

An outstanding work tracing Marx's influence in Asia is Trevor Ling's *Buddha, Marx, and God: Some Aspects of Religion in the Modern World* (St. Martin's Press, 1966). The bourgeois milieu of nineteenth-century Europe is sketched with vivid anecdotes and contrasted with that of Asia. Much of Marx's writing is journalistic polemic against various social thinkers in Germany, especially Bauer, Hess, Stirner, besides a more identifiable figure like Feuerbach. *From Hegel to Marx* by Sidney Hook (University of Michigan Press, 1962) is a helpful handbook on this background. An interesting view of Marx and other socialist options, written during the Depression in America, can be found in the theological critique *Moral Man and Immoral Society* by Reinhold Niebuhr (Scribner's, 1932).

The Collected Essays, Journalism, and Letters of George Orwell, ed. Sonia Orwell and Ian Angus, 4 vols. (Harcourt Brace, 1968), give a lively history of the era, mostly in terms of liberalism and socialism. See James Connors, "'Who Dies If England Live?': Christianity and the Moral Vision of George Orwell," in Warren Wagar, ed., *The Secular Mind: Transformations of Faith in Modern Europe* (Holmes and Meier, 1982), for a summary of Orwell's quarrel with the authoritarian Christian churches. In addition to a chapter on Silone, R. W. B. Lewis' *The Picaresque Saint* (Lippincott, 1959) suggests some further readings in modern fiction on the theme of the secular saint.

2. **Freudian Legacy.** I would advise approaching Freud also by sampling complete shorter pieces, such as the articles on war, religion, Dostoevsky, and Michelangelo in Philip Rieff, ed., *Freud: Character and Culture* (Collier, 1963). Besides the major works cited in this chapter, *Psychoanalysis and Faith: The Letters of Sigmund Freud and Oskar Pfister,* ed. H. Meng and Ernst Freud (Basic Books, 1963), gives a little-known side of Freud, his friendship and flexibility in debate with this Swiss pastor. The best complete biographical picture can be attained by combining the eulogistic Ernest Jones, *The Life and Work of Sigmund Freud,* ed. and abr. Trilling and Marcus (Anchor, 1961); and the hostile, thoroughly researched *Freud and His Followers* by Paul Roazen (Meridian Books, 1974). Peter Breggin, "Psychotherapy as Applied Ethics," *Psychiatry* 34 (February 1971), pp. 59–74; and Peter Homans, *Theology after Freud: An Interpretative Inquiry* (Bobbs-Merrill, 1970), especially the chapters on Norman Brown and Rieff, suggests ways to construct a meta-ethics around the psychoanalytic contract.

The neo-Freudian experiment in combining Freud with Marx can be explored further in Erich Fromm's *Beyond the Chains of Illusion: My Encounter with Marx and Freud* (Simon and Schuster, 1962). I think Fromm's best single essay is "Psychoanalysis and Zen Buddhism," in D. T. Suzuki et al., *Zen Buddhism and Psychoanalysis* (Harper, 1960), a concise summary of his reinterpretation of Freud and a socioreligious critique of Zen. A densely written, profound attack against Freudian bourgeois individualism is Richard Lichtman's *The Production of Desire: The Integration of Psychoanalysis into Marxist Theory* (Free Press, 1982). Herbert Marcuse, *Eros and Civilization* (Beacon Press, 1966), sets down ground rules for appropriate social adaptations of Freud. For background about Koestler's ideological pilgrimage, see Sidney Pearson, *Arthur Koestler* (Twayne, 1978); and Koestler et al., *The God That Failed* (Harper, 1949), which includes an important autobiographical statement by Silone.

3. **Dewey and Nehru.** Nancy Sizer, "John Dewey's Ideas in China: 1919 to 1921," *Comparative Education Review* 10:3 (October 1966), pp. 390–404, is a succinct overview of the China Tour and its effects. Further political background is given in Barry Keenan, *The Dewey Experiment in China* (Harvard University Press, 1977). Robert Clopton and Tsuin-chen Ou translate two sets of lectures, those on education and on social and political philosophy, in *John Dewey: Lectures in China, 1919–1920* (University Press of Hawaii, 1973).

A standard guide through Dewey is the excellent anthology by Richard Bernstein, ed., *On Experience, Nature, and Freedom* (Bobbs-Merrill, 1960);

and the same author's brief *John Dewey* (Washington Square, 1967), a summary of major themes. See Dewey's rebuttal and autobiographical comments to the Festschrift volume of essays on various aspects of his work, in Paul Schilpp, ed., *The Philosophy of John Dewey* (Tudor, 1939). Further analysis of Dewey's natural piety concept, and the Dewey-Marx parallels and contrasts can be followed in John H. Randall, "The Religion of Shared Experience," in Sidney Ratner, ed., *The Philosopher of the Common Man* (Greenwood, 1968), pp. 106–45; and Jim Cork, "John Dewey and Karl Marx," in Sidney Hook, ed., *John Dewey: Philosopher of Science and Freedom* (Dial, 1950), pp. 331–50.

Nehru's prison journal selections, letters, political speeches, and numerous random efforts at constructing his own philosophy have not yet found the wide reading public they deserve. Sarvepalli Gopal, ed., *Jawaharlal Nehru: An Anthology* (Oxford University Press, 1980), with its clear topical arrangement, gives over six hundred pages of excerpts, illustrating Nehru's incredible range of interests. See also his *Toward Freedom: The Autobiography of Jawaharlal Nehru* (John Day, 1941); and Michael Brecher, *Nehru: A Political Biography* (Oxford University Press, 1959).

4. **General Humanist Context.** The Humanist label is at one moment absurdly inclusive, the next moment just a partisan trademark. One way to chart out the terrain is to page through back copies of the *Humanist* magazine, published by the American Humanist Association. Most of this specific group of ethical, scientific, or naturalistic Humanists are represented in the Paul Kurtz anthology, *The Humanist Alternative: Some Definitions of Humanism* (Prometheus Books, 1973). It is intriguing to compare two famous manifestos, promoted mostly by this same AMA leadership—published in 1933 and 1973: *Humanist Manifestos I and II,* ed. Paul Kurtz (Prometheus Books, 1973). Warren Smith, "Are You a Humanist? Some Authors Answer," *Humanist* 41 (1981), pp. 15–26, a reprint of the same article in 1951, presents endless qualifications of the label, as people like Russell, Santayana, Thomas Mann, Mailer, and Koestler apply it to themselves.

An imaginative way to circle around the Humanist phenomenon and avoid adopting any settled maps is to try the following. First, read Sam Keen's *Apology for Wonder* (Harper and Row, 1969), which extends the margins of what we usually denominate religious awe to include very wide variants. Second, study the many illustrations given in James Thrower, *The Alternative Tradition: Religion and the Rejection of Religion in the Ancient World.* Notice that Greece, Rome, China, and India all have an inchoate recusant tradition, a periphery of religious people who do not quite fit into the defined institutional religions. Third, observe the way Aldous Huxley in *The Perennial Philosophy* (Harper, 1945) assembles a mystical tradition cutting across the accepted boundaries among world religions. What is often called Humanist "natural" mysticism easily fits into Huxley's wide categories. Fourth, see W. C. Smith's analysis of the meeting between Western secularism and the religious dimension of a traditional society in "Secularity and the History of Religions," in Albert Schlitzer, C.S.C., ed., *The Spirit and Power of Christian Secularity* (Notre

Dame Press, 1969). Fifth, Owen Chadwich, *The Secularization of the European Mind in the Nineteenth Century* (Cambridge University Press, 1975), gives indispensable background for the rise of various socialist movements. There are chapters on worker attitudes and the rise of anticlericalism. Sixth, follow the debate closely between Ronald Hepburn and H. J. Blackham in H. J. Blackham et al., *Objections to Humansim* (Constable, 1963), as a model of mutually penetrating criticism and civility between a Christian theologian and a Humanist philosopher.

6

Judaic Torah

Moses Mendelssohn, father of the *Haskalah,* or Jewish Age of Reason, once began a letter: "Moses the Mensch writes to Herder the Mensch, and not the Jew to the Christian preacher." By the late eighteenth century, a friendship, a society, or even a spirituality based solely on common human nature seemed closer to realization than ever before. This was the era of Jefferson's self-evident human rights, of international litterateurs flocking to the same prestigious salons, and of adulation for moral giants like Ben Franklin in his Noble Savage beaverskin cap, Confucius, or Socrates, all of them too massive to fit the petty specifications of Christian or Judaic orthodoxy.

The next two intervening centuries of demoniac nationalism, battles for tenuous civil and social rights, then incredible pogroms and the Holocaust, make it difficult today to imagine the unclouded Haskalah dream of an earlier period. In the novel *Mr. Sammler's Planet* by Saul Bellow, deathcamp survivor Sammler tries to complete a biography of H. G. Wells, whose declining ability and popularity in his last years present a sharp image of the disillusioned eighteenth-century rationalist. Man of Reason, sex emancipator, articulate teacher, moulder of a new universal order, Wells in his final sickness, depressed horribly by the Second World War, could only curse everyone in sight. As a further example, Sartre's *Anti-Semite and Jew,* a courageous book written during the German Occupation, quickly disposes of the question of whether Jews are primarily Jews or human beings. Only the naive, abstract mind of an eighteenth-century democrat, says Sartre, could state the problem in this fallacious manner. "He has no eyes for the concrete syntheses with which history confronts him. He recognizes neither Jew, nor Arab, nor Negro, nor bourgeois, nor worker, but only man—man always the same in all times and all places."

Yet we shall find that Mendelssohn's carefully nuanced Humanism is no more implausible than that of Russell, Nehru, or other Humanists of the preceding chapter, most of whom tried to take honest account of actual tragic human situations confronting them. Gotthold Lessing, Mendelssohn's best Christian friend, based the character of an idealized wealthy Jewish seer in his dramatic poem *Nathan the Wise* on Mendelssohn's exceptionally humane and tolerant personality. Lessing's earlier tract, *Education of the Human Race,* had suggested a developmental pedagogy for mankind: infancy requires the concrete sanctions imposed by Judaic scriptures, later childhood depends on deferred spiritual reward motives offered by Christian scriptures, and utopian adulthood means living by Reason alone, dispensing with all props of divine revelation. In this developmental context, Lessing's *Nathan* introduces an impulsive Christian knight, the pragmatist Muslim Saladin, and a Jew, showing one another an extraordinary love and tolerance that seem to transcend all three sectarian traditions. At the exact center of this drama is the adapted Boccaccio parable of three rings, described by Lessing as "the kernel from which *Nathan* developed." Asked by Saladin to declare which of these three revealed religions is the greatest, Nathan tells of an opal ring, passed down perennially from father to worthiest son, a ring conferring the favor of God and humanity on whoever trusts its magic. At last, the ring stops with one father, who judges all three sons equally worthy. Unable to resolve this dilemma in any other way, he purchases two duplicate rings and bestows one secretly on each son. After the father's death, each son, believing himself the recipient of the original ring, claims the throne. Summoned to settle their quarrel, a judge suggests that all three let subsequent generations test out the power of each ring, so that at the end of time God himself can judge which was genuine. "Let each one believe his ring to be the true one. Possibly the father could no longer tolerate in his house the tyranny of just one ring." He loved all three sons equally, and would not alienate the other two by preferment. Imitate his unprejudiced affection. "Let each strive to match the others in eliciting the opal's magic in his ring."

In our ensuing chapters on the fissiparous Judaic-Muslim-Christian Western family of religions—three branches stemming from a single Hebraic source—it is helpful to focus on Nathan's vision of a shared humanity and ethic underlying all three traditions. Just a decade after

Nathan, and the deaths of both Lessing and Mendelssohn, legal equality was already achieved for French Jews by the Revolution, and began to touch the rest of Europe through the Napoleonic Wars. As the protective walls of many ghettos fell, the new challenge of Haskalah was met by a remarkable range of strategies to enhance or block the process of social and religious assimilation. Later divisions of the American Jewish immigrant community into Reform, Orthodox, and Conservative derive from this crisis in nineteenth-century Europe. We shall now trace some of the more creative radical and also traditional European Jewish responses to Haskalah. Then with these varied reactions in mind, we shall outline a Jewish spirituality of exile and messianic return.

The Haskalah Humanist

Pastor Pfister frequently searched beneath Freud's casual self-definition as a "godless Jew" to uncover there an implicit theist. For this Swiss Protestant believed that "one who lives for truth lives in God." "That was an excessively friendly thought on your part," Freud once wrote him in reply, "and it always reminds me of the monk who insisted on regarding Nathan as a thoroughly good Christian. I am a long way from being Nathan, but of course I cannot help remaining 'good' towards you. . . ." But Pfister tried to carry his argument one step further: "But you are no Jew. To me, in view of my unbounded admiration for Amos, Isaiah, Jeremiah, and the author of Job and Ecclesiastes, this is a matter of profound regret." It is clear that Pfister's Jew must accept the Judaic religious tradition as normative; whereas Freud's Jew can be religious or secular, for this use of the term refers principally to cultural and racial identity. This semantic confusion has been compounded by a long-standing Talmudic tradition of treating apostate Jews, even those with Christian baptism, as authentic Jews. Yet there is Israel's 1962 Supreme Court decision, confirming that religious and irreligious Jews have the right of migration into that State, but not a Polish Carmelite priest born of Jewish parents.

An immediate shocking result of Jewish emancipation was the swarm of nominal, sometimes genuine, conversions to established State churches. It is estimated that three-quarters of Berlin's Jewish population from 1800 to 1850 became Christian. "A baptismal certificate is the ticket of admission to European culture," Heinrich Heine admits, counting on his new Lutheran identity to facilitate the achievement of a doctorate. In a famous letter to the granddaughter of Moses

Mendelssohn, her father explains why Fanny and her brother Felix were raised Lutheran. Both her parents had been brought up as Jews, without being obliged to change the form of religion. "The outward form of religion . . . is historical and changeable like all human ordinances. . . . We have educated you and your brothers and sister in the Christian faith, because it is the creed acceptable to the majority of civilized people, and contains nothing that can lead you away from what is good, and much that guides you toward love, obedience, tolerance, and resignation."

Karl Marx, descendant of two rabbi grandfathers, grew up in this same milieu of recessive Jewishness. His entire family joined the National Lutheran Church, ostensibly so his father could practice law, a profession otherwise prohibited to Jews in that society. Marx's adult life shows the telltale signs of self-conscious resolute assimilation—a sprinkling of anti-Semitic humor, and an uncharacteristic silence about any bourgeois discrimination directed specifically against Jews. For example, he jokes about Jews emerging from the pores of Polish society, or an English vacation spot spoiled by too many Jews and fleas, or rabbinic legalism that makes "even the lavatory an object of divine regulation." In his early essay "On the Jewish Question," Marx attacks the proposal by his teacher Bauer that Jews first become atheists and then be granted full legal incorporation into the secular State. The true issue is not theological, says Marx, nor concerned with Sabbath Jews, but everyday Jews, whose worldly cult is money. "As soon as society succeeds in abolishing the empirical essence of Judaism—huckstering and its conditions—the Jew becomes impossible, because his consciousness no longer has an object. . . . The social emancipation of the Jew is the emancipation of society from Judaism." This meretricious Jewishness is just one pseudonym for decadent capitalist Christianity.

Marx later argues in *The Holy Family* for complete Jewish political equality, an apparent reversal of his previous dialectical critique. However, his position must be read closely before it is conscripted as a proof-text: "States which cannot yet politically emancipate the Jews must be rated by comparison with accomplished States, and must be considered undeveloped." He implies that Jewish civil rights, like all laissez-faire property rights, are a litmus test to ascertain in any society the extent to which the bourgeois revolution has completed its aims. To promote Jewish rights is simply to speed up this preliminary revolution, the results of which will later be overturned radically to produce the classless society.

There is stunning irony in blaming the Jew for Shylock and Fagin capitalists, and at the same time for masterminds behind the anarchist or Marxist conspiracies to sabotage capitalist society. Yet no doubt disproportionately large numbers of Jews during the last two centuries have consistently led or supported movements of the radical and moderate left. Various reasons have been alleged for this ideological preference. Secular messianism in the West draws on the legacy of ancient Hebrew prophecy, which demanded business equity, authentic worship, and community responsibility toward resident aliens and the poor. Moreover, ghetto isolation and the restriction of Jewish social rights even after legal emancipation barred most Jews from experience in practical politics, and thus tended to insulate many of their most gifted intellectuals within a world of utopian abstractions. Most of all, their marginal existence at the seams of overlapping cultures diverted loyalty from a single race or nation to the wider human fellowship of socialism or other cross-cultural Humanist creeds. One of the best examples of this uncompromising internationalism occurs in a letter by Rosa Luxemburg, Jewish founder of the German Communist party. She cannot tolerate the myopic social conscience of her girlfriend: "Why do you come with your particular Jewish sorrows? . . . I have no separate corner in my heart for the ghetto. I feel at home in the entire world wherever there are clouds and birds and human tears."

Conversion to the socially dominant State churches, or to radical, secular, at times anti-Semitic internationalism, are two plausible responses, then, to the Haskalah experience. The third reaction is more ambivalent. Tolerated simply as one denominational option among others in society, Jewish spiritual life might be reduced to a series of conventional duties, detached from the rest of meaningful daily existence and gradually eroded, misrepresented, discredited. Yet Jewish identity remains somehow intact, often accompanied by a nostalgia for lost essentials—a pronounced tendency in the lives of Freud and Kafka. In recent American Jewish fiction, this theme governs the stereotype of the assimilated secular Jew, simultaneously fleeing yet cherishing immigrant roots, the trashbin of discarded religious and ethnic history. Bernard Malamud's short story "Jewbird" offers a witty yet increasingly ominous exchange between the frozen-food salesman Cohen and a skinny Yiddish-speaking bird named Schwartz, the doppelgänger voice of his suppressed Jewish immigrant origins. Flying in the kitchen window, the bird begs a glass of schnapps or a piece of herring, and decides to remain a few months. Yet Schwartz has the fish stink of the ghetto about him, rocks back and forth in prayer like a pious Jew, and whines about persecution from anti-Semitic crows, eagles, and vultures. Though his family finds Schwartz quaint and cuddly, Cohen cannot handle all the nagging reminders of despicable Jewishness and, in a final rage, murders the bird.

"If I am Moses, then you are Joshua," Freud writes to Jung at the peak of their friendship, "and you will take possession of the promised land of psychiatry, which I shall be able to glimpse only from afar." This statement suggests three insights into the intricate emotions of Freud—first, the religious mythos inherent in his psychoanalytic vision; second, an uncanny lifelong identification with the prophetic liberator of his own Jewish people; third, his anxiety to free the psychoanalytic movement from its narrow Jewish leadership in Vienna and surrender it to a prominent international Gentile. Years later, Freud would deplore Jung's anti-Semitic condescension toward him, and witness the classics by two "subversive Jews," Freud and Marx, destroyed side by side in Nazi bonfires. Though an express atheist, and so attached to German language and culture that he felt that the Palestinian terrain idealized by Zionists had given the world nothing but sacred frenzies, Freud nevertheless remained proud of his Jewishness. His conversation was riddled with Yiddish idioms and anecdotes, and he once confided to his fiancée in a letter, written after meeting a quaint old merchant, resolutely unshaven to commemorate the destruction of the Temple: "Even if the form in which the old Jews were happy no longer offers us any shelter, something of the core, of the essence of this meaningful and life-affirming Judaism will not be absent from our home."

The forms of modified Jewish ritual were emphasized in Kafka's early family background but not in Freud's. Kafka complains later that his *bar mitzvah* ceremony, the annual family Passover meal, and obligatory synagogue attendance were all "a mere nothing, a joke—not even a joke." In a letter to Felice, who was working with young children in the Jewish People's Home, Kafka admits, "I wouldn't think of going to the synagogue. . . . As a boy I almost suffocated from the terrible boredom and pointlessness of hours in the synagogue; these were the rehearsals staged by hell for my later office life." Yet he wishes the children at this People's Home could be introduced to authentic Jewish culture and spirituality, not by liberal West European Jews of his own milieu, but by traditional Jews from Poland and the East. "I would give unconditional preference to the latter Home. . . . The quality corresponding to the values of East European Jews is something that cannot be imparted in a Home. . . . But it can be acquired, earned." This priceless attribute gets associated in Kafka's mind with Yiddish culture and language. Raised in a German-Jewish community surrounded by Czechs, Kafka learned to dislike the German words for mother and father. "*Mutter* unconsciously contains, together with Christian splendor, Christian coldness also. . . . I believe it is only memories of the ghetto that still preserve the Jewish family. . . ." Although he later found it too unpolished and monotonous, the Yiddish theater seemed at first to portray "a Judaism on which the beginnings of my own rested, . . . that would enlighten and carry me farther along in my own clumsy Judaism. . . ."

A crucial ingredient seems to elude all these apparently well-assimilated Jews, having climbed within just a few generations to eminence in business, the arts, medicine, and university faculties. Forceful reaffirmation of this missing center constitutes a fourth response to Haskalah—strict neo-Orthodox fidelity to the traditional ghetto verities of eastern Europe.

The *shtetl* or ghetto, viewed as both claustrophobic prison and romanticized sanctuary, existed for centuries as a self-sufficient town within a town. Neighboring families were interwoven into a small, tight community, and linked to other *shtetls* by trade, annual fairs, and itinerant preachers. The Russian *shtetl* in Marc Chagall's paintings usually radiates an aura of warmth and magic: a tearful rabbi in his prayer shawl or a beggar in the snow, their grief mitigated somehow by the presence of a peaceful cow or flower or violin. Again, there is a sense of hovering catastrophe that gives the gentle humor a bittersweet nuance in Joseph Stein's *Fiddler on the Roof,* a play based on selected Yiddish tales by Sholom Aleichem. "Because of our traditions, we've kept our balance for many, many years," says Tevye in the opening lines. "Everyone knows who he is and what God expects him to do!" Perhaps the heart of the *shtetl* experience can be summed up in the Yiddish word *mentsh.* To be a *mentsh* has resonances different from the proposal by Mendelssohn to Herder that they sidestep their Jewish and Christian particularity and communicate "Mensch to Mensch." It means compassion, reluctance to harm any living being, a sense of family and social responsibility, an openness to the complete spectrum of human life. *Mentshlekhkayt* approximates Buddhist *karuṇā* or Gandhi's *satyāgraha,* but it adds a distinctive concern for personal relationships and an unashamed capacity to weep.

Without hesitation, the *shtetl* can tell us what it means to be a Jew. Jews are the People of the Torah. The ideal of each *shtetl* Jew is to study, pray, and embody Torah. Moral standards, ritual observance, and the entire educational system in this close society are regulated by religious law, enforced by the believing community. Often mistranslated as Law, *Torah* means revealed teaching, which includes *halakhah*, or law. It is strictly defined as the Sinaitic covenant between God and his Chosen People, spelled out in the Mosaic Pentateuch, the first five books of the Bible. More inclusively, Torah covers first the entire Bible; second, its various authoritative commentaries and applications in the rabbinic *Talmud*; and third, its expression in legitimate custom and consensus of the Jewish community. Torah in rabbinic lore closely resembles Hindu *sanātana-dharma* or Buddhist *dhammata*. It is an architectural cosmic plan, the divine mind or will, even the personified consort or handmaid of God. By exemplary fidelity to Torah, the Jewish people help restore sacred order to the cosmos. If properly understood, some traditional Jewish observances show amazing imagination in their attempt to summon and celebrate the presence of Torah in the heart. The *mezuzah* box enclosing a significant Bible quotation on parchment fulfills God's command, "You shall write the words of Torah on the doorposts of your home and upon your gates." Similar small *tefillin* containers are strapped around the forehead and wrists while praying. Congregations bow to the sacred Torah scroll, kiss it, and sometimes even embrace and dance ecstatically with what Kafka called these "old headless dolls."

A basic thread running through centuries of rabbinic leadership has been the development of a halakhic shield around the Mosaic Torah, a numinous protective screen purifying the Jews and separating them from the non-Jewish world. The intent of intricate dietary and Sabbath restrictions, or of frequent blessings and formulaic prayers, is to transform even the most ordinary actions into a complete sacramental way of life, much like the *li* ceremonial mystique of Confucius. Yet this whole structure seemed threatened with utter collapse, once privileged halakhic civil and criminal law in the *shtetl* had been displaced by a single uniform secular code of law. Worse yet, liberal Jewish scholars had begun to question divine inspiration of the Talmud and even of the Pentateuch. As mentioned in the previous chapter, an attempt to secularize religious institutions in a tightly integrated traditional society risks destroying the Center from which everything else derives its meaning.

Thus, the response of many *shtetl* rabbis was to insist on exact adherence to as many traditional halakhic observances as possible in this new open society—unchanged patterns of worship, for example, segregated dietary regulations, and the use of Yiddish, perhaps even distinctive dress. To those quick to sell out their religious identities, "progress is the absolute and religion is governed by it; to us, religion is the absolute," writes Samson Hirsch in 1854. If German Jews had previously stayed aloof from European civilization, the fault lay not in their religion but in the tyranny that confined them to the ghetto and denied them access to wider culture. Rabbi for thirty-seven years at an Orthodox synagogue in Frankfurt, Hirsch taught his congregation to be Jews in synagogue, kitchen, and factory, and not to "throw Judaism into a corner for use only on Sabbaths and Festivals. . . . Judaism is not a mere adjunct to life: it comprises all of life. . . . It is only through unfaithfulness of the majority that the loyalty of the minority becomes a duty demanding so much sacrifice. . . ."

Many Orthodox rabbis dreamed of emigration to found new *shtetls* in America and in Zionist Palestine or Africa. In fact, some ultra-Orthodox communities today in the State of Israel resent secular Jewish dissent from their efforts to convert the State into one large religious *shtetl.* Isaac Bashevis Singer's short story "The Little Shoemakers" is a charming analysis of the precarious transplantation of *shtetl* orthodoxy from eastern Europe to New Jersey. After years of delay, old Abba the Shoemaker finally leaves home to join his emigrant sons and their Americanized families, but he experiences terrible disorientation. In their New Jersey synagogue, he finds the sexton clean-shaven, a candelabrum with electric lights, no faucet to purify his hands, a congregation wearing abbreviated prayer shawls like scarves. So his sons don skullcaps in his presence, return to the dietary laws, introduce Yiddish phrases, and eventually build a shoemaker's hut in their backyard, where Abba and his children occasionally repair shoes together, as they once did in Europe. He recovers his old happiness: "They had not become idolaters in Egypt. They had not forgotten their heritage, nor had they lost themselves among the unworthy."

The teaching of Moses Mendelssohn himself represents our fifth and final response to Haskalah. At first an inchoate movement he fostered and attempted to chart, Haskalah settled later into a liberal ideology that often departed from his own scrupulously moderate position. Most important, Mendelssohn saw himself trying to balance the claims of tradition and assimilation, without yielding to either extreme. His major work, *Jerusalem: On Religious Power and Judaism,* written in 1783, addresses his fellow Jews: "Adopt the mores and constitution of the country in which you find yourself, but be steadfast in upholding the religion of your fathers, too. Bear both burdens as well as you can." Should both prove incompatible, if the price for citizenship be deviation "from the Law which we still consider binding, then we sincerely regret having to renounce our claim to civil equality and union. . . ." The scope of his theology is paradoxically more centripetal yet more inclusive than that of the rabbinic establishment ranged against him.

Mendelssohn translated the Pentateuch into German to make it accessible, wrote a fresh commentary on it, and promoted a broader secular education for Jewish youth. He also demanded that authority to punish and ostracize be removed from Jewish leaders and entrusted only to the State. The centripetal effect of these measures was to relegate classical Talmudic commentary and learning to the sidelines, and to lop off historical excrescences so that the Pentateuchic Torah could regain its centrality. Furthermore, the *shtetl* rabbinic system of an exclusively religious education for everyone received its death blow. Mendelssohn's return to the principal Hebrew scriptures seems comparable to Luther's evangelical detour around decadent scholasticism and late medieval piety back to the New Testament, or later German Higher Critics' application of a method derived from secular sciences to both Jewish and Christian sources. On the other hand, his recovery of scripture is not so much a Protestant Jewish revolt against Talmudic orthodoxy as a legitimate exercise of Talmudic argument and commentary, simply initiating another school within the comprehensive rabbinic tradition.

The inclusive scope of Mendelssohn's thought can be demonstrated in his treatment of two important issues, religious tolerance and the nature of Torah. Since his book *Jerusalem* is directed principally to the Gentile community as a plea for tolerance of Jewish religious and civil rights, it is essential that he clarify the Jewish basis for tolerating the non-Jew. Mendelssohn distrusts proselytizing of any kind, especially an ersatz ecumenism that seeks to achieve one fold and one shepherd by enlisting everyone under a single formula. "The unifiers of faith would simply be collaborating in pinching off a bit from some concepts here and there, in enlarging the texture of words elsewhere, until they become so vague and loose that any ideas, regardless of their inner differences, could if necessary be squeezed in." His first axiom is a revolutionary insistence that "diversity is obviously the plan and goal of Providence." Not one among us thinks and feels exactly like someone else. "Why should we use masks to make ourselves unrecognizable to each other in the most important concerns of life, when God has given all of us our own distinctive faces for some good reason?" His famous letter to Prince Karl-Wilhelm offers the following conclusion: "Inasmuch as all people must have been destined by their Creator to attain salvation, no particular religion can be exclusively true. . . . A revelation that claims to be the only road to salvation cannot be true, for it is not in harmony with the intent of the all-merciful Creator."

Consistent with the earlier rabbinic tradition, Mendelssohn develops a theology of not one but two crucial covenants. The first one originates with God's promise to Noah after the Flood, in the eighth and ninth chapters of Genesis: "I now make my covenant with you and your descendents, and every living creature, . . . all that have come out of the ark." God then expounds a sevenfold moral law for every human being. This universal covenant before the time of Abraham, Moses, and the Chosen People is the eternal Torah or Natural Law, imprinted on the conscience of everyone, "with a script that is legible and intelligible at all times and in all places."

God in a second covenant at Sinai, then, adds no new doctrinal content to this earlier revelation, but instead singles out the Jewish people to enact sacred ceremonial *mitzvot,* or duties. The purpose of *mitzvot* is to "call wholesome and unadulterated ideas of God and his attributes continuously to the attention of the rest of mankind." The Torah prescribes the deed only and leaves each person to ponder the religious and moral significance behind each deed. "The great maxim of this constitution seems to have been: a people must be driven to action but merely stimulated to contemplation. . . . Eternal verities were to be associated solely with deeds and practices, and these were to take the place of symbols which . . . could lead to idolatry through misuse or misunderstanding." Consisting of a few written *mitzvot,* the Mosaic Torah most of all means "the living instructions from person to person and from mouth to mouth that were to explain, enlarge, limit, or define more clearly what, by wise intent and wise moderation, had been left undefined in the written Torah."

Mendelssohn's theology of Torah welded together a brilliant yet controversial synthesis, which shaped a challenging problematic for his later disciples in the Reform and Conservative traditions. First, his Age of Reason preference for Natural Law, universal human verities, and the Noachic covenant softened the radical particularity of Mosaic Torah, and rendered Jewish religious practice answerable to evolving, contested standards of consistency, compassion, and an inclusive tolerance. Second, his perception of the Mosaic Torah primarily as a cultus rather than an ethic and creed confirms widespread claims that the Judaic tradition lacks dogma or a pronounced theological consensus. Yet in any historical period that treats prayer and ritual as the mere frippery and cosmetics of true religion, the Jew that can be identified only by cultus tends readily to blend into a Unitarian or liberal Protestant. Third, Mendelssohn's return to the Pentateuch text is countered by his stress on an unwritten living Torah transmitted as a spiritual experience from master to disciple, a process characteristic of other esoteric religious traditions. Such a Torah is more protean and pervasive, less easily distinguishable from its secular gravitational field within each historical era.

Myth and Ritual of Exile

Galut, or exile, has been the essential Jewish condition through most of its history. Egypt before the Mosaic Exodus, captivity in Babylon after destruction of the First Temple, dispersal across the entire earth after Roman demolition of the Second Temple—these are prolonged stop-overs in the Diaspora residence abroad, with relatively fewer years of homecoming to the Promised Land. The fate of God's Chosen People, migrating from place to place, can be symbolized by the myth of the Wandering Jew, which in the nineteenth century alone allegedly inspired at least four hundred works of fiction in various European languages. With no permanent home, alienated and forever on the move, mistreated by everyone yet undaunted and mysteriously unharmed, this figure fascinates the imagination. He is branded with the scar described by Demian in Hesse's novel *Demian* as the ambivalent Abraxas sign or the mark of Cain on his forehead. Sinister, bold, powerful, purportedly condemned by God for some crime—"but that he's awarded a special decoration for his cowardice, a mark that protects him and puts the fear of God into all the others, that's quite odd, isn't it?"

The Diaspora geographic dispersal and its Galut spiritual counterpart, a sense of homelessness and abandonment, summons up an intense, ambivalent range of feelings, not only for Gentiles but for many Jews themselves. For example, the Western, or Wailing, Wall in Jerusalem has been the principal Jewish pilgrimage center for centuries. To pray and weep here, at the site of these few remnants from the Second Temple and its glory, is to grieve in solidarity with Jewish suffering everywhere. As a symbol of Galut, the ruined Temple may be perceived as a deplorable vacuum that can never be filled until the final *kibbutz galuyot,* or gathering-in of the exiles. "By the ruins of Babylon we sat down and wept when we remembered Zion," says Psalm 137. "How could we sing the Lord's song in a foreign land?" Some Jews even register a defiant messianic denial of the tragic event itself. One rare passage in the Zoharic literature, probably the most influential anthology of *Kabbalah* mysticism, says the Temple never suffered actual attack, its stones never fell into the hands of other nations. "God has treasured up the stones of Jerusalem and hidden them from the sight of men; a day will come when the ancient stones will be revealed and found in their former position" (2:240b). Furthermore, many medieval rabbis even taught that each Jew would never lose tenure to four cubits of ground in the final Israel.

Though sometimes handled by sheer denial, profound loss demands mostly to be displaced or transposed. Perhaps with this psychology in mind, one Midrashic commentary claims that the *Shekhinah,* God's immanent presence, despite its escape on whirring wings from the First Temple in Ezekiel's classic vision, has never departed from the Wailing Wall. A characteristic Zoharic passage suggests that the *Shekhinah,* once the Temple was destroyed, "took one last look at the Holy of Holies, and left home to accompany Israel into exile." The Galut experience, then, could signify God's continued presence among his people, but now as essentially a *Deus Absconditus,* using their tragedy as a providential occasion to diffuse them as leaven among the nations. Perhaps God wants them to depend more on the sacred teaching than on their teacher, or to uncover within the immediate community itself a new mode of his *Shekhinah.* This theme inspires one of the most audacious tales in the Talmud, "The Oven of Akhnai." Arguing with a group of rabbis about the correct application of Torah to Akhnai's case, Rabbi Eliezer is driven in exasperation to perform a few dazzling miracles to sanction his own interpretation. He even solicits a heavenly voice to say, "The Halakhah is always as Eliezer teaches it." But Rabbi Jeremiah pays no attention to God's voice, for he is certain that "Torah has already been given to us on the mountain. We pay no attention, even to heavenly voices, because God has commanded us to decide according to the majority." Rabbi Natan met the prophet Elijah later in the vicinity, who reported that God's reaction to the entire contest was only to laugh and exclaim, "My children have defeated me, my children have defeated me!" Here is a teacher glad to be overruled at the hands of his disciples, struggling by their own prayerful initiative to construe true teaching.

Keeping track of these rich resonances, we can be more sensitive to the Galut dimension in two significant Jewish rites, Passover and the Sabbath. The annual *pesah,* or Passover meal, the Feast of Deliverance, adheres to a set ritual framework, leaving room for many local accretions, which tend quickly to develop their own vindication as immemorial symbols. Its intent is to recount and reenact the liberation of Israel from Egypt—first the narrative of past slavery and salvation; then the meal eaten in haste, with a sense of impending departure; then final hymns of thanks, prayers for future liberation, and a welcome for Elijah, forerunner of the Messiah. The *haggadah* instructions expressly state, "In every generation, all Jews must regard themselves as though they personally were brought out of Egypt. . . . It was not our ancestors alone that the Holy One redeemed from Egypt, but he also redeemed us with them." Historically, this Passover in each home replaced the annual Jerusalem pilgrimage to gather as a single nation and celebrate *pesah* animal sacrifices in the Temple. Now the home is transformed into a portable temple; *matzah* substitutes for the sacrifices; a repentent heart, a ritual bath, and pre-*pesah* housecleaning purify the temple; and the head of the household becomes its ritual priest.

The mythical time of *pesah* is in-between, in the Galut desert experience. We are released from the Egypt of darkness, sin, alienation, and destined for the Jerusalem of completion, freedom, and eternal life. Like the finale of the *yom kippur* liturgy, *pesah* concludes with the cry "Next year in Jerusalem!" Moreover, the *matzoth* have been blessed earlier by a recitation of the Halachma Anya prayer: "This is the bread of affliction which our fathers ate in the land of Egypt. . . . This year we are here, next year we shall be in the land of Israel. This year we are in servitude, next year we shall be free!" The *pesah* meal occurs in springtime, generally at home, and during the night. A Targum paraphrase of Exodus 12:42 telescopes the entire history of Israel into this fourfold ritual night. There is first the primordial darkness out of which God created the cosmos, then the night he called Abraham, and the night of Egyptian Exodus. "The fourth night is when he reveals himself to redeem the people of Israel from among the nations. All the nights are called nights of watchfulness." An authentic Galut spirituality will always center on this Dark Night, the endless desert experience of Israel, and a hopeful, resolute watchfulness.

Two puzzling ritual details in the *pesah* deserve further attention. The first is the *afikomen,* a *matzah* portion broken off and hidden playfully, more or less for a later surprise dessert. The youngest children in the community soon search it out, and surrender it only if promised a reward. Some rabbinic commentators view this as a symbolic ransoming of the enslaved people. A more obvious exilic theme can be discerned in the *afikomen* ritual developed by some Mediterranean *pesah* traditions. Pieces of *matzah* are wrapped in a napkin and carried like a knapsack by the youngest child. "From where have you come?" "From Egypt," the child replies. "Where are you going?" "To Jerusalem." "What food will you eat on the way?" And the child responds by pointing to the *matzah* bundle.

Again, a mysterious additional cup of wine is set aside at the meal, and the door is later opened to admit or release a numinous power. This rite seems a clear act of hospitality directed toward Elijah, messianic precursor, wandering from home to home, his task to encourage exiles and test out their worth and readiness for the messianic era. It is also a symbolic sharing of wine and hospitality stretching out beyond the home enclosure, an opened door to express solidarity with Jews celebrating *pesah* throughout the Diaspora this very evening. Nevertheless, once the prayers and singing are over, the Jewish community feels its part of the convenant has been completed, and now awaits God to fulfill his.

Images of Exodus past and messianic future pervade not only the annual *pesah* but also weekly Sabbath observance. The Bible offers at least two rationales for the Sabbath. "Remember you were a servant in the land of Egypt," Deuteronomy states, "and the Lord your God liberated you; . . . therefore he commanded you to keep the Sabbath." On the other hand, Exodus says, "Remember the Sabbath, . . . for in six days the Lord made heaven and earth, . . . and rested on the seventh day." Each Friday evening, family members wash off the week's grime, dress in their finest clothes, bring out best plate and silverware, light candles, recollect themselves, and enter a twenty-four-hour period of prayer, leisure, companionship, and three unhurried substantial meals.

For the average person today, *Sabbath* still connotes fastidious "blue laws" and the tedium of enforced inactivity. Yet more accurately, it should be given principal credit for inspiring humane customs of a shorter work week, paid vacations, retirement pensions, and even the academic sabbatical research leave. "Not only has Israel kept the Sabbath," says Ahad ha-Am, "but the Sabbath has kept Israel." Foretaste of the messianic era, a sacrament reaffirming each separate family's membership in the wider Jewish community, a reminder of human dignity and the right to leisure and rest, this weekly holy day has helped to sustain many Jews through the other six days of Galut oppression. The Talmud observes that "if all Jews were properly to observe two Sabbaths in succession, Israel would be immediately redeemed." In other words, the achievement of ideal ritual anticipation by the entire community not only disposes Israel for liberation, but gives evidence that Israel is already liberated. For as Pascal observes, "Whoever searches for God has already found God."

The Sabbath has been described as a moment of eternity in time, a sanctuary to be entered for contemplation. Protective rituals bracket out these hours from other weekdays—for example, the *kiddush* blessing over wine to begin Sabbath, the *havdalah* blessing over wine to terminate the Sabbath. What is the imaginative link between this sacred space and the myth of God's restful contemplation of his own creative activity? Rilke in a letter to Benvenuta expounds his concept of *einsehen,* with perceptive parallels to the meditative Sabbath principle. Rilke tells of his delight simply to *in-see* a dog passing by, not to *in-spect,* which means "immediately coming out again on the other side of the dog, regarding it merely as a window to the humanity lying behind it." One should try to let oneself into the dog's very center, the point where it begins to be a dog, where "God would have sat down for a moment when the dog's creation was finished, in order to watch it under the influence of its first embarrassments and inspirations, and to know that it was good, that nothing was lacking, that it could not have been better made."

A few ingenuous ecologist critiques have seized upon God's mandate to Adam in the first chapter of Genesis, "Fill the earth and subdue it, rule over it. . . ." These phrases allegedly provide a demonic rationale for the West's exploitative, calculative plunder of the natural world. Should we concede this claim for the moment, then it is plausible to view God's day of rest and the Sabbath custom as a counterbalancing limitation placed on mankind's dominion exercised the other six workdays. In both *Forgotten Language* and *You Shall Be As Gods,* Erich Fromm perceives an eschatological ecology in the Sabbath concept. We celebrate human victory over the chains of time. Its ritual anticipates and acts out our entire messianic destiny: "man's development from prehistoric oneness, through the separateness and alienation which occur in the historical process, to the achievement of a new harmony, . . . the full unfolding of man's reason and consciousness." In Talmudic prescriptions for the Sabbath, *rest* must be reinterpreted as freedom, peace, harmony between one person and another, between human beings and nature. *Work* means disharmony and Galut, any creative or destructive interference with this equilibrium. The Sabbath is a hallowing of the ideal balance, a preview of paradise with its familiar biblical image of the lion and lamb together, human beings at peace with animals and the soil. "God is free and fully God only when he ceased to work. So is man fully man only when he does not work, when he is one with nature and his fellow man. That is why the Sabbath commandment is at one time motivated by God's rest, and at the other by the liberation from Egypt. . . . Rest is synonymous with freedom."

The Kabbalists, and notably many of the Hasidic masters, are responsible for the popular belief that everyone, at the instant of crossing the threshold into Sabbath time, is possessed by a special Sabbath-soul, a burst of light from the upper world descending into profane darkness. According to the Zoharic literature, "a wind blows from the world-to-come. . . . The holy Shelter of Peace descends and spreads her wings over Israel like a mother protecting her children. . . . She then bestows a new soul upon each person" (3:173a;1:48e). By performing the Sabbath *mitzvot* faithfully, you not only transform your own heart, but in a mystical sense, restore harmony between upper and lower worlds, and join God in completing his creation of the cosmos.

Galut is taken very seriously by the Kabbalists, who project it dramatically into divinity itself. Parallel to many Gnostic and Hindu myths of creation, this God-image creates the universe by a process of self-alienation—his *Shekhinah* light, broken through some primordial cosmic flaw and spilling out over the universe. Our everyday profane life is filled with these many scattered hidden sparks, yearning to be freed from their constricting shells and reunited to the Pleroma, a completed godhead. Hasidic spirituality aims to uncover these sacred particles within the here and now, and reverently release them. By each loving *mitzvah* you liberate Israel more fully from Galut and restore the exiled *Shekhinah*. The privileged Sabbath-soul or garment of light aids you to sacralize, on this day especially, what would otherwise remain secular, and to overlook none of the *Shekhinah* sparks imprisoned in the six profane workdays.

The Zion-Israel Dilemma

At a crucial moment in Chaim Potok's novel *The Chosen,* two American Orthodox Jewish families size up each other across battle lines on the issue of a Zionist State. Shocked by the unwillingness of the United States and other nations to assist Jewish refugees fleeing Nazi persecutions, scholar David Malter becomes an ardent Zionist after learning of the Holocaust: "Some Jews say we should wait for God to send the Messiah. We cannot wait for God. We must make our own Messiah. . . . Palestine must become a Jewish homeland." Yet the ultra-Orthodox Reb Saunders, a *zaddik* patriarch with roots in the Hasidic *shtetl* tradition, asks in rebuttal, "Ben-Gurion and his Goyim will build Eretz Israel? . . . When the Messiah comes, we will have Eretz Israel, a Holy Land, not a land contaminated by Jewish Goyim!" A secular Jewish State in Saunders' eyes is a sacrilege, a violation of the Torah. He thinks it "better to live in a land of true Goyim than to live in a land of Jewish Goyim!"

More complex than this duel between personalities suggests at first, the argument over Zion-Israel continues today between Diaspora and Israeli Jews, between Jewish and non-Jewish Israeli citizens, between Israeli Ashkenazim and Sephardim, between secular and religious Jews everywhere. Although the fictional Saunders and Malter never probe these issues further, we can extend their implicit debate here to clarify a few important concepts. First, the Messiah has been viewed throughout Jewish history as either an exclusively religious figure—a prophet, a transcendent spirit, perhaps God himself—or a combined religiopolitical revolutionary. The messianic phenomenon can be interpreted more as an immanent principle, too, referring to a future millennium of universal social justice and peace, or to the Chosen People themselves at their moment of final apotheosis. The messianic reality, however conceived, may intrude into the human situation as a transcendent gift, unmerited by *mitzvot*; on the other hand, it may be an outside or immanent force closely interdependent on *mitzvot*. The Kabbalists, as we have seen, attributed an almost magical power to human deeds. At any rate, the rabbinic tradition says that the moment people's lives are perfected, the messianic era will begin. Saunders apparently expects a personal savior Messiah, sharply dissociated from mere human efforts in the secular political arena. Malter's activist zeal to create his own Messiah, on the other hand, sounds at first like blasphemy to an ultra-Orthodox literalist, but such claims simply echo much of the Talmud's bold rhetoric whenever it stresses the importance of our own *mitzvot*.

It would be helpful, furthermore, to distinguish cautiously the following concepts: Galut from the Diaspora, eschatological Zion from the present State of Israel, and the religious Jew first from the secular Jew and second from the Goy or Gentile. Today there are Jewish and non-Jewish Israeli citizens; and Diaspora Jews living abroad as citizens or noncitizens of other lands. In Saunders' eyes, the first Israeli prime minister, an acknowledged nonreligious Jew, is thus religiously indistinguishable from a Gentile. Saunders thinks he can maintain his own Hasidic religious identity more faithfully as a Diaspora Jew, clearly segregated by dress and customs from the Gentile and assimilated Jewish majority, than as the Jewish citizen of a secular State that uses the rhetoric of cryptoreligious Jewish pretensions. Perhaps what disturbs Saunders most is the Zionists' apparent confusion of Galut with Diaspora. The Jew exists on earth in perpetual Galut or alienation from God, looking toward Zion or the moment of messianic religious salvation at the end of time. Whether a Diaspora Jew in New York or an Israeli citizen, one can never progress to a stage when Galut and Zion are not an indispensable dialectic in the human situation. The Israeli State mistakes itself for Zion, when at best it can only be a small foretaste of Zion. To revere it as Zion is thus a sacrilege.

There are other significant voices that must be introduced into this debate about Zion-Israel. The first is David Ben-Gurion himself, who even as an impoverished adolescent in his eastern European *shtetl,* determined to migrate to Palestine at the first opportunity. "Jews in the Diaspora as Jews are human debris," he would write later. A favorite contrast in his speeches is the image of a strong young Israeli pioneer, rebellious and creative—opposed to the Diaspora Jew, a neurotic cowardly parasite, cut off from the soil, oppressed and thus oppressing others, and furthermore, arousing the legitimate contempt of non-Jews. Ben-Gurion could never imagine this Diaspora as a holy mission to disseminate Jewish faith and moral ideals to the nations, an interpretation pandering to Gentiles and comfortably assimilated Diaspora Jews. "Jews should come to Israel," his *Memoirs* states bluntly. "In the Diaspora they cannot really be Jews without an artificial self-consciousness and tension that disappears completely from their lives once they arrive here. Outside Israel, the end result for a Jew inevitably is either the ghetto or assimilation. . . . We offer a full Jewish life and a full human life, which, if not richer economically than elsewhere, promises greater spiritual fulfillment." In an address to the Israeli Knesset in 1950, he admits that "the Diaspora has not ceased with the foundations of the State." Yet a few sentences later he implies that the *kibbutz galuyot* of the messianic era has clearly arrived. In effect, he hopes the Diaspora experience will soon wither away, a tragic episode in Israel's long history.

Martin Buber, another immigrant to Israeli, is a Zionist spokesman vastly different from Ben-Gurion. Four decades of the German Diaspora had left with him a genuine, creative bond to German soil and culture, shattered one day when he woke to find this contract between cultures terminated by the host State. As he observes in his 1939 essay "The End of German-Jewish Symbiosis," it had taken him long to grasp "the tragic character of fate in the Diaspora, the origin and annihilation of genuine syntheses." Gandhi once outraged Buber by urging that Jews offer a resigned *satyāgraha* response to Nazi pogroms. "The Palestine of the biblical conception is not a geographical tract. It is in their hearts," Gandhi wrote in 1938. "But if they must look to the Palestine of geography as their national home, it is wrong to enter it under the shadow of British guns. A religious act cannot be performed with the aid of the bayonet or the bomb." Buber's defense in his famous letter to Gandhi is eloquent: "Satyagraha means testimony. Testimony without acknowledgment, ineffective, unobserved martyrdom, . . . Who would venture to demand it? . . . We do not want to use force. . . . We believe that a man must sometimes use force to save himself, or even more, his children. . . . From the time when Britain conquered Palestine, I have not ceased to strive for the concluding of peace between Arab and Jew."

It is remarkable that as early as 1929, we find Buber precisely as he claimed, promoting at international Zionist meetings a binational State structure to be shared with the Palestinian Arabs, a platform he never abandoned, despite its mounting unpopularity later among most of his colleagues. He passionately wished for a Jewish strip of land as a sheer physical haven for refugee Jews. "Dispersion is bearable, it can even be purposeful," he tells Gandhi, "if somewhere there is an ingathering, a growing home center, a piece of earth from which the spirit of ingathering may work its way out to all the places of dispersion." Unlike Ben-Gurion, he expects Galut and Diaspora to perdure, and the State of Israel to stand only as a precondition for Zion. The nation-state is indispensable, but never alone sufficient. Beyond this, Buber hoped for eventual spiritual awakening, the renaissance of Hebrew Humanism, and a gradual dissolution of the classical nationalist State into a global "community of communities," an ideal network of *kibbutzim* in cross-cultural intercommunion.

The attitude of Reform Diaspora Jews toward the State of Israel began in an outright Haskalah gesture of repudiation. This approach has been transformed into a contemporary blend of Buber's and Ben-Gurion's positions—sometimes fervent but conditional loyalty, sometimes a bewildered deference to every major pronouncement of the Israeli government. The major price exacted by modern western Europe for Jewish political emancipation in the last century could be summed up in one revolutionary slogan, "To the Jews as a nation, nothing. To the Jews as individuals, everything!" They must forfeit every hint of dual citizenship in order to prove themselves primarily committed Germans or French, and only derivatively, members of the Jewish persuasion. Under these pressures, we are able to appreciate Mendelssohn's warning to his Jewish colleagues that they "must not take even a single step preparatory to a return to Palestine" unless God himself should intervene to lead them there. His book *Jerusalem* adopts what he calls the initial Mosaic Constitution, but finds it later undermined by the Davidic Monarchy, a perverse doomed political experiment "dazzled by the splendor of a neighboring court." There is much prophetic evidence in the Bible for this disparaging view of kingship. Contrast this revisionist appraisal of theocratic Israel with the following counter-revisionist approach to the later Roman-occupied Jewish nation: "On May 14, 1948, a new State was not found ex nihilo," Ben-Gurion tells the Israeli Knesset. "Rather, the crown was restored to its pristine splendor 1,813 years after the independence of Israel was destroyed. . . ."

Prayerbooks of Jewish Reform during the nineteenth century tended to alter traditional petitions and rituals yearning for a return to Jerusalem and the Temple. At the 1841 dedication of a synagogue in Charleston, South Carolina, the rabbi addressed his audience, "This synagogue is our Temple, this city our Jerusalem, this happy land our Palestine." Official statements issued by the Central Conference of American Rabbis originate with the Pittsburgh Platform of 1885: "We consider ourselves no longer a nation but a religious community, and therefore expect neither a return to Palestine nor a sacrificial worship under the administration of the sons of Aaron, nor the restoration of any of the laws concerning the Jewish State." In response to the Balfour Declaration of 1917, which promised British support for a Jewish Palestinian homeland, this Reform Conference repeated, "The ideal of the Jew is not the establishment of a Jewish State, not the reassertion of Jewish nationality which has long been outgrown." In no way are we prepared for their dramatic reversal in the Columbus Platform of 1937. After dismissing proverbial charges of dual political loyalty, and acknowledging the full responsibilities of American citizenship, the rabbis conclude, "We affirm the obligation of all Jewry to aid . . . in the rehabilitation of Palestine . . . as a Jewish homeland, by endeavoring to make it not only a haven of refuge for the oppressed, but also a center of Jewish culture and spiritual life."

Most platforms and constitutions lag behind or thrust outrageously ahead of their constituents' current beliefs. Yet apparently a seismic groundswell within the Jewish community prompted this unprecedented change in the Reform Jew's official self-definition. Dreams of Mendelssohn and the early Buber for Haskalah equity and universal fellowship had to be reconciled with the Holocaust fact and its possible future recurrence. The priestly mission of Diaspora Jews to the nations had to adjust itself to the scandal of so many unwanted insecure survivors.

Saul Bellow's *To Jerusalem and Back: A Personal Account* celebrates Israel's reversal of the Diaspora Jewish fate: once led to helpless slaughter, the Jews are now formidable fighters; landless in dispersal, they are now farmers who have turned desert into garden. Yet he is irritated that so many putative friends of Israel urge it to set the world a moral example and become "exceptionally exceptional. Perhaps the Jews have themselves created such expectations." He had noticed earlier in his trip that almost every immigrant had brought to Israel a different version of Paradise. The political scientist Leonard

Fein suggests that just as every revolution promises more than it produces, so Israel has disappointed us by proving itself just another nation-state, yet one that still promises continuously to give us Zion. We recognize why Jews like Reb Saunders feared that "if the dream was ever to be given concrete form, many would forget the distinction between place and dream, and having inherited the place would forget the dream." Zion is the aspiration that binds all Jews, Galut is the certainty that they can never fully realize this aspiration. "Just as Israel is not and cannot be Zion," says Fein, "so Exile is a situation of Jews wherever they are, whether in the Diaspora or in Israel itself. Jews who are in Israel are also, then, in Exile, or ought to be."

The spiritual consciousness of most contemporary Jews returns again and again to ponder the divine plan in Galut, the Holocaust, and the State of Israel. As noted in our discussion of Buddhist spirituality, the world views of present and future eschatology are not easy to reconcile. Many religious Jews seem convinced that the Galut-Zion dialectic needs to recover its biblical prophetic integrity—a messianic future eschatology. Perhaps one prophetic function of the Diaspora Jew's perduring existence is to give witness that the Jewish people are wider than any single political State, and that both Galut and Zion identity are wider than either Diaspora or Israeli homeland. Otherwise, Tel Aviv or even Charleston could be mistaken for the New Jerusalem. The transcendent religious dynamic could stop short and fixate on some political idol. And some Israeli Jews might be tempted to overlook what other Israeli Jews recognize as a Palestinian Diaspora within the contemporary State of Israel.

FURTHER READING

1. **Overview.** An indispensable handbook, with extended, accurate entries on all major Judaic ritual and theological concepts, is R. J. Zwi Werblowsky and Geoffrey Wigoder, eds., *The Encyclopedia of the Jewish Religion* (Holt, Rinehart and Winston, 1965). Beryl Cohon's *Judaism in Theory and Practice,* 3rd ed. (Bloch, 1968), is a solid standard introduction to contemporary Jewish religious life, especially in America. Paul Mendes-Flohr and Jehuda Reinharz, eds., *The Jew in the Modern World* (Oxford University Press, 1980) presents an outstanding selection of primary documents in modern Jewish history, with careful annotations on the context of each snippet. Passages on the Haskalah, Jewish identity, and Zionism are especially illuminating.

Three introductory books are useful in learning to read and interpret Judaic sources, especially the Talmud. Jacob Neusner's *Invitation to the Talmud: A Teaching Book* (Harper and Row, 1973) presents a few accessible passages and alerts the reader to basic hermeneutical principles. In addition to Buber's popular Hasidic anthologies and introductions, Gershom Scholem's *On the Kabbalah and Its Symbolism,* tr. Ralph Manheim (Schocken, 1965), surveys the history of Jewish mysticism and singles out characteristic themes, images, and myths, especially the *Golem* figure. Principal collections and genres, such as Wisdom literature, Responsa, Commandments, the Talmudic and Zoharic texts, are described and exemplified in Harry Gersh, *The Sacred Books of the Jews* (Stein and Day, 1968).

The best sources on contemporary Judaic thought are the journals published by various active American Jewish organizations. For example, *Commentary,* sponsored by the American Jewish Committee, and *Jewish Heritage,* by the B'nai B'rith, can be sampled in Norman Podhoretz, ed., *The Commentary Reader: Two Decades of Articles and Stories* (Atheneum, 1966), and Morris Adler, ed., *Jewish Heritage Reader* (Taplinger, 1965). Most highly recommended are the back issues of *Judaism,* published by the American Jewish Congress. The content is varied and scholarly, and the prose unusually keen and terse, as though rewritten by a single consciousness.

2. **Haskalah Background and Aftermath.** The transition from the sixteenth century to the French Revolution in Jewish-Gentile relations is well documented in Jacob Katz's *Exclusiveness and Tolerance* (Oxford University Press, 1961). For a reconstruction of *shtetl* life, see the articles on the *shtetl,* Marc Chagall, and Isaac Singer in *Jewish Heritage Reader;* and especially the introduction to Yiddish *mentshlekhkayt,* exemplified by the texts of five plays, in Joseph Landis, tr. and ed., *The Great Jewish Plays* (Horizon, 1972).

Alfred Jospe presents a concise anthology of Moses Mendelssohn's thought, including the complete, newly translated text of *Jerusalem* in *Jerusalem and Other Jewish Writings* (Schocken, 1969). The Mendelssohn-Lessing friendship is explored in Alexander Altman, *Moses Mendelssohn: A Biographical Study* (University of Alabama Press, 1973), and F. Andrew Brown's *Gotthold Ephraim Lessing* (Twayne, 1971). See the passable translation of *Nathan the Wise* by Bayard Morgan (Ungar, 1955). In addition to surveys of Mendelssohn's theology in Noah Rosenbloom, "Mendelssohn's Redefinition of Judaism—Tension and Solution," *Judaism* 21 (1972), pp. 477–89, and in Eva Jospe, "Moses Mendelssohn: Some Reflections on His Thought," *Judaism* 30 (1981), pp. 169–82, see especially Michael Morgan, "History and Modern Jewish Thought: Spinoza and Mendelssohn on the Ritual Law," ibid., pp. 467–78. Spinoza holds that Mosaic ritual Torah is invalidated since the fall of the Second Temple.

The preceding chapter's bibliography introduced many suggested Freud and Marx sources. Lawrence Stepelevitch, "Marx and the Jews," *Judaism* 23 (1974), pp. 150–60, gives further evidence of Marx's conscious anti-Semitism. See the articles on Freud and Kafka in the *Jewish Heritage Reader* cited above. Nahum Glatzer, ed., *I Am a Memory Come Alive: Autobiographical*

Writings by Franz Kafka (Schocken, 1974), is a valuable collation from diaries, letters, and other scattered sources, arranged chronologically, with a helpful thematic index.

3. **An Exilic Spirituality.** Nahum Glatzer, "Zion in Medieval Literature: Prose Works," in his *Essays in Jewish Thought* (University of Alabama Press, 1978), pp. 135–49, gives insightful passages from the Jewish mystics on this theme. A rich sampling of tales, arranged thematically, can be found in Louis Newman and Samuel Spitz, ed. and tr., *The Hasidic Anthology: Tales and Teachings of the Hasidim* (Schocken, 1972). Gershom Scholem presents a convincing case against Buber's tendency to suppress Hasidic data that do not fit his partisan theses—see "Martin Buber's Hasidism," in *The Commentary Reader,* pp. 451–66, as cited above.

Ruth Fredman, *The Passover Seder: Afikoman in Exile* (University of Pennsylvania Press, 1981), focuses on the Elijah and *afikomen* rites especially, interpreted by illuminating parallels in religious anthropology. Monford Harris explores the night image and ritual time in "The Passover Seder: On Entering the Order of History," *Judaism* 25 (1976), pp. 473–88. The entire issue of *Judaism* 31:1 (1982) is devoted to discussion of the Sabbath—see especially Elliot Ginsburg, "The Sabbath in the Kabbalah," pp. 26–36, which emphasizes the theme of mystical marriage between Israel and the Sabbath. Sabbath as foretaste of the messianic era is explored in Theodore Friedman, "The Sabbath: Anticipation of Redemption," *Judaism* 16 (1967), pp. 443–52.

4. **Zionism and the State of Israel.** After perusing the Ben-Gurion *Memoirs* (World, 1970), with his emphasis on the frontier myth and biblical mandate, study the evolution of his position in Zeev Tzahor, "David Ben-Gurion's Attitude toward the Diaspora," *Judaism* 32:1 (1983), pp. 9–22.

E. William Rollins and Harry Zohn, eds., *Men of Dialogue: Martin Buber and Albrecht Goes* (Funk and Wagnalls, 1969), offers various letters and articles that register changing relationships between the two cultures, Jewish and German. The heated dialogue between Gandhi and Buber can be pursued further in Buber's *Pointing the Way: Collected Essays* (Routledge and Paul, 1957). It is interesting to conjecture why Buber's binational constitution with the Arabs, and also his misgivings about Israeli idolatry, had such little influence—see Norman Levine, "The Tragedy of Bourgeois Cosmopolitanism: On Martin Buber's Politics," *Judaism* 30 (1981), pp. 427–33. Further materials can be consulted in the Buber symposium issue of *Judaism* 27:2 (1978) and in Paul Schilpp and Maurice Friedman, eds., *The Philosophy of Martin Buber* (Open Court, 1967), especially Buber's replies to his critics.

Two dissenting Jewish voices should be heard before we presume a consensus on the Holocaust or on proverbial Jewish this-worldliness. Deborah Lipstadt, "Invoking the Holocaust," *Judaism* 30 (1981), pp. 335–43, objects to excessive uses of this calamity to give a lachrymose theory of Jewish history. Bernard Bamberger, "Jewish Otherworldliness," *Judaism* 26 (1977), pp. 201–5, deliberately builds up a case against present eschatology.

Leonard Fein, "Israel or Zion," *Judaism* 22 (1973), pp. 7–17, argues very persuasively for the separation between the eschatological ideal and its flawed, partial embodiment in the nation-state of Israel. The same position recurs in David Polish, "The Tasks of Israel and Galut," *Judaism* 18 (1969), pp. 3–16; and by implication in Sholom Kahn, "Israeli, Hebrew, Jew: The Semantic Problem," *Judaism* 19 (1970), pp. 9–13. Joshua Haberman, "The Place of Israel in Reform Jewish Theology," *Judaism* 21 (1972), pp. 437–48, develops more extensively the evolution from Haskalah assimilation to support of the State of Israel.

7

Muslim Sharīʻah

Jerusalem is not the same Holy City for Jews, Christians, and Muslims. Pilgrims of one creed jostle unavoidably, at times militantly, against those of another. One tradition's stories and prayers repeatedly threaten to drown out those of another. Not far from the Jewish Wailing Wall stands the Byzantine Church of the Holy Sepulchre, memorializing the final days of Jesus' fateful journey to Jerusalem. Directly within view, built allegedly on the cornerstone of Solomon's Temple, and on the primordial site where Abraham was commanded to sacrifice his son, is the Muslim Dome of the Rock. It is said Muhammad appeared here on his Dantean night ride and ascension into Heaven.

It seems appropriate to introduce the Muslim tradition by an extended architectural metaphor. Its prophetic reassertion of monotheism suggests empty desert vistas and transcendent space. Its finest artistic language has proved to be the mosque and minaret. And even Sharīʻah, or divine law, is transmitted today in the popular mnemonic formula of Five Pillars. Moreover, the concept of ethnic domain in architecture persuades us that differing self-contained simulated worlds can occupy the same geographical place. During the Paleolithic Age, for instance, a mere arrangement of upright stones might have defined a sacred magic circle, succeeded perhaps by a Canaanite phallic shrine, and then a Jewish temple, all on the same patch of ground. In a similar way, Jews, Christians, and Muslims revere many of the same sacred places, prophets, covenants, and myths of creation and apocalypse. Yet the Muslim Abraham and Ishmael must never be mistaken for the

Abraham and Ishmael of Jewish scriptures, nor the Muslim Tawrāt and Injıl for Jewish Torah and Christian Gospel, nor the Muslim prophet Isa ibn Maryam for the Christian Jesus. Every religious tradition in this common Abrahamic family has its own unique configuration. We shall try to measure each according to its own vision, without straining to detect causes of willful or unconscious metamorphosis when a later prophet reinterprets an earlier one. The archaeological rubble from specific Jewish and Christian monuments seems less significant than the new Muslim edifice itself, built with inspired coherence and imagination from old remnants.

Despite recent enmity over the State of Israel, Muslim and Jewish traditionalists share extraordinary religious affinities. Pure monotheists and iconoclasts, both reject the notion of an incarnate God as sacrilegious, even self-contradictory. Their spirituality centers on the revealed will of God, essentially as interpreted by a line of respected legal scholars. In the last century, resisting European assimilation and colonialism, both have tried to preserve their own identity as a political and religious people. Each has grudgingly accepted various compromises with secularism, nationalism, and socialism in building modern nation-states. Heartened by these many parallels, the average Muslim is appalled to page through the Jew's own Torah text, or the Christian's New Testament. If God's patriarchs and prophets can be portrayed as liars, murderers, and fornicators, then this disedifying extant Torah must be a corrupt version of the Mosaic original. And the scandal of four Gospel texts, with their many disparities of detail, indicates similar human tampering with God's unambiguous revelation.

To discern and obey the will of Allāh, neither human reason alone nor the Mosaic and Christian revelations combined seem to have provided sufficient clarity. So Muhammad was chosen to mediate God's final and comprehensive self-disclosure in the Qur'an. The last of the prophets supersedes every preceding prophet. A few passages in the Qur'an expect Jews and Christians somehow to retain and yet reinterpret their specific traditions in light of this new corrective vision: "People of the Book, you shall not be guided until you observe Torah and Gospel and that which is revealed to you from your Lord" (5:68). In his final Qur'anic covenant, God links himself definitively, not to a single nation, but to his *ummah muslima,* the universal community of believers. Sharī'ah is his revealed Will. And *Din* or *Islam,* utter religious submission, even when the reasonableness of God's plan cannot be fathomed, must be the distinctive quality of mankind's response. Originally designating a path to water, *Sharī'ah* means the complete spiritual Way. Revealed by a compassionate God, it is the detailed blueprint for an integral social and individual human life. Its prescriptions cover all human activities: religious belief, duties of prayer and fasting, and every foreseeable personal and juridical responsibility within a society pervasively religious.

Later *'ulamā'* religious scholars would split into differing legal traditions, once they had to apply Sharī'ah principles to new historical circumstances. The cited Qur'anic injunction would come first, and then its interpretation within the context of evolving *ummah* consensus and of *ḥadīth* selections—those extra-Qur'anic sayings and customs of varying authenticity attributed to Muhammad. Presuming these various legal schools, we shall study the theological and ritual complementarity of Sunnī and Shī'ī traditions, conflicting stances on the viability of a modern nation-state, and a broad sweep of experiments in Muslim spirituality.

Rituals of Pilgrimage and Martyrdom

"We enjoined Abraham and Ishmael to cleanse our House for those who walk around it," says Allāh in the Qur'an, "for those who meditate in it, and kneel and prostrate themselves." Then Abraham and Ishmael built the Ka'bah and dedicated it with the prayer, "Lord, make us submissive to you; make of our descendants a nation that will submit to you. . . . Send them, Lord, an apostle of their own who shall declare to them your revelations, instruct them in the scriptures and wisdom, and purify them of sin" (2:125–30). This significant Qur'anic text shows the principal etiological story behind the Mecca Ka'bah, focus of the *ḥajj* pilgrimage, which remains a major ritual responsibility at least once a lifetime for every capable Muslim. Here we catch Abraham and his son in the process of rebuilding. Muslims believe that Adam constructed the first Ka'bah on earth, patterned after an angelic Ka'bah in Heaven, and at that time was given the sacred Black Stone, still revered today at a corner of the shrine. The last mention of Ishmael in the Jewish Book of Genesis occurs after Abraham, obeying God's command, deserts Ishmael and his mother Hagar in the wilderness, both of them seeking desperately for water. "What is the matter, Hagar. . . . Lift the child up and hold him in your arms," God tells Hagar, as he directs her to a well full of water, "because I will make him a great nation" (21:14–21). Years later, Abraham returns to search for his adult son, according to the Muslim epilogue to this story.

And digging near the Zamzam well, with mounting excitement and awe father and son together rediscover the ruins of Adam's ancient temple, symbolic Center of the earth.

The later apostle for whom Abraham and Ishmael yearn, of course, turns out to be Muhammad. In the year 630, after experiencing eight years of exile and military failure since the *hijrah* flight to Medina, Muhammad at last rode his camel in triumph into Mecca. As enemy clans watched in sullen helplessness, he tapped the Black Stone with his long camel-stick as he completed each circling, and then knocked down all three hundred and sixty idols standing in the courtyard. He would not rest until all polytheistic overlay had been stripped off the original Abrahamic faith. Next he entered the massive Ka'bah stone cube itself and began scrubbing images off the walls, uttering the *shahādah* prayer at each corner as an act of reconsecration, "There is no god but God, and Muhammad is his apostle." Departing then for Medina, he returned again two years later, with accurate foreboding that this would be his final pilgrimage. He brought with him a young disciple on the same camel, apparently so that the boy could observe each detail of Muhammad's pilgrimage ritual. For every prayer and gesture would be devoutly reenacted by later Muslim disciples.

Today the empty Ka'bah is decked in black cloth with gold Qur'anic arabesques, and surrounded by the splendid Great Mosque of nineteen arched gateways. Hub of a wheel with spokes radiating throughout the earth, it is the magnetic Center toward which all praying Muslims prostrate themselves five times daily, and where the *miḥrāb,* or prayer niche, in every mosque is pointed. Men must dress for the *ḥajj* in an unstitched *ahram* sheet, with one shoulder bare, a cloth that many will preserve afterward for their burial shroud. Women are expected to wear a white dress, without jewelry. As pilgrims approach the city of Mecca, a sacred space restricted to Muslims only, they enter a zone of special sanctuary and consecration. This is the moment to renew the *niia* vow—to abstain from sinful thoughts and actions throughout the *ḥajj*, especially from harm toward any living being. After circumambulation of the Ka'bah, one must then begin the remaining rites: a sevenfold circuit barefooted along the causeway stretching between tombs of Hagar and Ishmael; meditation from noon to sunset at Mount Arafat; a day at Mina on the Mecca outskirts to cast stones at three pillars; and the *'īd al-aḍḥā* animal sacrifices on the tenth day of the *ḥajj* month, a feast celebrated at that moment by Muslim households everywhere in solidarity with the pilgrims. Finally, after the optional shaving of head and beard, everyone is prompted to spend a few days in reflection and dedicated reentry, now bearing the honorary *ḥajjī* title, a green turban, or some other indication of completing the *ḥajj*.

Three overlapping religious motifs dominate the *ḥajj* liturgy. The most obvious is ritual participation in Abraham's submission to Allāh. There is first Abraham's own sacred Ka'bah, the precious water from Hagar's Zamzam well, and a nearby stone upon which Abraham purportedly stood to complete his task of construction. Pilgrims rush seven times down the causeway to imitate Hagar's forlorn search for water. Mina is the revered place where Abraham was told to sacrifice his son, where he resisted diabolic temptations to disobey, and then offered the ram-replacement sacrifice. The Mina pillars are said to represent Abraham's devils, phallic remnants perhaps from some polytheistic cultus. By stoning them in the old Semitic style of banishing evil, believers reaffirm their own *jihād* holy war against contemporary idolatry. The huge communal ceremony of animal slaughter at Mina crowns each *ḥajjī*'s effort to recover the firm unquestioning faith of Abraham.

The famous Black Stone of Mecca, worn smooth by centuries of pilgrim contact, is the only surviving relic from the original Ka'bah. It is also a remnant that touched the lips of Muhammad. Memory of the Prophet's two final pilgrimages to Mecca adds a meaningful second nuance to the Abrahamic theme. Muslims claim not merely the unwavering monotheistic faith of the patriarchs, but a faith long betrayed and now restored, purified and aggressively reasserted, in the face of rival religious counterfeits. Muhammad's return to Mecca gives the Ka'bah experience a willful and militant neo-Abrahamic dimension. In his *Caravan of Dreams,* Idries Shah tells of the many believers who insist on walking the final fifty miles from the Jidda airport or seaport to Mecca. Why must they walk? Perhaps some hesitate to pay the bus fare, yet others must fulfill a private vow. Though the exact means of Muhammad's entry is disputed, these people feel that "greater humility and piety attach to entering the Holy City afoot as Muhammad did, nearly fourteen hundred years ago. Though a conqueror, he walked thus with the Four Companions to Abraham's shrine, there to demolish the three hundred and more idols, and to establish the worship of one God alone among the people of this land."

On his final pilgrimage, the ninth of the month of Dhū al-Ḥijjah, Muhammad went to Mount Arafat, and wearily preached a concluding sermon there. At sundown he fell into ecstasy and received one of his last divine revelations. Muslims today stand in sustained meditative silence at this spot, and retrace Muhammad's footsteps as they complete the remaining *ḥajj* rituals, including a recommended visit to his tomb at Medina. The previous night on the plain of Arafat, spent camping out in thousands of tents, can transport a contemporary urban Muslim back to the simple nomadic origins of the first *ummah muslima*.

Besides the Abraham and Muhammad dimensions, the *ummah* constitutes a third religious motif in the *ḥajj*. Since *ḥajjī* identity is a customary prerequisite among candidates for Muslim leadership back home, it is not surprising to meet strong uniformity of doctrine, ritual, and even architectural style flowing consistently from the Mecca source to the farthest Muslim outreaches. Two weeks of intensive religious renewal, the precisely monitored public liturgies, the sermons, the conversations with pilgrims from other nations—these experiences the *ḥajjī* transmits back home to help tighten a worldwide Muslim consensus. *Ḥajj* celebrates not only the origins and heroic continuity of Muslim history but its present diversity and solidarity as a community, especially at the moment of *'īd al-aḍḥā* sacrifice. Malcolm X in his autobiography gives an especially poignant account of this *ummah* experience, which shattered his previous Black Muslim racist ideology: "White, black, brown, red, and yellow people, blue eyes and blond hair, and my kinky red hair—all together, as brothers! . . . All ate as one, and slept as one. Everything about the pilgrimage atmosphere accented the Oneness of Man under One God. . . . America needs to understand Islam, because this is the one religion that erases from its society the race problem."

These words of Malcolm X state the remarkable Qur'anic ideal, even though Muslims complain of persistent abuses within their own societies—myths of Arab supremacy, for example, and of subtle color discriminations pervading African and Indian folklore, long before their accentuation by racist colonial powers. There is a tenth-century *ḥadīth,* based on the contested testimony of Anas, recounting Muhammad's attempts to challenge the color prejudice of his own early community. A poor Black confides to Muhammad the fear that his ugly color will ban him from Paradise, for no Muslim family will permit him to marry their daughter. Sent next day by Muhammad to the devout home of an especially beautiful daughter, the Black delivers a solemn message to her father, "The Prophet has given me your daughter as my wife." Rudely dismissed by the father, he is later accepted with misgivings through the renewed intervention of Muhammad, who then proceeds to raise money for the husband's dowry. Before wedding formalities can take place, the Black leaves for a *jihād* battle, and dies bravely. His corpse is tended by Muhammad himself, who wipes the dust from his friend's face and witnesses his soul entering Paradise. The body is then carried back to his reluctant in-laws, with the vindictive message, "Allāh has already married him to a better woman than yours!"

In the *ḥajj,* Muslims "journey to the Center, to the house of God," says Seyyed Nasr in ***Ideals and Realities of Islam,*** to do penance and seek forgiveness for sins. In returning home, they are expected to live devout lives, and bring "the purity and grace (*barakah*) of the house of God with them. Something of the Center is thus disseminated in the periphery . . . to unify the Muslim community and spread the purity which lies at its heart to the limbs and organs." In counterpoint to this converging, retentive gravitational pull represented by the *ḥajj,* we can distinguish a number of divergent and often recusant forces, active around the periphery. To overlook these counterforces would be to mistake a bland uniform stereotype for the complex variegated Muslim reality. Perhaps the first reason these tendencies survive is the relatively meager festival life decreed by official Muslim calenders. Only the tenth day of *ḥajj* and the joyous conclusion of *ramaḍān* fast are mandatory traditions. Perhaps Muhammad did not want to risk *shirk,* or idolatrous abuse, in attempts to Islamize prevalent folk customs. Yet those unable to put up with such austerity have managed ever since to smuggle in various alien feasts, such as *nawrūz* or the Persian New Year, the spring fertility festival of ancient Egypt, and the various *mawlids,* or birth and death dates of regional prophets and saints, especially the feast of Muhammad himself on the *mawlid al-nabī.*

A further reason behind this creative diversity is the widespread critique of patent *ḥajj* distortions. Recent Muslim reformers in Southeast Asia, for instance, acknowledge with distress that most of the poor can never afford the *ḥajj.* People would mortgage or auction essential family property, squander most of the funds on a single Mecca junket, then return claiming their local *ummah* should support and fawn over them. Tourist companies had been launching vigorous *ḥajj* advertising campaigns, even offering commissions to renowned *ḥajjīs* for enlisting new candidates. Many pilgrims returned, expecting to enjoy a life of contemplative withdrawal, perhaps to preside at most local religious events, but no longer to do physical labor—perhaps in unconscious emulation of their Buddhist *bhikkhu* neighbors, dependent on laity to fill the monks' begging bowls. Yet both the Qur'an and *ḥadīth* demand egalitarianism, without social discrepancies, pretentious titles, or a parisitic priestly caste. Elsewhere in the Muslim world, too, complaints recur against Wahhābī fundamentalist control of the Mecca holy places, notably their alleged efforts to conscript vulnerable Muslim visitors into rigid Wahhābī orthodoxy or a current local Saudi version of Arab nationalism. At various times in Muslim history, pilgrim detours to regional shrines in Iraq, Iran, and North Africa have threatened to tap the principal flow to Mecca.

The most important reason for Muslim religious disparities today is the bitter historical schism that became prominent within two decades after Muhammad's death, Sunnī-Shī'ī quarrels over the *ummah's* nature and leadership. The Sunnī majority today attribute infallible authority to the consensus hammered out by the first Muslim generation, for Muhammad in one *ḥadīth* promised, "My community will never agree in error." They back the *ummah*'s selected line of caliphs as legitimate *ummah* leaders. Yet a movement of political-religious dissent had gradually taken shape by the time of 'Alī, Muhammad's cousin and son-in-law, the fourth caliph. New non-Arab converts resented the Arab nepotism of previous caliphs, and religious idealists craved a charismatic moral leader like Muhammad, rather than some decadent political dynasty in Medina or Damascus just like that of any non-Muslim nation. Refusing to endorse this debased *sunna,* or tradition, the Shī'īs developed their own apocalyptic version of a pure authentic *sunna* transmitted underground through a succession of holy *Imams,* who alone possessed the gift of infallible spiritual authority. This sequence extends from Muhammad to 'alī to Husan and Husayn, and then to their brief line of descendants, the last of which, the Hidden *Imam,* disappeared, yet will return someday as messianic liberator. "Perhaps the most outstanding feature of Shī'īsm," says Iranian political scientist Hamid Enayat, "is an attitude of mind which refuses to admit that majority opinion is necessarily true or right, and—which is its converse—a rationalized defense of the moral excellence of an embattled minority." Shī'īs (partisans) condition their consent to any civil or religious law by a subversive proviso, demanding that the law conform to the will of this Hidden *Imam*. Consent can be withdrawn suddenly, vindicated by sure immediate appeal to this elusive spiritual authority.

If the unitive majority tradition is best symbolized by the *ḥajj,* then the centrifugal minority can be most vividly illustrated by the Shī'ī *muḥarram* liturgy. The tragic defeat of the House of 'Alī, especially the martyrdom of his son, the third *Imam* Husayn, has always touched the deepest Muslim feelings in Iran, Iraq, Pakistan, and India. At the battle of Karbala in Iraq, Husayn contested the claims of Yazid to the caliphate, and after witnessing the thirst, starvation, and slaughter of his besieged troops and family, one by one, he was brutally stoned to death and decapitated. This catastrophe is immortalized in Husayn's shrine at Karbala, a renowned center of pilgrimage, and in the famous *ta'ziyah,* or Passion Play.

Muḥarram rites extend for ten days, from New Year's to *'āshūrā',* a span similar to the Jewish High Holy Days, ending in *asor* or *yom kippur,* Day of Atonement. *'Āshūrā'* combines *kippur* communal repentence with New Year overtones of mourning the old year's death, consecrating the new. In Muslim Northwest Africa, this day is associated with sacred bonfires, derived from primal agrarian rites, and memorial liturgies for the dead. It is hard to imagine a more appropriate atmosphere for the Shī'ī *'āshūrā'* reenactment of Husayn's martyrdom, with its fierce outpouring of grief. Not just their individual lives, but chronicles of official Muslim history, have not been what God wanted his people to be. They cry to Allāh in repentence and for retribution, for return of the *Imam-Mahdi,* for a recapitulation of Muhammad's idealized reign over his first community.

During Shī'ī *muḥarram* rites, cafés and places of public entertainment close down in many cities, and black flags appear everywhere. The media restrict themselves mostly to Qur'an readings and other explicitly religious coverage. Many wear mourning garments, fast, and do not shave. Though local adaptations vary widely, the *ta'ziyah* usually occurs in two forms—women and children enact or give a dramatic reading of the long epic in private gatherings, the narrators at times moving from home to home; whereas most men assemble in streets for a graphic public drama and procession. The public *ta'ziyah* drama, of course, portrays Husayn's personal faith, his motives for rebellion, the unequal battles between soldiers on horseback at Karbala, his last exchange with each of his dying family, and finally the gory head displayed before grieving crowds. There is the somber parade of huge funeral floats, and a symbolic burial of Husayn's coffin. Many individual families construct their own papier-mâché coffin, and bury it or cremate it in a ritual bonfire. It is expected that a few zealots each year will goad themselves into a frenzy of self-mutilation with whips or swords, straining by actual bloodshed to identify with Husayn's passion and death. Muslims in the streets and at home sob openly, striking their breast or head, keening in a rhythmic cadence pattern, *"Yā 'Alī, Ai Husayn, Husayn Shah!"*

Some versions of the *ta'ziyah* epic grope far beyond Husayn's lifetime to trace scenes from the wider sweep of Muslim salvation-history. In one early episode, for example, the angel Gabriel visits the Hebrew patriarch Jacob, inconsolable over the loss of his son Joseph, and introduces an angel troop to perform an instant preview of Husayn's later martyrdom. Jacob gains new perspective on his own suffering, compared with the enormity of Husayn's. Or some lamentations by Husayn at Karbala turn into broad apocalyptic forecasts of injustice, perhaps within more recent eras: "They are going to kill me mercilessly, for no other crime or guilt than that I happen to be a prophet's grandson. . . . All are gone! In this land of trials there is no one compassionate enough to befriend and protect the household of the Apostle of God." One version concludes with the remark by an anonymous elderly Muslim, as the bleeding head is paraded past him, "On those lips have I seen the lips of the Apostle of Allāh!" The epilogue to another version has proven singularly offensive to Sunnī orthodoxy. After Husayn's death, Muhammad at Allāh's command entrusts him with the key to Paradise, lifting him to such dizzy heights that he becomes exclusive mediator for all mankind: "Deliver from the flames of hell everyone who has shed a single tear for you, . . . achieved a pilgrimage to your shrine, or composed tragic verse for you. Bear everyone with you to Paradise!"

Muslim history abounds with tales of conquest and glory, and at times seems to endorse the Jewish Deuteronomist conjecture that armies loyal to God cannot lose battles. Experiences like the Shī'ī *muḥarram* contribute a crucial Job-like tragic demurral to Muslim triumphalism. *Muḥarram* recalls the easily overlooked years of desolate misunderstanding in Muhammad's earlier life, notably his prayers to learn the religious rationale behind a decade of military defeats at Medina. Ritual participation in the Husayn event is a pledge of readiness to die someday his kind of death in the midst of a hostile world, the death of a courageous Muslim witness to the faith. At the same time, it carries each believer back to the religious wellspring of the Shī'ī community's existence.

Shī'ī *muḥarram* spirituality, of course, can never be smoothly reconciled with exacting Wahhābī Sunnī iconoclasm, which even refuses to encourage Mecca pilgrims to visit Muhammad's Medina tomb at the close of the *ḥajj*. Popular imagination might be tempted to forget that Muhammad, after all, is merely a human being. Wahhābīs prefer to direct attention to the famous Sūfī satire about a caretaker of some local shrine, whose son Nasruddin set off to travel around the world on his donkey. When the animal died in the rarefied mountain air of Kashmir, the boy dropped down heartbroken in quiet meditation, after raising a mound over the grave. Pilgrims crossing the steep trails eventually generated a myth of the Silent Mourning Dervish. They concluded the relics must have been remarkably holy to evoke so much devotion. Soon a rich man built a dome over the grave, and others began to add it to their list of pilgrim centers. When Nasruddin's father arrived to investigate this rival shrine, he confessed to his son that their family shrine had also been erected thirty years before over a donkey's grave.

The Muslim Political Vision

We observed in an earlier chapter how Burmese and Sinhalese postcolonial regimes reached out for any available Buddhist, socialist, nationalist ideology to harness recently released centrifugal ethnic forces into an emergent nation-state. Today it is almost impossible to keep pace with the huge diversity of new nations sanctioned by an appeal to traditional Muslim verities. Both insurgent and incumbent parties often label their cause a classical *jihād,* invoke the messianic *Mahdi* or Hidden *Imam* instead of the Buddhist Maitreya, or the Golden Age of the first four caliphs instead of Gandhi's Rāma-Rāj or U Nu's Wishing Tree millennium.

Fatah, the largest Palestinian guerilla organization, for example, has taken its identity from the Muslim term for a *jihād* conquest, and most Palestinian Liberation Army brigades name themselves after historical Muslim victories against Christian Crusaders, Mongols, and Zoroastrian Persians. The *ḥajj,* too, once held subtle political implications for Gamal Nasser, principal figure behind Egypt's series of Pan-Arab and Pan-Islamic alliances. "As I stood before the Kaaba, with my thoughts wandering around every part of the world which Islam has reached," Nasser writes in his *Philosophy of the Revolution,* "I realized . . . the journey to the Kaaba should no longer be construed as an admission card to paradise, or as a crude attempt to buy forgiveness of sins after leading a dissipated life. The Pilgrimage should have a potential political power." He pressed the king of Saudi Arabia to transform it into an annual session of international Muslim leaders in science, finance, politics—an Islamic Parliament of Mecca, cooperating beyond national loyalties, "submissive to the Divine Will, but immutable in difficulties and implacable with its enemies."

The Ayatollah Khomeini, by permitting Iranian disciples to designate him *imam,* has played on crucial religious ambiguities in the title—its generic sense of leader, but also the specific Shī'ī evocation of an authoritative Hidden *Imam.* Two speeches delivered from his French residence in exile a month before and after *muḥarram* rites of 1979 illustrate his skillful blend of the religious and the political: "It is as if the blood of our martyrs were a continuation of the blood of the Karbala martyrs. . . . Just as their pure blood brought to an end the tyrannical rule of Yazid, the blood of our martyrs has shattered the tyrannical monarchy of the Pahlavis." *Muḥarram* is described as "a divine sword in the hands of the soldiers of Islam," to be wielded against "this stinking carrion of monarchy, . . . usurpatory and contrary to both the law of the land and the Sharī'ah. . . . An Islamic State is not the protector of capitalists and big landlords."

Muhammad has been called his own Constantine, in contrast to the underground apolitical minority Christian sects that took three centuries to develop into the sole established Church of the Constantinian Roman Empire. Buddhists or Christians have never been identified as a people, in the same way we speak of the *'am Yisra'el* or the *ummah muslima.* We have seen that many ultra-Orthodox Israeli Jews yearn to incorporate the *halaḳḥa* into constitutional law in modern Israel. Similarly, Muslim traditionalists—by Constitution in Pakistan and Iran, or by gradual parliamentary pressures in Malaysia, for example—want Sharī'ah enshrined as the law of the land. Faced with potential regimes based on *halaḳḥa* or Sharī'ah, the citizens of religious minorities are predictably fearful. They foresee a tangle of civil disabilities, discrimination, and government-sponsored school and media campaigns to proselytize and belittle them—no matter what patronizing concessions the Bible or Qur'an might boast to protect resident aliens or so-called People of the Book.

The Indian poet-philosopher Mohammed Iqbal, a principal inspiration for the separatist Muslim State of Pakistan, defines Islam as both an ethical ideal and a social polity. Islam "is organically related to the social order it has created. The rejection of the one will eventually involve rejection of the other. Therefore, the construction of a polity on national lines, if it means a displacement of the Islamic principle of solidarity, is simply unthinkable to a Muslim." Arguing with the same logic as Zionist Martin Buber, Iqbal wanted to carve a special northwest Indian State for refugee Muslims threatened by Hindu assimilation. If European Haskalah was the bane of *shtetl* Jewish orthodoxy, Muslim traditionalists found their nemesis in Western colonialism, European-style education, laissez-faire democracy, but especially in governments patterned on the Ataturk reform in Turkey, a modern secular State with a disestablished historical caliphate.

Classical Arabic and other ancient Islamic languages lack dichotomous terms such as *secular-religious* or *church-state,* probably because Muslims have always viewed religious and political authority as indistinguishable. The complaint of Khomeini makes sense, then, that scholarly Orientalist and imperialist *Time* magazine versions of Islam sell back to Muslims a pastoral, quiescent, and otherworldly image of themselves, which then enervates them so that they permit the West to loot Muslim resources and productivity. "They have tried with their propaganda and insinuations to present Islam as a petty, limited affair," he warns *'ulamā'* leaders in his best-known work, *Islamic*

Government, "and persuade us that the only duty of the Fuqaha and Ulama is to give their opinion on legal problems. . . . Wake up! Pay some attention to reality and the questions of the day." Under Muhammad's leadership, a free and virtuous society came into being, with everyone bowing before its might. "But why should they bow before *you,* whose only activity is offering opinions on points of law?" The naive American press, with its own tradition of Church-State separation, continues to disparage Khomeini as a cleric meddling in politics. "This is why they call us political mullahs, but was not our Prophet also political?"

In recent postcolonial Muslim efforts to form viable political communities, we can sort out three representative approaches. The first has been disastrously minimized. It is a strain of fierce atavistic local and individual nomadic autonomy, often a passive-aggressive deadweight, a threat to every sanguine urbanized ideologue. In his shrewd Sudanese story "The Doum Tree of Wad Hamid," Taieb Salih introduces the casual, assured voice of an elderly village sage, trying to correct any misapprehensions that might be carried away by his young tourist auditor, stung by savage flies and distressed at the lack of hospitals, roads, and most other essentials of modern life. "We are thickskinned people," the old man tells him. "We have become used to this hard life, in fact we like it, and ask no people to subject themselves to the difficulties of our life." The roads periodically cast up some new stranger at the door, like an odd shred of seaweed. Then his auditor learns the significance of the villagers' prized ancient Doum Tree, a shrine and repository of local history.

Bureaucrats from the distant White Colonial capital once tried to remove this Doum Tree in order to install a community water pump for a utopian agricultural project, but were quickly frightened off. "One day they told us that the government which had driven out imperialism had been replaced by an even bigger and noisier government. . . . Two years passed without our knowing what form the government had taken, Black or White." The new Black regime, as though anxious to make citizens aware of its presence, attempted to install a steamer stopping place alongside the Tree, and after the ensuing riot of villagers, locked a number of them in jail. The dissenters were freed and applauded a month later, after newspapers, citing the Doum Tree rebellion as a "symbol of the nation's awakening," had succeeded in toppling this tyrannical coalition. Yet the entire village remains indifferent to both government approval and disapproval: "Our life returned to what it had been—no waterpump, no agricultural scheme, no stopping place for the steamer. But we kept our Doum Tree. . . ." Near the tale's conclusion, we discover that Wad Hamid, at whose tomb near the sacred Tree villagers go frequently to pray, had once been enslaved by a cruel infidel who would not allow him to say his Muslim prayers openly. Aiding his miraculous escape from this tyranny, God led him here to found this very village, and to transmit a legacy of fierce religious autonomy, wary of all institutional control.

The second Muslim response to the search for political legitimation is a fundamental return to the Sharī'ah. The Qur'an already seems to anticipate all the more recent political insights of Europe, and only imperialism and the accidents of history have impeded Islam's triumphant embodiment. This is the olympian certainty of Khomeini's *Islamic Government* treatise: "Our only basis of reference is the time of the Prophet and the Imam Ali. . . . The entire system of government and administration, together with the necessary laws, lies ready for you." Iran must rid itself of infatuation with Western constitutional government, and never stoop to borrow its system of laws. For example, "if the administration of the country calls for taxes, Islam has made the necessary provisions; and if laws are needed, Islam has established them all." The burden of V. S. Naipaul's hostile critique *Among the Believers: An Islamic Journey,* written in 1981, is that Muslim political leaders in Iran, Pakistan, Malaysia, and Indonesia have thus far offered their followers only religious passion, without a constructive political and economic program. For people of limited skill, money, and grasp of the world, Islam "is their way of getting even with the world. It serves their grief, their feeling of inadequacy, their social rage and racial hate." Their prayers smolder with malevolence, whispering about Islam endangered, enemies from the West, the need for a *jihād* bloodbath. In Pakistan specifically, acclaimed throughout the world *ummah* as the first pure Islamic State, modeled on the reign of Muhammad and the first four caliphs, citizens seem united solely by their conviction that the materialistic Western world must be pulled down. To replace it, Naipaul found only a handful of religious negatives—no alcohol, bank interest, or feminine immodesty; and after General Mohammed Zia's coup, no law courts or political parties or dissent. "The faith was asserted because only the faith seemed to be whole; and in the vacuum only the army could rule." He thinks Pakistanis blame their failures almost exclusively on Western imperialism and on their own deficient faith in political solutions already revealed by the Sharī'ah.

It seems unfair to select Pakistan as a Muslim showcase, with its inherited weak economy, overpopulation, and disastrous civil wars—these have siphoned most energy away from religious renewal, with mere national survival at stake. The House of Saud is perhaps more representative, although the last few Saudi kings have quietly sidestepped efforts to get a written constitution, which would have limited their legislative powers. Though large oil revenues demand sophisticated decisions about economic planning and fiscal regulation, all policy derives in theory from the Sharī'ah, formulated by the king in consultation with the *'ulamā'*. If people press for security, justice, due process, science, where shall they find it? "It is there," King Amir Faisal once answered. "Everything is there, inscribed in the Islamic Sharī'ah." Head of the large Saudi clan, principal tribal *shaykh,* religious chairman of the *'ulamā'*, the king at present has an opportunity to embody the Muslim political-religious ideal: flexible political realism, combined paradoxically with Wahhābī traditionalism.

Two liberal Muslims are spokesmen for a third Muslim approach to this modern legitimation crisis. Achmad Sukarno and Mohammed Ali Jinnah, first presidents of the Indonesian Republic and of Pakistan. Sensitive to the religious and ethnic pluralism in their respective societies, both favored the secular State model, yet both employed an inclusive Muslim vocabulary to win a broad base of Muslim support without alienating other groups. For Sukarno, a Sharī'ah-State could only mean "a dictatorship over minorities," the stifling of political initiative by doddering *'ulamā'* conservatives. Yet he was convinced that Islam's spirit would be reinvigorated, once it had the chance to develop freely and competitively. "We accept the separation of State and religion, but we will inflame the whole people with the fire of Islam, so that all the delegates in parliament will be Muslims." The era of the first four caliphs might prove a fine historical example, but not an immutable law for the present era. "What have we absorbed of Allah's Word and the Prophet's Sunna? Not its spark or flame," he writes in 1936, "but the ashes, dust, asbestos. . . . Ashes that take the form of Islamic mouthings and Islamic piety without devotion." Islamic rhetoric needed to be translated into moral progress, scientific thought, social justice. A bold eclectic, trying to create a durable alloy of socialism, nationalism "broad as the air," and an Islam "flexible like rubber," Sukarno eventually lost the presidency because of his reluctance to outlaw the Communist party from his wide synthesis.

Although he adhered faithfully to the daily fivefold *ṣalāt* prayers and the *ramaḍān* fast, Sukarno had alienated his official traditionalist Muslim support as early as 1940, after he wrote an essay entitled "Society in the Camel Age and Society in the Airplane Age," which concluded with a parable that provoked instant controversy. His stepdaughter Ratna complained one day that the dog had contaminated a bowl at their well by drinking from it. Sukarno suggested she wash the bowl with soap and creolin. She hesitated to comply because Muhammad requires that the bowl be washed seven times, at least once with earth. Sukarno convinced her by explaining that people had no soap and creolin during Muhammad's time, so she could not have been told literally to use either item. His strict Muslim opponents seized on this anecdote as confirmation of Sukarno's arrogant freethinking in the field of religion, his disdain for mystery and tradition, his inability to achieve personal Islamic submission. They felt that Sukarno, not the Sharī'ah, needs the reform.

Utterly removed from the flamboyant confidence of Sukarno, and often uncomfortable in the presence of his zealous traditionalist Muslim colleagues, Jinnah simply wanted a State "where the principles of Islamic social justic could find free play." His loyalty to Sharī'ah was conscientiously minimal and tacit, and he usually spoke of Islam less exclusively as a religious faith than as a unique social system, nationality, and civilization. Like Gandhi, he took pains to guard the rights of every religious minority, and slapped down all rumors of religious authoritarianism or a totalist State. "Man has indeed been called God's Caliph in the Qur'an," Jinnah told the Muslim League in 1939, and this means "to behave toward others as God behaves toward mankind. In the widest sense of the word, this duty is . . . love and toleration toward all other human beings." His ethics of social justice can be epitomized in a few lines from the Qur'an: "Righteousness does not consist in whether you face toward the east or the west. The righteous are those who believe in Allah and the Last Day, . . . who for the love of Allah give their wealth to kinsfolk, orphans, the needy, wayfarers, and beggars, and for the redemption of captives" (2:177).

Sharī'ah Roots of Sūfī Spirituality

Besides a Muslim activist ethos for marketplace, court, and caucus, and even a fallback ideology for the dispossessed and resentful, there is also a Muslim ascesis designed for contemplatives. Muhammad was not just a warrior statesman, but also a unique ecstatic, often praying far into the night. Allāh tells him, "All night keep vigil, wrapped up in your mantle, . . . and with measured tones recite the Qur'an, for we are about to address you words of surpassing gravity. It is in the watches of the night that impressions are strongest and words most eloquent; in the daytime you are hard-pressed with work" (73:1).

Each Muslim who follows mere Sharī'ah essentials will achieve salvation, but a deeper inward path is open to anyone wishing to go further. In addition to *ḥajj* and *ramaḍān,* the other three Pillars of Islam are the *ṣalāt* daily prayer, the *shahādah* creed, and the *zakāt* alms. If lived in depth, every Sharī'ah injunction invites an ordinary believer beyond the literal ritual deed to a more comprehensive spiritual discipline. "The ṣalāt means to awaken from one's dream of forgetfulness and remember God always," says Seyyed Nasr. "The fast means to die to one's passionate self and be born in purity. The pilgrimage means to journey from the surface to the center of one's being, for, as many Sūfīs have said, the heart is the spiritual Kaa'bah. The zakat also implies spiritual generosity and nobility. . . . Sharī'ah is the necessary and sufficient basis for the spiritual life."

The spirituality Nasr describes here in his *Ideals and Realities of Islam* is popularly called Sufism. I shall use the term *Sufist* then, to designate not only various monastic or political brotherhoods in Muslim history, nor just a specific elitist style of mysticism under a trained *shaykh* guide, but the broad spectrum of experiments in Muslim spirituality. What all approaches share is veneration for the Qur'an, Sharī'ah, and Muhammad's example as somehow normative. In other words, Sufism is the interiorization of Islam—an inclusive esoteric tradition, basically egalitarian, with room for a spiritual elite, but always authentically Islamic. "To kiss the threshold of the Sharī'ah" is one Sūfī master's depiction of a Muslim's first duty in aspiring to the mystical Way, even though we realize many Sūfīs initiated their way of life as rebellion against excessive legalism and aridity in the Sharī'ah scholasticism of their day. "Sometimes Truth knocks at my door for forty days," says another master, "but I do not permit it to enter my heart unless it brings two witnesses, the Qur'an and the Prophetic tradition."

We must now try to identify this distinct imprint of the Qur'an and Muhammad's character upon Muslim spirituality. The most appropriate Christian analogue to the Qur'an is not the New Testament but the person of Jesus, incarnate Word of God. For the recited and written Qur'an on earth replicates the Eternal Qur'an, Uncreated Word of Allāh. It is thus incomparable to any other book, absolutely untranslatable, a text to be handled and read with awe, only after the strictest ritual self-purification. Each personal copy of the Qur'an participates somehow in the event and divine source of Muhammad's own Qur'anic experience, Allāh's self-disclosure through the mediation of Gabriel. The textual wording is not so much discursive content as an evocative presentational symbol with an aura of sustained religious exaltation. The *tajwīd* recitative performance by a good *ḥāfiz* has power to stir even hearers like myself, lacking knowledge of Arabic. To pray the

Qur'an ideally, just as in the *ṣalāt* liturgy, it is best to measure out sacred space—with or without a prayer rug—at home, in a mosque, or any other selected area. Then you perform the prescribed ablutions, recollect yourself meditatively and turn toward Mecca. A zone of holy ground emerges, a prayer space with boundaries to exclude profane and evil forces.

Allāh's revelation has reached its final shape in the historical recitation of the Qur'an to Muhammad. This is the climactic numinous moment to be reexperienced in a genuine but modestly derivative way by each Muslim praying the Qur'an. According to an important *ḥadīth,* Muhammad assures us the "Qur'an has been revealed in seven forms. Each verse has an inner and outer meaning." If a person's Qur'anic experience is profoundly open, then, Allāh might give insight into fresh aspects of this original polysemous disclosure to Muhammad, and prolong that moment of prophecy. Such a belief accounts for specific techniques associated historically with Sūfī mysticism. Many chant and dance out Qur'anic *mantras* to induce trance, repeat a meditative litany of Allāh's attributes listed in the Qur'an, and engage in the number mysticism of Jewish and Christian Kabbalists—decoding concealed wisdom or predicting apocalyptic events by computing the mysterious numerical value of Qur'anic words or pages. Renowned Sūfī theologians have devised an intricate hermeneutics to uncover secret allegorical and spiritual meanings in the text. In a culture where mystics delve into the hidden meanings of Qur'anic words and even the numerological significance of letters in a word, there has developed a beautiful art of Qur'anic calligraphy, which tries to achieve a visual effect as stunning as the audial experience of God's Word. Script becomes a sort of visual sacrament, symmetrical and pure, sharing in the very speech and writing of God himself. It adorns mosques, minarets, prayer rugs, and personal jewelry, and melts into creative flora, lace filigree, and more abstract geometrical designs.

In earlier chapters, we have explored the various conjectured motives for iconoclasm. There is the moral iconoclasm of the classical Hebrew prophets, reinterpreted by most contemporary Humanists as a challenge against every pseudoreligion that undermines human maturity. There is the paradoxical apophatic way, favored perennially by world mystics, and also the disciplined aniconic caution of early Theravāda Buddhists, fearing the mortal Gautama would otherwise be inflated into another Hindu *avatāra.* In addition to all these convincing reasons, the Muslim reluctance to use human and animal images apparently has further motives behind it. First, resplendent monumental art had become associated with exploitative privileged classes, whereas

Muslims from the beginning tried to eliminate luxury and caste from their self-expression. Second, unable perhaps to compete with rival civilizations in their skill at religious painting and sculpture, Muslims decided simply to change the game rules. Third, identifying themselves mostly with the mobile international mercantile class of the Middle Ages, Muslims developed a sober bourgeois morality, utilitarian and impatient with the ornamental, aesthetic, or venturesome, unless these could serve some obvious didactic function. Fourth, we realize that abstract and nonobjective contemporary schools of art dismiss recognizable images in order to stress color masses, pattern, and direct emotional impact. Similarly, the Muslim religious sensibility might have strained unconsciously to achieve an immediate spiritual evocation, without reminding the viewer of other experiences. Fifth and most important, to concentrate on the Qur'an as their exclusive sacred icon, Muslims determined to eliminate all other symbols that might drain or divert religious energies from Allāh's mighty Qur'anic summons.

"To regain delight in my reading of the Qur'an," says the Sūfī Khawwas, "I approach it as though Muhammad were announcing it to me, then Gabriel announcing it to Muhammad, and finally as though it were God himself speaking." Besides this Qur'anic emphasis, we have noted that the second principal motif in Muslim spirituality is identification with the life and person of Muhammad. "For those who look to Allāh, there is a good example in Allāh's apostle," says the Qur'an (33:21). The popular religious imagination has surely fallen in love with the Prophet, for streams of prayer, poetry, and song extol his gentleness, sunlike face, and handsome black hair—"Your name is beautiful. You are beautiful, Muhammad." His name is almost numinous, the common basis for oaths, the Muslim pattern for names of most males. But a genuine Muslim saint must prove strictly and exhaustively human to be a plausible model for mankind—not a God-Man, not a withdrawn celibate. Muhammad "is Man, Man, Man, and not God," as Ismail al-Faruqi insists. He had to pass through every phase of our life, sharing all affliction and joy, to show us the way. This comprehensive human being is often denigrated as a barbarous polygamist and imperialist by non-Muslim critics. Yet Muslims view him as a tender exemplary father and husband, and find his military campaigns a paradigm of all morally just warfare, especially in his compassionate treatment of prisoners and the readiness to forgive enemies, once they had been defeated.

The manner and extent of this emulation has led to many quarrels within the *ummah*. Influential scholastic theologian and mystic al-Ghazali expects disciples to imitate Muhammad "in all his comings and goings, motions and rests, even in his manner of eating, rising, sleeping, and speaking." He then picks a few loving, punctilious examples, which parallel the impassioned *guru* emulation practiced by many Hindu *bhaktas*. Like Muhammad, "begin with the right foot when you put on your shoes. Eat with your right hand. In cutting fingernails, begin with the forefinger of your right hand, and end with the thumb; begin with the right little toe and end with the left little toe." It is easy to parody this piety of the itsy-bitsy, but we can discern in it the momentous weight of the past, a badge of group solidarity in minuscule but perceptible detail, and a ceremonial sacralization of ordinary life, much like Confucian *li* and Jewish dietary ritual.

The focus of most Sūfī meditation, however, is not these externals, but Muhammad's vivid *mi'rāj,* his literal or visionary night ride from Mecca to Jerusalem and ascent into Heaven. This popular story can be traced to a few controversial Qur'an passages, difficult to construe with certainty. Allāh, says the first *surah,* made him "go by night from the sacred temple to the farther temple, . . . that we might show him some of our signs" (17:1). The second *surah* refers ambiguously to Gabriel or Muhammad: "He stood on the uppermost horizon. . . . He saw some of his Lord's greatest signs" (53:7ff.). From these two *surahs,* a number of *ḥadīth* anecdotes, the eight-century Muhammad biography by Ibn Ishaq, and a few later accounts, we can outline the basic narrative.

Muhammad is awakened one night by angels near the Ka'bah, who split open his body, take out his heart, and purify it in Zamzam water. Then placing him on a winged horse called Borak, Gabriel carries him to the Temple in Jerusalem, where Muhammad greets an assembly of prophets, including Abraham, Moses, and Jesus, and leads them in prayer. He and Gabriel next climb a ladder to Heaven and gain entry only after Gabriel vouches that Muhammad has been given a special divine mission. Rising up through the seven Heavens, Muhammad at each level meets a different prophet from the past, each repeating the same questions to Gabriel, "Who is with you?" and "Was he called?" After Gabriel's reaffirmation, each figure always concludes, "Please welcome Muhammad; his coming here is good." The two companions progress upward from Adam, through Jesus and John the Baptist, Jacob's son Joseph, Enoch, Aaron, Moses, and finally to Abraham at the entrance to Paradise. The finale to more popular versions of this tale presents a flash encounter with Allāh, followed by a debate with Moses about the number of required *ṣalāt* periods to be imposed daily on all Muslims. Allāh asks fifty at first, but Moses tells Muhammad, "I tried people before you . . . and it did not have the desired effect." So Muhammad returns to Allāh again and again, at Moses' nagging, and gets the burden reduced. Eventually he is ashamed to ask that it be curtailed further than five times daily. A divine voice finally calls out, "I have established my divine commands, and have made them easy to my servants."

Like every great creative narrative, the *miʻrāj* of Muhammad accomplishes many purposes. In the version recounted here, it gives tangible four-dimensional structure to Muhammad's otherwise private ineffable visions, from which the Qur'an emerged. His experience had a vertical cosmic scope to it, and a horizontal range back through history. Second, his inaugural call to be a prophet is symbolized graphically by an angelic incision, a baptism into the Abrahamic Ka'bah-Zamzam heritage, a shamanic winged horse and ladder to enter wider unconscious realms, and ritual reaffirmation in his naming and mission throughout the courts of Heaven. Third, step by step, he sets up continuity with Jesus, Moses, and others, and reinterprets the entire prophetic historical past. In the act of opening doors and welcoming him, each prophet at that moment surrenders some previous status. In Jerusalem it is Muhammad who leads them all in prayer. Fourth, we have an etiological sketch that foresees and answers Muslim complaints about the *ṣalāt* obligation, contrasted with relatively lighter Jewish prayer duties.

Miʻrāj stories and such Christian epics as the *Purgatory of Saint Patrick* probably influenced the structure of Dante's *Divine Comedy* cosmic journey. But as we would anticipate from Dantean aggressive Christian theology, Muhammad ends up disemboweled in the *inferno* as a contemptible schismatic. On the other hand, the ordinary Muslim at prayer and many Sūfī ecstatics have consistently interpreted their own spiritual longing and delight as a participation in Muhammad's *miʻrāj* experience. Abu Yazid al-Bistami was the first of many Sūfī masters to use *miʻrāj* imagery to describe his own religious visions and thus to introduce a new literary genre. "I dreamed I ascended to the heavens," Bastami begins, and as his flight on a green bird lifts him through one angelic realm after another, he identifies them with graduated psychological stages (*maqām*) and stations (*hal*) of the familiar purgative-illuminative-unitive odyssey toward God. At one pause in this climb, he cries out, "O Lord, with my egotism I cannot reach you nor escape from my selfhood. What am I to do?" God answers, "O Abu Yazid, you must win release from your thou-ness by following my beloved Muhammad. Smear your eyes with the dust of his feet and follow him continuously." Muhammad once appeared in a dream to the early Sūfī Fariduddin Attar, and complained, "Do you love me?" And he responded, "Forgive me, but the love of God has kept me busy from loving you." Yet Muhammad came back with the rebuttal, "Whoever loves God, loves me." Many Sūfī theologians were convinced that the ordinary spiritual Way proceeded by a series of self-denying identifications—first with one's spiritual guide, then with Muhammad (*fanā' fir-Rasūl*), and finally with Allāh (*fanā' fi-Allāh*).

It is clearly possible to commit *shirk*, or idolatry, in veneration of Muhammad. He has been viewed as the archetype of perfect humanity, as we have mentioned, but Ibn 'Arabi boldly identifies him with the cosmic rational principle, embodied as a creative dynamic Light within every historical prophet and saint. Husayn al-Hallaj, hanged in the tenth century allegedly for the blasphemous claim "I am God," wrote with reckless effusiveness, too, about Muhammad: "All the lights of the prophets proceeded from his light. He was before all, his name the first in the book of Fate. He was known before all began, and will endure beyond the end of all." We recognize the tendency in all esoteric traditions to draw on the rhetoric of pantheism or panentheism to evoke the unitive impact of ecstatic wisdom and love. Surely the self-annihilation described in *fanā' fir-Rasūl* and *fanā' fi-Allāh* experiences is intended as shocking hyperbole. Muslim theologians within two or three centuries after Muhammad's death tried to clarify the crucial distinction between *waḥdat al-shuhūd* and *waḥdat al-wujūd*. Between the phenomenon of experiential union, which most mystics affirm; and the fact of monistic ontological identity, which every Muslim monotheist must deny.

It is surprising to discover in the *Mathnawī-i Ma'nawī* of Rumi, renowned poet of lyrical rapture, a less inflated but shrewd estimate of Muhammad's place in any spirituality that is authentically Muslim. He divides the *shahādah* creed into two affirmations: "There is no god but God"; then the second, "And Muhammad is his apostle." To believe only the first half could lead to pantheism, a fusion and confusion of all world creeds. The second is calculated to destroy this first temptation, limit the inclusiveness of Islam, and set it off from other professions of faith. The historical reality of Muhammad is a divine test for every believer. The only true esoteric spiritual Way for a Muslim must be anchored in the central exoteric Sharī'ah.

FURTHER READING

1. **Descriptive Bibliography.** Besides his description of the field in "Islam," from Charles J. Adams, ed., *A Reader's Guide to the Great Religions* (Free Press, 1965), pp. 287–318, Adams' other books and articles on Islam are al-

ways well written and authoritative. Extensive updating can be found in the section on Islam in David Littlefield, *An Annotated Guide to Books in English for Non-Specialists* (Libraries Unlimited, 1977), pp. 139–69; John Taylor, "Islamic Religion," in Derek Hopwood and Diana Grimmund-Jones, eds., *Middle East and Islam: A Bibliographical Introduction* (Inter Documentation Company, 1972), pp. 102–17; and Penelope Johnstone, "Islam: Bibliographical Survey," *Journal of Ecumenical Studies* 16 (1979), pp. 313–20.

2. **Introductions.** The best known Qur'an translation is by N. J. Dawood (Penguin, 1981), though its controversial rearrangement of *surahs* into their conjectured chronological order makes it a difficult reference tool. Two samplers of Qur'an excerpts, *ḥadīth,* Sūfī verses, both arranged thematically, might be useful: John Alden Williams, ed., *Themes of Islamic Civilization* (University of California Press, 1971), and Arthur Arberry, ed., *Aspects of Islamic Civilization: As Depicted in the Original Texts* (University of Michigan Press, 1967).

A dated but helpful encyclopedia, especially on the topics of *ḥajj, mi'rāj,* and *muḥarram,* is Thomas Hughes, *A Dictionary of Islam* (W. H. Allen 1935). Kenneth Cragg's *The House of Islam,* 2nd ed. (Dickenson, 1975), is a concise, accurate overview. Richard Antoun, "Social Organization and the Life Cycle in an Arab Village," *Ethnology* 6:3 (July 1967), pp. 294–308, can help readers visualize how an average rural Muslim family incorporates its religious beliefs. Sometimes it seems the very interpreters of Islam have prejudiced the reader against their subject, which appears desiccated and fanatical. Muslims themselves have analyzed this phenomenon, which they call imperialistic Orientalism. See Donald Little, "Three Arab Critiques of Orientalism," *Muslim World* 69 (1979), pp. 110–30, and "Islam and the Orientalists," in Elie Kedourie, *Islam in the Modern World* (Mansell, 1980).

A superb introductory study on the Abrahamic family of religions, F. E. Peters' *Children of Abraham: Judaism, Christianity, Islam* (Princeton University Press, 1982), sifts out their unique configuration yet their basic similarities. This triadic theme is illustrated graphically by Thomas Indinopulos, "Jerusalem the Blessed: The Shrines of Three Faiths," *Christian Century* 15 (April 12, 1978), pp. 386–91. Two lively analyses of the possible grounds for misunderstanding between Muslims and Christians can be found in Zafar Ansari, "Some Reflections on Islamic Bases for Dialogue with Jews and Christians," *Journal of Ecumenical Studies* 14 (1977), pp. 433–47; and Kenneth Cragg, "Being Christian and Being Muslim: A Personal Debate," *Religion* 10 (Autumn 1980), pp. 196–208.

3. **Ḥajj and Muḥarram.** Background on Muslim differences, expecially the Sunnī-Shī'ī conflict, can be found in Fazlur Rahman's *Islam* (Holt, Rinehart and Winston, 1966); and especially the Shī'ī-slanted explanation in Hamid Enayat, *Modern Islamic Political Thought* (University of Texas Press, 1982), and in the articulate books of Seyyed Nasr. See Nasr's *Ideals and Realities of Islam* (Praeger, 1967); *Islamic Life and Thought* (State University of New York Press, 1981); and "Religion and Arab Culture," *Cahiers d'Histoire Mondiale* 14 (1972), pp. 702–13. Hava Lazarus-Yafeh, "Muslim Festivals,"

Numen 25 (1978), pp. 52–64, discusses possible reasons for the paucity of celebrations.

A fine book on the legendary origins and historical development of the *ḥajj,* with illustrations drawn mostly from earlier sources, is Emel Esin, *Mecca the Blessed, Madinah the Radiant* (Crown, 1963). Besides Esin's description of the contemporary rites, see Alex Haley, ed., *The Aubiography of Malcolm X* (Grove, 1966), especially the Mecca chapter; and "Pilgrimage to Mecca" in Idries Shah, ed., *Caravan of Dreams* (Octagon, 1968). Erich Isaac discusses some of the rival pilgrimage shrines in "The Pilgrimage to Mecca," *Geographical Review* 63 (July 1973), pp. 405–9. Criticisms of *ḥajj* abuses can be found in Narifumi Maeda, "The Aftereffects of Hajj and Kaan Buat," *Journal of Southeast Asian Studies* 6 (September 1975), pp. 178–85, and Raymond Scupin, "The Social Significance of the Hajj for Thai Muslims," *Muslim World* 72:1 (January 1982), pp. 25–33.

Muḥarram accounts and *ta'ziyah* excerpts are given in Earle Waugh, "Muharram Rites: Community Death and Rebirth," from Frank Reynolds and Earle Waugh, eds., *Religious Encounters with Death* (Penn State University Press, 1977), pp. 200–13, and "Religious Symbolism and Social Change: The Drama of Husain" by Gustav Thaiss in Nikki Keddie, ed., *Scholars, Saints, and Sufis* (University of California Press, 1972), pp. 349–66. See the more popular version in Royston Pike's *The Strange Ways of Man* (Hart, 1967), entitled "The Passion Play of the Muslim Martyrs," pp. 180–9.

4. **The Political Implications.** The best introduction to current crises in political legitimation is a set of three articles in Michael Curtis, ed., *Religion and Politics in the Middle East* (Westview, 1981)—Bernard Lewis, "The Return of Islam," pp. 9–30; Hrair Dekmejian, "The Anatomy of Islamic Revival," pp. 31–42; and Mervin Verbit, "The Political Character of Judaism and Islam: Some Comparisons," pp. 69–76. V. S. Naipaul's *Among the Believers: An Islamic Journey* (Knopf, 1981) is a stimulating polemic. More balanced, with an updated account of developments in Turkey and Russia, is Edward Mortimer's *Faith and Power: The Politics of Islam* (Random House, 1982). Complete this survey by consulting John Eposito, ed., *Islam and Development: Religion and Sociopolitical Change* (Syracuse University Press, 1980); Mohammed Ayoob, ed., *The Politics of Islamic Reassertion* (St. Martin's Press, 1981); and Alexander Cudsi and Ali Dessouki, eds., *Islam and Power* (Johns Hopkins University Press, 1981).

An excellent biography of Sukarno is Bernhard Dahm's *Sukarno and the Struggle for Indonesian Independence,* tr. and rev. Mary Heidhues (Cornell University Press, 1969). Abdul Lateef, *The Great Leader: Mohammed Ali Jinnah* (Lion Press, 1965), gives a crude anthology of excerpts from Jinnah's speeches in the final section. Imam Khomeini's essay "Islamic Government" and other speeches are collected in Hamid Algar, ed., *Islam and Revolution* (Mizan, 1981). Algar's commentary is helpful, but I must disagree with his claim that "the word *imam* applied to Khomeini has its general and original sense of leader, and not the particular and technical sense it has acquired when applied to the Twelve Imams. . . . " (p. 10). It strains credulity to insist that hidden overtones have been intentionally excluded in this explosive political-religious atmosphere.

5. **Muslim Spirituality.** Annemarie Schimmel's *Mystical Dimensions of Islam* (University of North Carolina Press, 1975) is a trove of fine citations from Sūfī masters, with helpful indices. See R. Caspar's survey of current approaches in "Muslim Mysticism: Tendencies in Recent Research," from Merlin Swartz, ed., *Studies on Islam* (Oxford University Press, 1981), pp. 164–84.

An attractive brief collection of Sūfī apothegms can be found in Catharine Hughes, ed., *The Secret Shrine: Islamic Mystical Reflections* (Seabury, 1974). Idries Shah's many books of Sūfī tales are readily available, but notice R. C. Zaehner's caution in his convincingly argued essay "Why Not Islam?," *Religious Studies* 11 (1975), pp. 167–79. He complains of Shah as an "egregious populariser," who makes Sufism look like Vedānta, or worse yet, a form of Zen Buddhism. David Brewster distinguishes between Ascetics, Affectives, Ecstatics, Orthodox, and Monists in his suggestions on reading the Sūfī masters—"The Study of Sufism: Towards a Methodology," *Religion* 6:1 (Spring 1976), pp. 31–47. Two illustrative Muslim lives are set side by side in Ira Lapidus, "Adulthood in Islam: Religious Maturity in the Islamic Tradition," *Daedalus* (Spring 1976), pp. 93–101. Sūfī lawyer-theolgian al-Ghazali is compared with Ibn Khaldun, a politician-judge, as embodiments of Muslim spiritual values.

James Royster, "Mohammed as Teacher and Exemplar," *Muslim World* 68:4 (October 1978), gives vivid examples of Muhammad's life as paradigm. The *mi'rāj* is developed as a theme in the following three articles: Earle Waugh, "Following the Beloved: Mohammed as Model in the Sufi Tradition," in Frank Reynolds and Donald Capps, eds., *The Biographical Process* (Mouton, 1976), pp. 63–86; J. R. Porter, "Mohammed's Journey to Heaven," *Numen* 20 (1974), pp. 64–80; and Nazeer El-Azma, "Some Notes on the Impact of the Story of the Miraj on Sufi Literature," *Muslim World* 63:2 (April 1973), pp. 93–104. The last article includes a valuable translation of al-Bistami's vision.

Leonard Librande, "The Calligraphy of the Quran: How It Functions for Muslims," *Religion* 9 (Spring 1979), pp. 36–58, and Marshall Hodgson, "Islam and Image," *History of Relgions* 3:2 (Winter 1964), pp. 220–60—both give a superb approach to the Qur'an as icon in an otherwise iconoclastic context.

8

Christian Spirit

After the recapture of Jerusalem in 1187 by Saladin, urbane Muslim leader portrayed in Lessing's *Nathan the Wise,* a series of militant popes prodded reluctant armies of western Europe to join in three final Crusades, each progressively more disastrous. As the Fifth Crusade took shape, Saladin's nephew Malek el-Kamel, sultan of Egypt, found two surprisingly different religious adversaries ranged against him, Innocent III and Francis of Assisi. Of the two, Pope Innocent seemed easier to account for—majestic Catholic caliph, presiding over a Christendom that seemed almost a mirror image of the extensive *ummah muslima* empire surrounding Europe. Christian warriors, like their Muslim counterparts, perceived this war as a *jihād.* Innocent revived his predecessors' Crusade Indulgence, extended to all liberators of Jerusalem, and many preachers reasserted Bernard of Clairvaux's promise that death in battle as a soldier of Christ meant the grace and glory of martyrdom.

God the Creator "has established two high luminaries in the sky of the universal Church—papacy ruling over souls, and royalty ruling over bodies," Innocent warns the Rectors of Tuscany during his first year in office. "As the moon receives its light from the sun, . . . so the royal power draws all its luster and prestige from the papal power." Quick to test out this claim to supremacy, he boldly intervened in European politics whenever the Church's integrity seemed threatened. Describing himself as "less than God but more than man, and one who shall judge all others, but himself be judged by no other human being,"

Innocent was able to choose and depose kings, streamline canon law, shield his clergy from lay control, and even inspire an army to stamp out the Albigensian heretics. He convoked the Fourth Lateran Council in 1215, which almost as an afterthought to salutary measures of administrative church reform, tightened discriminatory laws against Jewish residents, now required to wear distinctive dress. At the head of what some Christians still think the apogee of a united Christendom, Innocent died shortly after assuming personal command of the Crusade for Jerusalem.

A few years later, two clownish figures in gray tunics crossed barefoot through Muslim fortifications in Egypt and asked for an interview with Malek el-Kamel. Mingling with Crusaders for some time before this in an attempt to domesticate them into apostles for peace, and predicting the failure of this military offensive, Francis of Assisi and Brother Illuminato had found everyone deaf to the sultan's reasonable peace overtures. Unlike the warrior pope, Francis was ready to meet Malek face to face, with hopes not to slay but convert him. From his own point of view, Malek was surprised to find in Francis an authentic prophet, a sort of Christian Sūfī ascetic, and kept him for days of engrossing religious conversation. We are told that Francis had prepared himself for a martyrdom vastly different from the average *jihād* casualty. He eventually challenged the sultan's court theologians to a histrionic ordeal by fire: "If I am burnt up, impute it to my sins. If my God protects me, acknowledge him as true Lord and Savior of everyone." Malek, expressing a pious desire that Allāh would reveal his will impartially to both Christian and Muslim, dismissed Francis and Illuminato with permission to visit Christian shrines in Muslim territory. Within five years, Francis on Monte Verna would experience a stigmatic ecstasy, the imprint of a radical identification with the suffering and death of Jesus, surely the mystical culmination to his quest for martyrdom in Egypt.

It must be conceded that Innocent's horizons were probably more unworldly and self-doubting, and Francis' more timebound and conventional than my two simplified portraits thus far suggest. But let Innocent typify the institutional Christian, Francis the charismatic, prophetic Christian. Innocent shall stand for Christ's Kingdom embodied in, if not identified with, the triumphalist Church Militant; and Francis for the martyr transformed into the monk, a witness to Christ's final Kingdom that transcends and passes judgment on every provisional human utopia, including the Church. Soon the more radical disciples of Francis, calling themselves Franciscan Spirituals, would expand the traditional monastic vow of poverty into a socialist denunciation of all private ownership in society. At the same time, disciples of Joachim of Fiore, condemned at the Fourth Lateran, would continue to proclaim an approaching Age of Aquarius, a reign of love and the Holy Spirit to replace an institutional Church that seemed smothered in canon law and clericalism.

We shall now extend the scope of this typology and search for the theology and political wisdom implied behind various historical attempts to institutionalize the Christian charism. In two succinct corollaries to this discussion, we shall investigate a few major themes in the Christology and spirituality common to most Christians, despite their sectarian differences.

Christian Political Wisdom

Muhammad proved to be his own Constantine, I remarked before, whereas underground Christian currents, first in Jewish Diaspora communities, then throughout Roman society, took three centuries to congeal into the single established Church of the empire. The Gospels consistently highlight Jesus' repudiation of a political crown. In his ministry to the oppressed and needy in all social classes, he tried in vain to transform popular hopes for an insurrectionist Messiah into the lofty Deutero-Isaiah dream of a martyr pacifist, totally expendable for others. The Gospel of John concludes that Jesus, denounced unjustly before Roman authorities as a political seditionist, at last assured Pilate, "my kingdom does not belong to this world." In its moral teaching, the New Testament never gives a detailed Torah or Sharī'ah blueprint for constructing a distinctively Christian society. The Pax Romana and stunning network of Roman law and communications are welcomed as a providential backdrop for worldwide dispersal of the Gospel. Acts of the Apostles, written in part to show that Christian faith and loyal Roman citizenship can be compatible, takes for granted that Paul's demand for a trial in Rome will place him before the most reliable civil forum on earth.

Since the first Christians expected an immediate cataclysm and return of Christ, many seemed content to be minimal, quiescent citizens, taking advantage of Rome as the best temporary expedient to hold a perishing world together. Yet are Christians obliged to pray for Caesar? During the late second century, when Christians were persecuted for being antisocial atheists, unwilling to tolerate the gods of their fellow citizens, Tertullian explains their few grudging motives for honoring the emperor. Christians should pray for him because Jesus said to pray for persecutors and enemies. Moreover, the current emperor at least seems more tolerable than some potential alternative even more blasphemous. Finally, "a Christian is the enemy of no person, least of all the emperor, established in power by the Christian's own God," he says in *Ad Scapulam*. Empire and emperor must both be respected, but only "as long as this age endures." This provisionary eschatological outlook undermines the secure surface of each present loyalty.

In the pre-Constantinian era, and during later Christian history, two significant scriptural texts provide the basis for Christian debate about the limits of political loyalty. There is first the thirteenth chapter of Paul's Epistle to the Romans: "Let every person submit to the governing authorities. There is no authority except by an act of God, and the existing authorities are instituted by him. Consequently anyone who rebels against authority is resisting a divine institution. . . . Pay tax and toll, reverence and respect, toward those to whom they are due." This text has generated an interesting progeny of interpreters, each speaking from a different political experience. Gripped by fear of anarchy and convinced that princes, not ecclesiastics, are the more trustworthy bastions of order, Luther reads this passage as a strict religious vindication of secular authority. On the other hand, a subversive esoteric interpretation, given in Origen's second-century apologetics, trims down Paul's admonition as if intended for the ordinary citizen, but not for the revolutionary spiritual elite.

A message sharply divergent from this Epistle appears in the thirteenth chapter of Revelations, garish and cryptic, written most likely toward the end of the first century, during the reign of Domitian. Loathsome beasts assume political power and demand to be worshiped as gods, mouthing bombast and blasphemy, at war against God's people, "deluding all inhabitants of the earth, making them erect an image in honor of the beast. . . . Rich and poor, slave and free, had to be branded . . . with the mark of the beast." This test is usually decoded according to Apocalyptic genre conventions as an opaque attack against the current persecutory regimes of Nero and Domitian. The State is now a satanic power, only to be combated and endured. Both passages from Romans and Revelations in juxtaposition, then, indicate a dramatic, inclusive paradox. Paul's earlier sanguine estimate of cooperation with Rome soon succumbs to a martyr's sense of alienation. Or the Epistle embodies an acculturated Greco-Roman, world-affirming, middle-class perception of the empire; whereas the Book of Revelations emerges from a militant Jewish separatist tradition, speaking for the marginal and slave proletariat.

Or the State in New Testament writings is represented comprehensively at its zenith and at its demonic nadir—both plausible alternatives.

Reactionary, progressive, and radical political platforms within the Christian political tradition have turned repeatedly to the Bible and earliest Christian communities for persuasive religious legitimation. These positions are often sorted into conventional Orthodox-Catholic-Protestant polities, present-future eschatologies, insurgent-incumbent ideologies, or Troeltsch church-sect dichotomies. It seems less distorting simply to call them three recurrent types of Christian legitimation. Each can be designated a legitimate form of Christian Humanism—*Humanism* meaning the concern to humanize the world, to secure and extend human values; *Christian* meaning a focus on Jesus Christ as the divine-human prototype, and an endorsement of Christian scriptures as somehow normative.

The first position, Christian integralism, is prepared at its most militant to understate the Humanist factor for the sake of a uniform, uncompromising Christian identity. The second, Christian democracy or Christian socialism, aiming for a Humanism that is open and pluralistic, tries to preserve both dimensions in balance. I shall call the third position prophetic Christian *kenoticism*. It is ready to minimize or surrender the Christian label, relegated to the silent realm of vision and motive. It fosters radical commitment to whatever seems the most authentic Humanist program, whether it be Marxist or some other form of revolutionary socialism. As a dramatic oversimplification of the contrast between a religious integralist polarity and its two alternatives, we can cite Dostoevski's famous credo, written in prison: "If anyone proved to me that Christ was outside the truth, and it really meant that truth was outside Christ, then I should prefer to remain with Christ than with truth." In contrast, there is Meister Eckhart's belief, no less passionate: "Truth—so noble a thing, that could 'God' turn aside from it, I would cling to truth and let 'God' go."

The Roman Empire of Constantine and Theodosius offers the clearest scenario of our first position, Christian integralism. State-supported temples, public worship by the entire community, religious life intertwined with every other aspect of life—this inherited Roman Way was modified by Constantine's substitution of his new Christian faith for the old Greco-Roman henotheism. By the middle of the fourth century, a once-persecuted Church had now become persecutor, demolishing non-Christian temples, imposing the death penalty on those who still persisted in offering pagan sacrifice. As protectors of the Church, subsequent emperors enforced canon law and theological orthodoxy, and gradually moved bishops into prominent rank in the civil bureaucracy. Although western Europe developed a volatile combination of papal-royal jurisdictions, each given coequal status in Augustine's *City of God,* the Byzantine East preserved a relatively smooth symbiosis, so that it is hard to determine which dominated the other, the Church or the State. With the emergence of nationalism and the sovereign State, this Pax Christiana dream split into an assortment of Latin Catholics, Orthodox Greco-Slavs, and Protestant Anglo-Saxons—an entire national Church often adopting the almost incidental religious identity of its ruler.

Familiar with the national Church pattern—Anglican in England, Roman Catholic in Spain, Lutheran in Sweden—nine of the thirteen American colonies passed laws to endorse their own respective established churches. Some colonies restricted public office only to certified members of this privileged Church, some extended religious liberty to include all Protestants, but not Catholics or Jews. New England Puritans viewed themselves as the New Israel, a Christian Bible Commonwealth, and not in any sense a pluralistic democracy. "Theocracy is the best form of government in the Commonwealth as well as in the Church," says John Cotton. "It is better that the Commonwealth be fashioned to the setting forth of God's house, which is his Church, than to accommodate the Church frame to the civil State."

One of the most literate modern apologists for an integralist Christian State is T. S. Eliot, who once described himself as classicist in literature, royalist in politics, and Anglo-Catholic in religion. Written at the approach of World War II, *The Idea of a Christian Society* summons every legitimate resource to confront Nazi neopaganism. Eliot wants a tough Christian social alternative, not an anemic secular liberal democracy. This means "a religious-social community, a society with a political philosophy founded upon the Christian faith," not "a mere congeries of private and independent sects." Eliot does not so much argue for an established Church, but rules out the possibility of disestablishing the Anglican State Church, as he knows it. The effect on people would be catastrophic—a "visible and dramatic withdrawal of the Church from the affairs of the nation, the deliberate recognition of two standards and ways of life, the Church's abandonment of all those who are not by their wholehearted profession within the fold." The ideal Christian State is intended not just for saints or the devout leisure class, but especially for those "whose Christianity is communal before being individual. . . . It would engage the cooperation of many whose Christianity was spectral or superstitious or feigned, and of many whose motives were primarily worldly or selfish. It would require constant reform."

It is difficult to decide if Eliot's anxiety that the State should exert totalist responsibility stems from the taint of polemics against totalitarian adversaries. Or perhaps he has inflated the dream of a lost medieval Christian synthesis, an era of limited historical religious horizons, of accidental religious and racial concurrence. Nevertheless, his conclusions are unmistakably integralist. No absolute conscientious objector will be tolerated in this Christian State. Moreover, we cannot be "Christian in some social relations and non-Christian in others. . . . To accept two ways of life in the same society, one for the Christian and another for the rest, would be for the Church to abandon its task of evangelizing the world." Earlier, in his *After Strange Gods* lectures at the Univeristy of Virginia in 1933, the moment of Hitler's rise to power, Eliot seems obsessed by the aesthetics of homogeneity. "Adulterate" is an attribute incompatible with the ideal State. "What is still more important is unity of religious background; and reasons of race and religion combine to make any large number of free-thinking Jews undesirable."

We catch echoes of Dostoevski's Grand Inquisitor in Eliot's compassion for the minimalist Christian groundling, and notably in his scheme to build a uniform communal ant-heap where people will be happy and protected after surrendering much of their religious freedom. "Rome and the sword of Caesar" are the two basic weapons that Ivan in *The Brothers Karamazov* attributes to this satanic figment of his creative imagination, actually the Inquisitor rebel concealed in Ivan's own heart. Dostoevski, like most other Orthodox Slavophiles, believes that Caesaro-Papism in the West has alienated sensitive religious minds and driven them into the arms of totalitarian atheists. As Prince Myshkin explains to his audience in *The Idiot:* "The pope usurped an earthly throne, and took up the sword. . . . Socialism, like its brother atheism, springs from despair in opposition to Catholicism. . . . Our Christ, whom we have preserved and they have not even known, must shine forth in opposition to the West, . . . and carry our Russian civilization to them."

This same Slavophile ideal lies behind Solzhenitsyn's controversial Harvard Address in 1978, in which he excoriates the West's depleted will, spiritual immaturity, its fixation on secularity, legalism, and consumer goods. By contrast, through extreme suffering, the Russian soul "has now achieved a spiritual development of such intensity that . . . it has produced stronger, deeper, and more interesting characters than those generated by standardized Western well-being." Though the political composition of Solzhenitsyn's utopia is never spelled out, it still employs the rhetoric of Christian homogenity and restricted civil rights, especially freedom of speech. The backside of Dostoevski's Slavophile zeal is an angry intolerance against Humanist atheists, Roman Catholics, Jews, Poles, and Germans.

The most spirited protest against Caesaro-Papism, and especially against the worldly Christian, communal rather than individual, that Eliot makes room for in his national Church, occurs in Kierkegaard's *Attack upon Christendom* broadsides. "Christianity," he says, "must be inversely proportionate to number." A pure sectarian idealist, he hunts in vain for even one authentic Christian in the nineteenth-century established Danish Church: "Christendom has slyly done away with Christianity by the affirmation that we are all Christians. . . . Resolutely to reject religion is something passionate. . . . The widespread, most pernicious sort of indifferentism is to hold a particular religion, but watered down and garbled into mere twaddle, lived without passion." Each Sunday, we meet a ridiculous anomaly in the pulpit—affluent, pampered State functionaries that play at Christianity. They preach a Gospel of renunciation, poverty, readiness to suffer for Christ, whereas the sacred words are rendered fraudulent by the louder preaching of their lives. If Christ returns, he shall find "Christian States and nations, a Christian world, thousands of mercantile priests—but faith, what Jesus understands by faith, will that be found on earth?" Though it may sound insane in a world where everyone is Christian simply as a matter of course, Kierkegaard refuses to call himself yet a Christian, hoping to make others wonder if perhaps they might be Christians even less than he. "My task," he concludes, "is to revise the definition of a Christian."

Besides integralism, the second attempt at religious legitimation has been the formation of explicit Christian political parties, notably the flourishing Christian Democratic movement that offered a stable rallying ideology in the moral chaos of Europe after World War II. Chancellor Konrad Adenauer's *Memoirs* explains the origin of his own Christian Democratic Union as follows: "Only a great party with its roots in Christian-Western thinking and ethics could educate the German People for their resurgence, and build a strong dike against the atheist dictatorship of communism." Germans because of their particular culture and history seemed all too inclined to submit to the power of the State. Yet Western Christian civilization had created and transmitted a distinctive political heritage: "recognition of an order based on law and binding upon everyone, rejection of State omnipotence and narrow

State egotism, affirmation of the solidarity of all people and nations and their concomitant responsibilities, defence of the Bonum Commune of an international order, rejection of pernicious race theories, respect for the dignity and God-given liberty of the individual."

This human-rights manifesto, based on Adenauer's Catholic background in natural law ethics and more recent papal encyclicals, seemed broad enough to attract most segments of German society—with the obvious exception of doctrinaire integralists, whether Christian, Communist, or National Socialist. "Hence, the new party had to be a Christian party, and one that would embrace all denominations, Protestant and Catholic Germans. Indeed all who knew and valued the importance of Christianity in Europe whould be able to join—and it goes without saying that this also applied to our Jewish fellow-citizens." Like De Gaspari, Schuman, and many other Christian Democrats of his era, Adenauer labored to clear away the wreckage left by nationalist fragmentation and build a European unity based on a common Christian heritage. The chancellor was wily enough a politician, too, to realize that "the best way to counteract the isolationist tendencies in the United States was to keep underlining our allegiance to Western civilization, to the democratic view of life and politics, and the ideal of Christianity, and to stress our community with America."

His socialist adversaries perceived Adenauer's party as a snug camouflaged Christian version of the old bourgeois conservatives. "In my view," he concedes readily, "there was need for a just social order that would enable every person to acquire property for himself and his family. I was convinced it was unnecessary to nationalize. . . . The concentration of political and economic power in the hands of the State was, I thought, likely to lead to undue dependence on the State." A more radical style of Christian Democracy, nuanced and Chileanized, can be discovered in the fragile career of Eduardo Frei, president of Chile for six stormy years before the dramatic accession of Allende's leftist regime in 1970. In his Notre Dame University address of 1963, he described his Christian Democracy party as "nonconfessional. . . . Inspired by a philosophy which in the end is confirmed by natural right, its call goes to all—Catholics, people of other faiths, or with none at all." As third alternative to the right and Marxist left, he offered a Democratic left, attracting support from many progressives, but especially from business and Church conservatives, alarmed at the impending candidacy of Allende, gathering momentum offstage.

"There are two principal roads—Capitalism and Communism," Frei once observed. "Neither suffices because neither understands the sacred quality of man." Capitalism dehumanizes a person by making work the overpowering feature of life, and Communism by making the State superior to the individual's rights. Unfortunately, his proposals for land redistribution, expropriation of foreign-controlled industry, and tax and education reforms proved eventually too sluggish a program for his clients on the left, too disruptive to the right.

It is important to correlate the evolution of Frei's political thought with an unexpected "opening to the left" by Chile's Catholic hierarchy. The humane social philosophy of figures like Jacques Maritain had left its mark gradually on the seminaries. During the sixties, Pope John's *Mater et Magistra,* the decrees on religious freedom and acculturation at the Second Vatican Council, Pope Paul's *Populorum Progressio,* and especially the consensus of one hundred fifty Latin American bishops at Medellín confirmed demands for radical transformation in society. The Chilean bishops were no longer dominated by Archbishop Caro of Santiago, who censured Frei's Falange Nacional party twenty years before, for "fighting the Franco regime, the most Catholic in the world, . . . and believing in diplomatic and commercial relations with Russia."

Frei was remarkably alert to this long-overdue shift in official Catholic self-definition: a new Christian "development ethos," replacing the old "deviation . . . passed on to the Latin American Catholic by what we might call the Spanish stream of spirituality." The former Catholic political mystique at its worst meant resignation to human misery and fixed social and economic structures as sanctioned somehow by God's will, indifference to material progress and contempt for business and manual occupations, and the rationalization of existing government abuses as a consequence of Adam's Fall. In effect, society was pervaded by a pious "disregard for practical effectiveness and the functional value of good intentions." The new Aggiornamento, on the other hand, a "spirituality of economic development," permits resignation only to the inevitable, not until every effort has been expended to improve the full scope of human life, including its natural, physical conditions. "The handling of money does not in itself degrade anyone," Frei insists repeatedly. Unlike nepotism, genuine government charity consists in conferring posts on the most competent, not on those most grateful or in need. Political change should not be intimidating, for "Christian morality is a morality of specific replies to specific problems, which are always different, and this requires a dynamism that continuously adapts the Christian reply to problems of existence."

Colonial and exploitative regimes often preempt the Christian label as a rationale to instill the compliance Frei has associated with otherworldly regression. Against these governments, sometimes the wisest Christian legitimation for dissent requires people to discard Christian shibboleths altogether, even the vocabulary of parliamentary democracy, moderate reform, Alliance for Progress, and all other weasel words misused to emasculate the prophetic forces of revolution. This is the third style of Christian Humanism, exact antithesis to the triumphalist Christendom affirmed by Eliot and pilloried by Kierkegaard. Following the prophetic self-renunciatory pattern of Christ's *kenosis*—"he made himself nothing, he became a servant"—it searches for practical secular coalitions with any true revolutionary Humanist.

The character of Father Rivas, clumsy ex-priest, the Paraguayan Marxist terrorist in Graham Greene's *Honorary Consul,* exemplifies the agonized, abortive attempt to release oneself and others from the narcolepsy of cultural Catholicism. When he tries to persuade his wife that their marriage, although unrecognized by the official Church, is truly valid, she can only respond with church-mouse docility, "If you say so, Father." He reprimands her gently, "I wish you would not call me Father all the time. I am your husband, Marta, your husband." Her final rejoinder underlines the endless depressing misunderstanding between them: "I would be so proud if just once I could see you as you used to be, dressed at the altar, turning to bless us, Father." We learn that Rivas left the Church after his denunciation by police to the archbishop for a sermon about "Father Torres who was shot with the guerrillas in Colombia. I only said that unlike Sodom the Church did sometimes produce one just man, so perhaps she would not be destroyed like Sodom." Rivas refuses in conscience to continue preaching "Sell all and give to the poor" before front pews of starving children, with the archbishop far off, "rendering unto Caesar," dining in splendor with the military elite of Paraguay.

The one just martyr referred to in Greene's novel is Camilo Torres, who once explained his laicization as "taking off my cassock to be more truly a priest." In the fight against hunger, poverty, illiteracy, and lack of shelter and public services, he declared himself "prepared to fight together with the Communists for our common goals. . . . I do not want to be identified with the Communists alone, and thus, I have always sought to work together not only with them but with independent revolutionaries and those of other ideologies." Torres believed that Christians should not be anti-anything, just pro-humanity. "I am not an anti-Communist, because this Communist charge hounds nonconformists among my compatriots, whether they be Communists or not."

This controversial motif of Christian-Marxist collaboration and other strategies of radical social activism have been explored resourcefully by recent Latin American theologians of liberation. Their major preoccupation is to educate the poor in decision making and participatory management, and thus overcome a legacy of otherwordly fatalism. Second, they expect any theologian not merely to reflect and react, but to engage in praxis: to trace empirical sources of each specific exploitative institution, prophetically to desacralize and delegitimize current social injustices. Third, they issue a dialectical critique against most alternative European theologies, as self-vindicating projections by a secure academic elite, often celibate and bourgeois, insulated from rural poverty because of their proximity to posh metropolitan power centers. The closing peroration in most ecclesiastical documents on any social issue exhorts all parties to Christian love and nonviolence, almost at any price. The effect is to paralyze most constructive reform and soothe each reactionary conscience. Fourth, as Uruguayan theologian Juan Segundo argues, Jesus was indeed a revolutionary, not so much against the Roman Empire as against the oppressive Scribes and Pharisees. "They, and not the Empire, imposed intolerable burdens on the weak and dispensed themselves from them, thus establishing the true socio-political structure of Israel." To that extent, then, the countertheology of Jesus proves to be overtly but not exclusively political.

Rarely does a revolutionist, once settled in power, retain the earlier promise of insurgent aspiration. Though his achievement still draws a predictable range of critics, the ideals of Kenneth Kaunda seem to have stayed intact through two arduous decades. The now-legendary first president of Zambia, he continues to advocate a socialist secular State, postcolonial reconciliation, racial and religious pluralism, and a practical but conscientious reinterpretation of the Gandhian nonviolent ideal. "We have been African nationalists, we have been Pan-Africanists, and now we must be international and think of man everywhere," he once told Zambia's new delegates to a Pan-African Congress. "We are not concerned solely with rights of Africans, but with the inalienable rights of all men." The devastating imprint left by African colonialism, as Kaunda records it, matches the scars Frei observed in Latin America. "Colonialism, for all its benefits, devalued man," he writes in *A Humanist in Africa,* published in 1966, his second year in office. "It created elite societies in which men's worth was determined by an irrelevant biological detail—skin pigmentation." They set out to destroy our self-confidence, convincing us that we were "primitive, backward, and degraded, and but for their presence among us, would be living like animals." Too many victims were left with a withering *bwana* complex, still looking over their shoulder for the white man's approval.

Daily Bible reader, son of a Presbyterian missionary, Kaunda assesses his mission-school education and his brief later teaching career there as essentially an experience of friendship and kindness. At the same time, in childhood he resented the padded church seats reserved for European missionaries, but "my father, who had been working for the mission longer than most of them, had to sit on a wooden bench like the rest of the African congregation. I demanded to know whether it would be the same in Heaven." With the introduction of Christian preachers into Africa, we got a "half-way sort of personal security and peace at the highest price, the price of losing liberty. One Zulu priest has said, 'When Europeans came, they had the Bible and we had the land, but now we have the Bible and they have the land.' I share this with him, but . . . Christ has an undoubted place in my heart."

People with self-respect pounded out of them by aggressive colonialism need most of all to restore faith in their own possibilities. "This is why a Humanist outlook accords well with our temperament," says Kaunda, "while grim Marxism and the narrow Christianity which preaches endlessly about the depravity of Man does not. . . . We have seen something of the very best Christianity, thank God; I myself have benefited from it." Yet he conjectures that the reason for a growing Muslim impact upon Africa is its reinforcement of belief in oneself without denying a dependence upon Allāh. Perhaps a Humanism truly inclusive and communal, not selfishly individualistic, may eventually become Africa's contribution to the imperialistic First World, which too often talks with condescension about all it has to teach others. "Let the West have its technology and Asia its mysticism! Africa's gift to world culture must be in the realm of human relationships." Recognizing the advantages of technology, Kaunda still questions how his nation can embrace them without being trapped by consumerism and losing its soul. His litmus test for an advanced civilization consists of one question: "How does that society treat its old people, and indeed, all its members who are not useful and productive in the narrowest sense? . . . How can we humanize our politics in Zambia so that the humblest and least well-endowed of our citizens occupies a central place in the government's concern?"

Kaunda's model human being, of course, is the person of Jesus Christ. His description of Christ explicitly combines quotations from Gandhi and Teilhard de Chardin: a nonviolent activist Christ at the heart of an unfolding cosmos, in which "man is thrusting like an underground seed upwards toward the light." For Kaunda, Jesus is "the

Man against whom all men must measure themselves when they try to live the life of love." A pronounced characteristic of Jesus is that he does not judge people according to their accidental group membership. "To him each man, woman, and child, irrespective of color, is unique, endowed with ultimate worth and dignity. . . . Every man is unrepeatable, . . . intended to be an end in himself." The dedicated Christian activist, then, is foremost a "servant of man, . . . an instrument of the love of Christ which challenges men to become their true selves. . . . In this sense, Christian practice is not a particular brand of action appearing alongside other endeavors. Rather, it blends with the efforts of men. . . ." In other words, Christian specificity no longer clings to the privilege of a separate party or ideology.

Two Christ Images

The Christian Humanism of Kaunda, indebted to Teilhard and Gandhi, attempts to keep two traditional Christ motifs in balance—the sovereign emanating Cosmic Christ, and the renunciatory servant Christ. This composite Christ of glory and of the cross probably represents the Christology of most believers. The first image, too profound to be preempted merely as an integralist rationale, derives from a number of Pauline texts such as the following: "We are created in Christ Jesus. . . . God put everything in subjection beneath the feet of Christ, and appointed him supreme head of the Church, his body, which holds within it the fullness of him who himself receives the entire fullness of God" (Eph. 2:10;1:23). In the second image, prototype of Christian kenoticism, Christ "emptied himself, . . . and in obedience accepted even death on a cross. . . . The divine nature was his from the first, yet he did not cling to his equality with God" (Phil. 2:6–8).

The immanent Cosmic Christ finds superb expression in the novels of Dostoevski. Zossima in *The Brothers Karamazov* once paused on a warm July night, so quiet that he could hear the plash of fish and identify each separate bird call. "Every blade of grass," he tells his peasant friend on their forest journey, "every insect, ant, and golden bee, all so marvellously know their path. . . . Christ has been with them even before us. . . . The Word is for all; all creation, every leaf is striving toward the Lord, singing glory to God, weeping to Christ, even unconsciously." For this reason Zossima, Alyosha, and so many other mystics of the soil drop down in reverence to kiss the earth, beg its forgiveness, celebrate a solidarity with all living creatures, even the unseen spirit world. "All is like an ocean," says Zossima, "flowing and blending. Touch it in one place and it reverberates at the other end of the world. . . . We have been given a mysterious, inward sense of our living bond with the other world, higher and heavenly." In self-conscious auctorial comments scattered throughout this novel, Dostoevski complains that his protagonist Alyosha probably seems undefined, a sickly, ecstatic, poorly developed creature. Yet such an alleged artistic flaw, after all, should be expected, granted the perverse ingenuity of most human beings to depict more plausible demons than saints. Characters like Alyosha and Myshkin seem to skirt the edge of frenzied ecstasy, epilepsy, schizophrenia, almost as if Dostoevski cannot discover numinosity at the center of human life, but only at its outer limits, trailing off into the subhuman or superhuman.

This same tendency to dematerialize human nature can be observed in many of the most treasured ancient icons portraying the Christ story. We noticed that earliest Buddhists approached Buddha with awesome aniconic restraint, and their later images often prefer stylized, elongated human Buddhas and *dharmakāya* giants. A similar taste prevailed among the first Christians. Conditioned by a strict aniconic Jewish tradition, and left numb by the riot of henotheistic images in popular Greco-Roman culture, many Christians learned an initial mistrust of statuary in the round and of realistic portraits. Instead they turned to sacred words and letters, various cross symbols without the corpus, the cruciform architectural pattern of a basilica, a simple fish or lamb design. Only gradually did they accustom themselves to sculptured flat reliefs, painted icons, frescoes, and mosaics, which often focused on a Christ towering in final judgment or, paradoxically, a massive madonna holding the Christ child with a toy world in his hands. The icon painter intends to evoke a mysterious otherworldly Christ that transcends the ordinary human form: a two-dimensional distended body, puppetlike ritual gestures, weightless garments, eyes fixed in a glare, a diaphanous haze of light and color.

In the Christian Near East, icons are treated even today with a reverence that western Europe customarily reserves for relics of a saint or the true cross. Mounted as a banner, the icon has even led troops into battle; set in a folding jeweled frame, it has become a receptacle of power to heal the sick. An icon of Christ, for instance, mirrors and somehow participates in the sacred person it depicts. In this sense, a prayerful affirmation of Christ's iconic presentation can be linked closely to the central Christian belief that God became genuinely incarnate in Jesus. During the eighth-century Christian iconoclastic controversy, John of Damascus argues in his *Defense of Holy Images,* "It is not divine beauty which is rendered by the painter's brush, but the human form. Therefore, if the Son of God truly became man and appeared in man's nature, why should his image not be made?" All material reality has been sanctified by the Spirit, and bears within itself the potentiality to become the flesh of God incarnate. In Saint Athanasius' arresting turn of phrase, our very flesh is now Logos-ified (*logotheises*), permeated by the Logos or divine Word. Maximus the Confessor concludes that Incarnation (*sarkosis*) implies Divinization (*theosis*). Simeon the New Theologian in his tenth-century *Divine Hymns of Love* offers an even more dramatic image: "We become Christ's limbs, and he becomes our limbs. . . . Unworthy though I am, my hand and foot are Christ. I move my hand, and it is completely Christ, for God's divinity is united inseparably to me. I move my foot, and it glows like God himself!"

"God becomes human so that humanity might become divine"—this delicate paradox of Orthodox *theosis* can invite simplistic distortion, especially if translated literally from poetry and myth into an ontology. Alan Watts's *Myth and Ritual in Christianity,* for example, adopts a Hindu Advaitin version of *theosis,* perceiving Jesus as a transhistorical *avatāra,* no more unique than Kṛṣṇa or the *dharmakāya* Buddha. Christ "is man, but not *a* man," he argues. "The Incarnation of God is not something which comes to pass in a single, particular individual alone. Theological, as distinct from mythological, Christianity has always wanted to insist that such an Incarnation occurred only with respect to the historical individual called Jesus of Nazareth. It has confused the true uniqueness of the Incarnation with mere historical abnormality." With consistency, Watts reduces all instances of "each, a, or this particular person" to sheet *māyā* ego-illusion. He diagnoses the Christian obsession over Christ's uniqueness as a symptom of acute cultural insularity, unaware of comparable incarnation myths elsewhere. The Old Israel's racial exclusiveness survives as the New Israel's inferiority complex of spiritual exclusiveness. *Theosis* means an option eternally present to transcend one's individual ego and realize a fundamental *Brahman-Ātman* unitive experience. Following a similar logic, Jung reinterprets Christ's Incarnation into a myth about our potential self-transformation, establishing a bridge between the numinous Unconscious and conscious life. "Only then can 'God be born.' . . . By this act of incarnation, man—that is, his ego—is inwardly replaced by 'God', and God becomes outwardly man."

A shocking corrective to this dematerialized universal Christ-principle is the unmistakably vulnerable humanity of the kenotic Christ. Not generic mankind, but a unique individual man named Jesus of Nazareth shed his blood on a particular square foot of ground at an unrepeatable instant of linear time. According to the most testable historical affirmation in the ancient creeds, "he suffered under Pontius Pilate, was crucified, died, and was buried." It is fashionable to denigrate the sentimental, overly explicit Christ-image of Western late Gothic—an inconsolable pietà or a flayed crucified corpse. Yet this art at least confronts us on occasion with the scandal experienced by his disciples right after the crucifixion, when Easter could only have seemed an implausible miracle. In Dostoevski's *The Idiot,* Myshkin describes the effect of such a painting hung above the doorway in Rogozhin's room. "Why, this is a painting that might make some people lose their faith!" he exclaims. It represents Christ at the moment of removal from the cross, "a face which still retains much warmth and life. Nothing is rigid in it yet, and the suffering seems to continue in the face of the dead man as if he were still feeling it." The body is mangled and swollen from the beatings. How could the apostles and women standing there believe, "gazing on the cadaver, that this martyr would be resurrected?"

The film script for Ingmar Bergman's *Winter Light* asks for a crucifix carved in this artistic style, opposite a vestry window, where the Lutheran Pastor Tomas struggles in silence to surmount his flu delirium and Dark Night of faith. "The mouth opens in a scream," Bergman specifies, "the arms are grotesquely twisted, the hands convulsively clutch the nails, the brow is bloody beneath the thorns, and the body arches outward, as if trying to tear itself away from the wood." Almost unconscious of their meaning, Tomas repeats the words of dereliction attributed in Mark's Gospel to Jesus on the cross, "God, my God, why have you abandoned me?" Later, Algot the sacristan, stricken with severe arthritis, shares with Tomas his recent insight into Christ's passion. More acute than mere physical torture, the mental sufferings of Christ are perhaps more readily comprehensible, for they resemble most of our own: "His disciples abandoned him, the whole lot of them. And he was left alone. . . . He cried out, 'God, my God, why have you abandoned me?'. . . The moment before he died, Christ was seized with a great doubt. Surely that must have been his most monstrous suffering of all? I mean God's silence." It remains ambiguous whether Tomas merely hears Algot out as a pious neurotic or now glimpes fresh religious meaning in his own depression.

The Christian imagination is challenged to perceive separately—and only then attempt to juxtapose—this desolate cry of Christ, and his final Johannine shout of triumph, "It is achieved!" More important, how can a timebound death in Jerusalem of one exlusive individual be correlated with the salvation of people at every time and place by the inclusive Lord of history? Artists strain outrageously to suggest the cosmic implications of his death. Some crucifixion paintings depict a skull beneath the cross, at times even identified as the remains of Adam, with Christ's blood dripping on the skull. Golgotha in legend becomes Adam's burial place, Christ's agony in the garden is transferred to the Garden of Eden. The cross that redeems mankind is extended down to cut into the earth's center as an *axis mundi* connecting Heaven and earth. There is a tenth-century Constantinople triptych of the crucifixion, the cross at its base transfixing a contorted troll, probably a river or mountain god symbol of Hades. An especially popular motif in the earliest centuries is Christ's journey to the underworld, reenacting the pattern of most Orpheus and Hercules myths—a gauntlet of ordeals, liberation of captives, a savior returning from darkness with the gift of immortality for all mankind. Iconography shows the wounded Christ battling with devils, a tradition that later culminates in the famous Harrowing of Hell mystery plays, or baptizing and preaching to Old Testament saints, now released from prison. This myth is developed graphically in early apocryphal literature, notably the Acts of Thomas, Apocalypse of Peter, and Gospel of Nicodemus.

Neglected by most contemporary theology and preaching, the credal symbol of Christ's Descent into Hell, as commonly interpreted during the first three centuries, implies a kaleidoscopic Christology of both glory and the cross. Later eras would use this myth as a springboard to debate whether Christ's divine nature alone or the divine nature united to his human soul entered Hell; and whether he visited purgatory, limbo, or the fires of the damned. Such issues today seem relatively trivial. The phrase *descendit ad inferna*—later, *ad inferos*—made its first appearance as a late addition to the old Roman Symbol of Faith. The spatial myth referred to is certainly *she'ol,* Jewish realm of the dead. In the early fifth century, Tyrannius Rufinus' *Commentary on the Apostles' Creed* judged this clause a recent insertion, perhaps intended merely to expand the previous words about Christ's death and burial.

Two striking complementary interpretations are given to the Descent myth in the second and third centuries. Irenaeus, Miletus, and Hippolytus use it to express Christ's conquest over death, devils, and the underworld. Responding to dualistic Gnostic critics, they argue that Christ rules every aspect of existence, even the demonic. Furthermore, Clement and Origen view the Descent as confirmation of the Gospel's universal scope, preached by Christ to noble Greek Humanists and Old Testament saints still awaiting the Messiah in *she'ol.*

The second principal meaning of the Descent has already been indicated by Rufinus. Unsettled at the grisly abasement of Christ by his tormentors, Docetists reduced his death to the mere appearance of decay. In rebuttal, by acknowledging Christ's passage through the common abode of the dead, and the spatial separation between his body and soul for three days, the Christian tradition adheres emphatically to the full human reality of his death. To die a human death means that Christ plunged himself into the utmost pain, darkness, and loneliness, the experience of every mortal being-unto-death. Midpoint in his rite of passage between death and resurrection, the nadir of Descent transforms itself into a beginning Ascent to glory, his theophany as cosmic savior.

The Way and the Spirit

The preceding chapter concluded with an attempt to anchor an esoteric Sūfī path within the historical exoteric tradition of Sharī'ah, Muhammad, and the Qur'an. Otherwise, Muslim spirituality might melt away into Advaitin Vedānta, or the eclectic transhistorical *philosophia perennis* reservoir articulated by such persuasive exponents as Jung, Coomaraswamy, Aldous Huxley, and Watts. Can we discover distinctive exoteric roots, too, for a Christian spirituality? A clear-cut differentiating note does recur in the accounts of some mystics. For example, the unitive vision described throughout the world by pantheists and panentheists has its singluar Christian counterpart in the *panenchristism* already cited in Dostoevski and early Fathers of the Church. "Mighty Matter," Teilhard prays according to the grammar of this tradition, "the hand of God, the flesh of Christ. . . . I acclaim you as the divine milieu, . . . ocean stirred by the Spirit, clay moulded and infused with life by the incarnate Word!"

The perennial apophatic Way and Dark Night of mystics has its own Christian variant, too, though the exoteric context is often left obscure. We readily associate widespread experience today of God's absence, eclipse, or nothingness with the Deus Absconditus of Luther and Pascal, Kierkegaard's Divine Incognito, and Nietzsche's Death of the Gods. Luther adds a significant Christian nuance to what seems an account of his own Dark Night, given in the *Explanations of Ninety-five Theses.* After quoting his favorite mystic, Tauler, he says, "At such a time God appears terribly angry and alongside him the whole creation. . . . All that remains is the naked desire for help and a terrible groaning, for one does not know where to turn for help. In this instance, the person is stretched out with Christ."

The Christian mystic's incorporation into Christ's own Dark Night is a motif developed mostly by implication in John of the Cross. Such a Night is painful and frightful because the mind's habitual functions are strained beyond their limits to grapple with unfamiliar divine light, paradoxically the instant of profoundest religious vision. God's action upon each believer is a calculated spiritual weaning—he drops you from his arms and forces you to walk alone. The *Dark Night of the Soul* calls this a severe wounding, loss, and burial, "the shadow of death and torments of Hell." Thus, groping beyond familiar concepts and images into trackless space, we undergo a rite-de-passage abandonment that is actually the incomprehensible depths of God. The prototype of every human Dark Night is the Descent of Christ into Hell, a model and grace available to any Christian contemplative choosing to reenact the death of Christ.

In two pivotal doctrines, Christians have essentially reshaped their rich Jewish spiritual heritage. First is the following of Christ as the Way; the second, a *bhakti*-like surrender to the grace of the Holy Spirit, rather than a fidelity to the letter of the Mosaic Torah. Interweaving both these themes, Paul's central teaching in Romans and Galatians gives the prayer of every Christian a pronounced Trinitarian stamp. Our lives oriented toward God the Father, we are the redeemed brothers and sisters of Jesus Christ, with the Holy Spirit enabling us to cry, "Abba, Father!" It is not even certain how best to pray, but through our inarticulate groans the Spirit himself prays for us. "We are Christ's fellow heirs if we share his sufferings now in order to share his splendor hereafter. . . . Given the Spirit as firstfruits of the coming harvest, we groan inwardly while waiting for God to make us his children. . . . We are discharged from the Law, to serve God in the new way of the Spirit, in contrast to the old way of a written code" (Rom. 7–8).

The Christian Way, then, means loving discipleship first of all, following in the footsteps of the evangelical Christ. We have watched many devout Buddhists imitate Gautama's conjectured posture and *mudrās* in meditation, and strive to recover his *samādhi* experience somehow by praying near landmarks like the Bo Tree and Deer Park. The Muslim *ḥajjī* usually hopes to duplicate all the recorded rituals and spiritual attitudes of Muhammad as the prophet moved in his final pilgrimage from the Ka'bah to Mount Arafat. In the Christian disciple, spiritual identification and imitation assume an astonishing range of forms. Most popular of all Christian formal prayers, the Our Father is recited to assimilate the mind of Christ, communing with God his Father. Jesus asked that the Last Supper, presage of his death, be reenacted "in remembrance of me," so that later followers could experience his real sacramental presence among them. The purpose of monastic vows is to mirror the circumstances of Christ's committed faith—the simple routine labor and contemplative quiet of his thirty hidden years, or the final public ministry of preaching and teaching.

The stigmata of Saint Francis, we suggested earlier, and also his craving for martyrdom in Muslim Egypt, were both gestures of ecstatic identification with the suffering and death of Jesus. The earliest Christians could imagine no more exemplary imitation of their founder than the shaping of one's very death to vindicate once more in public the cause for which Jesus was martyred. Luke in Acts of the Apostles assigns to proto-martyr Stephen the same final words of forgiveness and surrender attributed by Luke's Gospel to Jesus. Within a few decades, this subtle spirituality of martyrdom had already adopted the style of a more self-conscious apologetics. The *Martyrdom of Saint Polycarp,* for example, tries to superimpose as many Gospel details as possible on the account of this bishop's famous trial and death. "By almost every step leading up to his death," its preface states, "the Lord intended to show us anew the type of martyrdom narrated in the Gospel."

The specific behavior of Jesus toward children, outcast sinners, religious authorities, the very adverbs and adjectives used by the Gospels to surmise his implicit attitudes—these are the indispensable sacred particulars for devout contemplation and imitation by the saints. The autobiography of Ignatius Loyola, for instance, recounts his earliest sickbed reveries, based first on books of medieval romance, then on biographies of Christ and the saints. "If Saints Francis and Dominic could do this, then so can I!" he repeated to himself with a touch of macho competitiveness. Later, during an actual barefoot pilgrimage to Jerusalem, now able to act out his fantasies of imitating Jesus, he records his fascination with Christ's stone footprints allegedly left behind on Mount Olivet. Ignatius had to bribe the Muslim guards to let him return twice in order to calculate precisely the direction faced by each footprint.

Among the techniques recommended for meditation and Christian transformation in the *Spiritual Exercises,* a book drawn from his own experiences, Ignatius asks the reader to imagine Joseph and the pregnant Mary, for instance, on the road from Nazareth to Bethlehem. "Consider its length and breadth, and whether such a road is level, or passes through valleys or over hills." The contemplative aim here is to enter the Gospel scenario as imaginatively as possible, gain loving familiarity with every character there, and "pray for joy with Christ in joy, . . . or for pain and tears with Christ in torment." A far more literal imitation of Christ has been encouraged by the spirituality of Charles de Foucauld, a contemplative outcast living among Muslim Sahara nomads. According to his journal, he finds delight living under the sky and walking over the very land where Christ once lived. And the Gospels can be distilled into this one simple directive of Christ: "Follow me. Do what I did. In every situation ask yourself, what would our Lord have done? Then do that. This is your only rule, but it is absolutely binding on you."

Besides the following of Christ, I have mentioned that a second principal theme in Christian spirituality is the gratuitous gift of the Spirit. Paradoxically, the Way of Christ is not merely a teaching but itself a person: Christ, the *Way*. According to Taoists, the *tao-te* can be represented as a doctrine introduced from the outside, but it is most of all a force endemic to each individual, an uncoiling spring sacred and potentially directive. Similarly, the Christian *Spirit* is not just an inspiring moral ideal but a *Pneuma* or *Élan,* a numinous enabling presence that radiates strength and joy. "God's grace not only indicates what ought to be done," says Augustine in his commentary on Pauline dogma, "but helps make possible the achievement of what it indicates. . . . God has willed that his saints should not glory in their own strength but in himself. . . . What else but his own gifts does God crown when he crowns our merits?" His tract *On the Gift of Perseverance,* after citing Paul's phrase about "crying out 'Abba' in the Spirit," adds an important proviso: "This 'crying' is also the gift of God. . . . What a mistake to believe our seeking, asking, knocking is of ourselves, and not given to us."

This receptivity to the Spirit must not be mistaken for invertebrate passivity. In the language of Being, Heidegger describes this attitude as an alert listening, hearkening, openness to reality. Its most patent antithesis survives the dated polemical labels of Pharisaism and Pelagianism, and can be smoked out in the immature religious practice of all world religious traditions. The persecuted whiskey priest in Greene's *The Power and the Glory* names it aptly the "habit of piety," and suspects that God might be closer to the now-acknowledged wino and fornicator in himself than to the once-insulated holy priest, circled by churchy admirers. Cora Tull, the twice-born Christian caricatured in Faulkner's *As I Lay Dying,* is endowed with the clichés and metronomic cadence pattern of the self-soothing believer: "I have tried to live right in the sight of God and man, for the honor and comfort of my Christian husband and the love and respect of my Christian children. So that when I lay me down in the consciousness of my duty and reward I will be surrounded by loving faces, carrying the farewell kiss of each of my loved ones into my reward." Cora admits that sometimes she is assailed just momentarily by religious doubt. "But always the Lord restores my faith and reveals to me his bounteous love for his creatures."

The substance of the Jesus Prayer, a simple ritual formula in traditional Orthodox Hesychast spirituality, undercuts this sterile religious pride. The words are "Lord Jesus Christ, Son of God, have mercy on me, a sinner." In usual practice, the words are treated as a *mantra,* prayed with awesome concentration at first, then repeated thousands of times day and night, until they sink deep into consciousness as a sort of incessant background music. Simeon the New Theologian tells of a young man who could move easily in and out of an ecstatic trance while forever murmuring this prayer in the deepest regions of his mind. Yet he managed to pay close attention to his daily responsibilities as a government clerk, without explicit devotional interruptions. Fourteenth-century Gregory of Sinai anticipates a phase when the mind, left to itself, becomes too weary to focus on the prayer's meaning, and so eventually finds itself content to let the prayer pray itself. "One should appeal to the Lord quietly and without agitation, . . . until the mind, receiving force from the Spirit, firmly prays within on its own." This spiritual discipline seems a challenging blend of receptivity and energetic self-preparation.

Closer to the Orthodox Hesychasts than he might ever have recognized, Martin Luther renews the Pauline and Augustinian distinction between crucial gifts of the Spirit and their demonic misuse. One of his Pentecost sermons tracks down those who boast presumptuously that they possess the Spirit. The danger is to become too secure. "The pious Christian is still flesh and blood like other people. . . . There will always be mingled in us purity and imperfection; we must be conscious both of the Holy Spirit's presence and our own sins." Every human being must remain *simul justus et peccator.*

In a quaint, touching set of instructions for his friend Peter the Barber, *Simple Advice on How to Pray,* Luther manages to distill most essentials in the Christian prayer tradition. Remember that you are not just standing or kneeling by yourself, but also the whole Christian Church and all good Christians with you, in one united prayer." This confidence in the communion of saints leaves no room for groveling fatalism. Luther concedes that he often browses "so richly on one single thought that I can let go all other petitions in the Our Father. For when that happens, the Holy Spirit himself is speaking. And one word of his is worth a thousand of our own prayers." Though some spiritualities disdain this ingenuous style of petitionary prayer, there is a robust directness and trusting personal familiarity about Luther's approach that approximates what Jesus no doubt experienced in saying "Abba, Father!" The enabling presence of the Spirit means both Son and Spirit commune with the Father through our inarticulate groans, as Paul assures us in Romans: "God willed that we be shaped according to the image of his Son, . . . and searching our inmost being, knows what the Spirit means, because the Spirit pleads for God's people in God's own way."

FURTHER READING

1. **Overview.** A useful recent bibliography can be found in the Jaroslav Pelikan updating of H. H. Walsh, 'Christianity" in Charles Adams., ed., *A Reader's Guide to the Great Religions,* 2nd ed. (Free Press, 1977), pp. 345–406. *The New English Bible* (Oxford University Press, 1970) seems preferable for literate accuracy in its translation. Other massive encyclopedic tools are John Willis, S.J., *The Teachings of the Church Fathers* (Herder, 1966), a broad anthology of snippets arranged thematically; Hubert Jedin and John Dolan, eds., *History of the Church* (Crossroad, 1965–81), 10 vols.; and Karl Rahner et al., eds., *Sacramentum Mundi: An Encyclopedia of Theology* (Herder, 1968–70), 6 vols.

2. **Christian Political Wisdom.** The attitude of Jesus and the early Church to political authority is traced in Alan Richardson, *The Political Christ* (Westminster, 1973); and Francis X. Murphy, C.SS.R., *Politics and the Early Christian* (Desclee, 1967), which covers the period up to Augustine. Two excellent editorials on "The Dialectic of Romans 13:1–7 and Revelations 13" occur in *Journal of Church and State* 18–19 (1976–77), pp. 433–43, 5–20.

Sidney Ehler and John Morrall, eds., *Church and State through the Centuries* (Newman, 1954), gives most of the major historical documents and commentaries on this topic. A popular fivefold typology showing various styles of interaction between Christianity and the surrounding culture can be found in H. Richard Niebuhr, *Christ and Culture* (Harper, 1951). Thomas Parker's *Christianity and the State in the Light of History* (Black, 1955) has an especially fine chapter on the pre-Constantinian Church. The western European Church-State controversy is surveyed concisely in Albert Mirgeler, *Mutations of Western Christianity,* tr. Edward Quinn (Herder, 1964). See the contrasting Byzantine scenario portrayed by Stefan Zankov, "Nation and Church in the Orthodox Lands of Eastern Europe" in Kenneth Latourette et al., eds., *Church and Community* (Allen and Unwin, 1938), pp. 129–68; and the more recent Kallistos Ware, "Christian Theology in the East: 600–1453" in Hubert Cunliffe-Jones, *A History of Christian Doctrine* (Fortress, 1978), pp.

181–226, especially the section on the political background behind the Iconoclast Controversy.

It is interesting to speculate on the sincerity of Constantine's religious conversion and on the manner in which Christians adjusted to sudden State endorsement. Both the following articles give persuasive reasons in support of his sincerity: Henry Chadwick, "Conversion in Constantine the Great" in Derek Baker, ed., *Religious Motivation: Biographical and Sociological Problems for the Church Historian* (Blackwell, 1978), pp. 1–15; and Massey Shepherd, "Before and After Constantine" in Jerald Brauer, ed., *The Impact of the Church upon Its Culture* (University of Chicago Press, 1968), pp. 17–38.

The relationship between Francis of Assisi and Innocent III is explored by Giulio Basetti-Sani, O.F.M., "Francis of Assisi" in Roger Auber, ed., *Prophets in the Church* (Concilium Series—Paulist, 1968), pp. 9–26; and especially by Thomas Renna, "Pope Innocent III and Francis of Assisi" in his *Church and State in Medieval Europe: 1050-1314* (Kendall-Hunt, 1974), pp. 65–120. James Powell, ed., *Innocent III: Vicar of Christ or Lord of the World?* (Heath, 1963), gives a provocative selection of documents on the complex policies and personality of this pope. Michael de la Bedoyere's *Francis: A Biography of the Saint of Assisi* (Harper and Row, 1962) mixes salt with sugar in presenting heroic fact.

Christian political options in Latin American are surveyed in Daniel Levine, ed., *Churches and Politics in Latin America* (Sage, 1980). Brian Smith, "Christians and Marxists in Allende's Chile: Lessons for Western Europe" in Suzanne Berger, ed., *Religion in West European Politics* (Frank Cass, 1982), pp. 108–26, studies the Catholic hierarchy's cautious support and gradual disaffection toward the Allende regime. Paul Lehmann's *The Transfiguration of Politics* (Harper and Row, 1975) devotes a chapter to the thought of Che Guevara, Camilo Torres, and other revolutionary figures. Marred by its eulogistic style, *The Last, Best Hope: Eduardo Frei and Chilean Democracy* (Random House, 1967) still manages to capture vintage Frei in his own words. A good sampling of liberation theology at its most succinct and literate is *The Mystical and Political Dimension of the Christian Faith,* eds., Claude Geffre and Gustavo Gutierrez (Concilium Series—Herder, 1974). The articles by Segundo, Gutierrez, Galilea, and Dussel are most insightful.

A quick survey of Church-State vicissitudes in the United States, especially during the colonial period, can be found in the editorials "Church-State Relations in the Modern World," pp. 121–28, and "The Secular State," pp. 169–78, *Journal of Church and State* 6–7 (1964–65). A copy of the Solzhenitsyn address should be examined in *Solzhenitsyn at Harvard* (Ethics and Public Policy Center, 1980). The eighteen commentaries that follow the speech reveal a wide range of implicit political theology among the critics. In addition to Adenauer's *Memoirs,* consult Terence Prittie, *Konrad Adenauer: 1876–1967* (Cowles, 1971). In addition to Kaunda's *A Humanist in Africa,* consult Fergus Macpherson, *Kenneth Kaunda of Zambia: The Times and the Man* (Oxford University Press, 1974).

3. **Christology.** The biblical context, especially a text such as Philippians 2:6–11, is admirably explicated in Reginald Fuller, *Foundations of New Testament Christology* (Scribner's, 1965). Some of the earliest patristic theories are surveyed in Gustaf Wingren, *Man and the Incarnation: A Study in the Biblical Theology of Irenaeus,* tr. Ross Mackenzie (Oliver and Boyd, 1959); and Gustaf Aulen, *Christus Victor: An Historical Study of the Three Main Types of the Idea of the Atonement,* tr. A. G. Hebert (SPCK Press, 1953).

On the Descent into Hell theme, see John N. D. Kelly, *Early Christian Creeds,* 2nd ed. (Longmans Green, 1960), and especially his notes and translation—*Rufinus: A Commentary on the Apostles' Creed* (Longmans Green, 1955). Compare the attitudes of ten theologians, from Clement to Aquinas, in Ralph Turner, *"Descendit ad Inferos:* Medieval Views on Christ's Descent into Hell and the Salvation of the Ancient Just," *Journal of the History of Ideas* 27(April–June 1966), pp. 173–93. The best concise introduction to a study of this motif is Herbert Vorgrimler's "The Significance of Christ's Descent into Hell" in Edward Schillebeeckx, O.P., *Who Is Jesus of Nazareth?* (Concilium Series—Paulist, 1966), pp. 147–60. The Dark Night implications of this doctrine are suggested imaginatively in Hans Urs Von Balthasar, *The God Question and Modern Man,* tr. Hilda Graef (Seabury, 1967), pp. 92–111.

Albert Moore's *Iconography of Religions* (Fortress, 1977) gives superb illustrations and commentary on the Christ figure in Christian art. Kurt Weitzmann et al., eds., *The Icon* (Knopf, 1982), devotes separate articles to the icon art of various Slavic cultures. See especially Venetia Newall, "Icons as Symbols of Power" in Ellis Davidson, *Symbols of Power* (Folklore Society, 1977).

4. **Spirituality.** On the topic of apophatic mysticism or the *Via Negativa,* see Richard Kroner, "Negative Theology," *Speculation and Revelation in the Age of Christian Philosophy* (Westminster, 1959), pp. 132–49; and Vladimir Lossky, *The Vision of God,* tr. Asheleigh Moorhouse (Faith Press, 1963), pp. 99–137.

Richard Wood, O.P., ed., *Understanding Mysticism* (Doubleday, 1980), is a fine collection of articles giving psychological, sociological, and philosophical appraisals. The Orthodox and Roman Catholic mystics are represented by brief passages in F. C. Happold, ed., *Mysticism: A Study and an Anthology* (Penguin, 1979), and David Fleming, S.M., ed., *The Fire and the Cloud: An Anthology of Catholic Spirituality* (Paulist, 1978).

Anne Fremantle, ed., *The Protestant Mystics* (Little, Brown, 1964), ranges through the seventeenth-century Metaphysical poets, Van Gogh, C. S. Lewis, and many other imgainative possibilities. The effect of this anthology is to expand one's traditional concept of the mystic. Hugh Kerr, ed., *A Compend of Luther's Theology* (Westminster, 1943), gives selected paragraphs from Luther in thematic arrangement. A convincing case for the presence of a mystical dimension in Protestant spirituality is mounted by Gordon Rupp, "Protestant Spirituality in the First Age of the Reformation" in G. J. Cuming and Derek Baker, eds., *Popular Belief and Practice* (Cambridge University Press, 1972), pp. 155–70.

Conclusion:

Reflections on a Method

Religious traditions are similar because of shared human history and our circumscribed capacity to express the inexpressible. They are dissimilar mostly because each sacred revelation bears the stamp of a *personal equation*—the finite linguistic system, cultural bias, and individual character-armor shaping each prophetic imagination through which the sacred is mediated. We are struck by astonishing parallels among the eight spiritualities selected for the present study. Drawn from every creed, countless people of spiritual sensitivity cherish a common experience of wonder and mystery, live by essentially the same moral consensus, adopt analogous techniques to institutionalize and reanimate periodically their originating group charism, split into fundamentalist-liberal polarities in response to the dilemmas of secularity, and offer similar patterns of religious legitimation, especially for contemporary postcolonial societies. World mystics recount experiences of the same apophatic Dark Night and of quests marked by the metaphors of flight, combat, or spiritual courtship. Utopia in most traditions is a city ruled by ideal justice, a communion banquet with the gods, a garden reuniting nature and all livings beings, a *nirvāṇa* of homecoming and definitive rebirth.

Moses Mendelssohn cautioned, on the other hand, against a specious ecumenism that tries to blur the contours of each distinctive human face, for God has charted a unique path for every person. A subtle syncretist like Gandhi, too, tried not to flatten out appropriate religious differences. Ready to tolerate the great world faiths as facets of a single "religion which underlies all religions," Gandhi was forced to admit that neither Vedas, Bible, nor Qur'an, all touched by human imperfection, possess the complete truth attributable to God alone. Moreover, "no two persons I know have had identical conceptions of God. Therefore, there will perhaps always be different religions answering to different temperaments and climatic conditions." Still, such diversity of faith must never obscure Gandhi's one pivotal paradox: "If you reach the heart of your own religion, you have reached the heart of the others, too."

In summary, let this celebration of religious heterogeneity by Gandhi and Mendelssohn stand as the first of five methodological assumptions that have provided conscious direction to our present study. In each world religious tradition, we have tried to locate esoteric universals within their unique respective exoteric contexts. As the best literary regionalists have always demonstrated, immersion in radical local particularity is the most accurate point of access to the transcendent human verities.

Our second assumption follows as an immediate corollary to the first: within each religious tradition, waive all simplified encyclopedic overviews. Instead, track down a few significant rites, saints, or motifs in depth, and then register their massive spiritual implications. This seems the wisest method to close in on anything so complex and elusive as a specific religious weltanschauung—the import of stupa and Bodhisattva to Buddhists, for instance, of *ḥajj* to Muslims, or of Marx to Humanists. The neo-Platonist Longinus knew how to treat each perceived object as a potential moment of expanding comprehension. And some of the best literary critics grasp intuitively a single image or scene in a text, and expand this circle of significance until it reaches out to encompass the whole work, then the implied vision pervading an artist's corpus, and finally the trends of an entire era. Ideally, this same microcosm-macrocosm correlation, too, should animate approaches to the great world spiritualities.

The third principle sanctions a flexible interdisciplinary strategy to take accurate religious soundings. Each of us perceives as a comprehensive human being, of course, not merely in the role of a formal theologian. It is essential to distinguish between the vital religious impulse disguised beneath a modest human pseudonym and the extinct impulse mummified beneath an overt religious label. If such discernment seems rare for the devout insider, it is still more rare for an outsider. Interpreted in isolation, sacred scriptures and official sectarian documents often project an unreal portrait belied by the actual religious life of a people. Our abstract simplifications must be checked out against the living exponents of each tradition—against their significant religious behavior recorded, for instance, in popular literature, iconography, or biography, and scrutinized by psychology, anthropology, and all the other human sciences. Nehru once addressed the Lok Sabha on divorce customs in early Hindu history, and suggested an admirable interdisciplinary method to ascertain the spiritual values prevalent in any evolving society. "You should not read some rigid enactments, like the commandments of Manu. . . . Take one of our old plays, the *Mrich-chakatika*. . . . See the tender humanity found in the play. In it there is no rigid puritanism," but tolerance, generosity, and refinement. "The test of an individual is how he treats his wife, his son, or his neighbor. How he behaves toward another, how he functions in a social relationship."

A fourth presumption draws attention to the moral dialectic running like a tragic geological fault through every human construct, even our loftiest spiritualities. No ideal is so noble that it cannot be debased by demonic ingenuity to rationalize a life in direct betrayal of the ideal. Even the truth, says Kierkegaard, can become a lie on the lips of some people. If religious faith implies a fallible creed, code, and cultus response to the Absolute, then we must expect to find creed habitually threatened by dogmatism, code by legalism, cultus by empty ritualism. It takes extraordinary faith to discover the Church as body and bride of Christ in Greene's or Updike's tepid suburban Christian congregations, or the flawless *ummah muslima* in Najib Mahfuz's squalid Egyptian "Mosque in the Alley." Surely an honest assessment of the major world faiths must record not just their glory but also at least their potential shame. In exploring each spirituality, I have consistently stressed its moral splendor of vision, but have not silenced prophetic cries within the tradition itself, struggling to winnow the authentic Tao, Dharma, or Spirit from its counterfeits.

The final methodological assumption can be called a *hermeneutical reversal.* A major artistic classic, for example, does not so much stand in need of judgment as stand in judgment over you. It demands an opening and volte-face of consciousness. Brushing aside the stock criteria of assessment, your whole unconscious agenda, it levies this sharp challenge: how are your spiritual horizons now affected by this fresh heightened realization of what it means to be dead or alive, or dead in the midst of life?

The narrator in Carlos Castaneda's popular Don Juan series stumbles again and again because he neglects this hermeneutical axiom. Attempting to explain sophistries of genealogy and biography to a shaman of apparently inferior education, this religious anthropologist instead is forced to answer unsettling questions about his own personal history. He patronizes the old man by affirming their equal status, whereas Don Juan replies, "We are not equals. I am a hunter and warrior, but you are a pimp." A confessed academic drone, the narrator concedes that Don Juan consistently "reversed the roles; I was the stupid one." After four years of subsequent apprenticeship under Don Juan, he acknowledges himself still a mere spiritual beginner. His scientific studies in religion had been "forgotten or at least redirected into channels that were worlds apart from my original intention." In other words, the appropriate approach to a faith other than your own is not that of detached olympian critic, but a limited fallible participant-observer, ready to listen with reverence and be touched, perhaps altered, open to constant reassessment of your own unfathomed *personal equation.*

INDEX

Index

Boldface numbers indicate the definition or first significant use of a term. Boldface primary entries indicate chapter titles; subheadings entered under each chapter title give a précis guide.